RADIANT

Thanks to Sara Loudon, Dawn Darby and Kathleen Hannula for their proofreading and suggestions for improvement.

Published by Canon Press
P.O. Box 8729, Moscow, Idaho 83843
800.488.2034 | www.canonpress.com

Cover design by James Engerbretson
Cover illustration "Darlene Deibler Rose at Kampili" by Forrest Dickison
Interior design by Valerie Anne Bost

Printed in the United States of America.

Library of Congress Cataloging-in-Publication Data is forthcoming.

15 16 17 18 19 20 21 22   9 8 7 6 5 4 3 2 1

RADIANT

FIFTY REMARKABLE WOMEN IN CHURCH HISTORY

Richard M. Hannula

canonpress
Moscow, Idaho

To my wife

CONTENTS

REFORMATION AND BEYOND ══ 93
STANDING FOR THE GOSPEL

MISSIONS REAWAKENED ══ 181
MISSIONARIES AND CONVERTS

20TH AND 21ST CENTURIES ═══ 237
TRIAL AND TRIUMPH
OF THE WORLDWIDE CHURCH

FOR FURTHER READING ═══ 315

INTRODUCTION

Those who look to him are radiant;
their faces are never covered with shame.
—Psalm 34:5

From the days when Mary and Martha opened their home to Jesus, the Christian church has relied on the steadfast faith and tireless work of women. Women were the last to leave the scene of Christ's crucifixion and the first to proclaim His resurrection. Lydia, a successful businesswoman, was the first person in Philippi to turn to Christ through the Apostle Paul's preaching. Her home became Paul's headquarters and the location of the first Christian church in the region. Priscilla and her husband helped Paul found the church in Ephesus and led Apollos to a deeper understanding of the Holy Spirit's work in the hearts of believers. The Roman philosopher Celsus mocked the fast-growing Christian faith in the Roman Empire saying women spread Christianity "by gossiping Christ at the laundry."

In the fourth century, Libanius, the famous pagan orator who assisted Emperor Julian's efforts to revive paganism in the empire, was forced to say, "Good heavens! What remarkable women are found among the Christians."

Stories of the heroes of the church's past can touch the hearts and minds of believers in powerful ways. It is the Bible's own way of communicating truth by setting before us flesh and blood examples of God's people. The role played by women, through the power of the Holy Spirit, in the conversion of souls from every nation, tribe, people and language is not as well known as it should be. The following sketches trace the witness of women through two thousand years of church history—from brave souls who died as martyrs in the arena to zealous medieval queens leading their husbands and their subjects to Jesus—from Western missionaries forsaking the comforts of home to bring the gospel to the four corners of the globe to native women in remote lands, pointing their fellow tribesmen to Christ.

These short sketches simply scratch the surface of the women's lives. Effort was made to honestly depict them in the midst of their unique time and circumstances. However, it was not possible within a few pages to thoroughly explore their strengths and weaknesses, faith and doubts, truths and errors. To learn much more about these Christian women, follow the trail marked out in "For Further Reading" at the end of the book. It is my hope that the reader—boy or girl, man or woman—will be inspired, by the grace of God, to follow in their steps as they followed in Christ's.

EARLY CHURCH

PERSECUTION AND EXPANSION

Dufing the first three hundred years of the church, Christians experienced seasons of calm and periods of storm. Under some Roman emperors and governors who believed that devotion to paganism meant loyalty to the government they suffered intense persecution. Christians who refused to bow down to the pagan gods of Rome suffered cruel public deaths as enemies of the state. Perpetua and Crispina were two of hundreds of women who died for Christ in the arena. At other times, the state left Christians largely alone, and the faith was often advanced by influential women from the great aristocratic families of the empire.

After Emperor Constantine made Christianity legal in the empire, mothers like Monica and Anthusa were free to raise their children in the Christian faith without interference from the government. When the Roman Empire collapsed, women played a prominent role in bringing the good news of Christ to the far-flung peoples that the Romans called "barbarians."

1 PERPETUA
Not in Her Own Power, but in God's, 181–203

In 202, the Roman governor at Carthage in North Africa ordered the arrest of Christians. Among those rounded up was Perpetua, the young mother of a one-year-old boy. She came from a noble family—her father was a pagan and her mother a Christian. Her husband was no longer around, either he had died or he had abandoned her because of her Christian beliefs. At that time, Christians could escape punishment by offering a sacrifice to the emperor as a god. After her arrest, Perpetua was held with four Christian friends, including her pastor, Saturus, in a private home under a strong guard. Her father came and pleaded with her to deny Christianity. "For the sake of your child and our family," he said with tears in his eyes, "reject Christ."

Perpetua pointed to a pitcher sitting on a shelf and said, "Father, can that pitcher change its name?"

"No," her father answered.

"Neither can I call myself anything else than what I am—a Christian."

Her determined reply made his heart pound and his cheeks flush red. Grabbing her by the shoulders, he shook her, demanding that she renounce her faith. "I am a Christian," she said.

Seeing that his daughter could not be persuaded either by plead-ings or threats, he went away, hanging his head.

A few days later, guards moved Perpetua and her friends from the house and cast them into the dungeon of a large prison. The heat and stench from the prisoners packed together like cord wood was nearly unbearable. "Oh, the horror and darkness," Perpetua said, "I have never been in such a place."

Soldiers cursed and whipped the prisoners at will, but worse than the physical torture was Perpetua's concern for her baby. After a few days, the chief jailer moved them to a less crowded section of the prison, and a friend brought her infant son to her. She thanked God for the ability to nurse her fam-ished child. Then she directed her friend to place her son in the care of her mother.

After several days, word spread that the Christian prison-ers would soon stand trial. Perpetua's father came to her in prison, his face pale and drawn, and his eyes red and swollen. "Daughter," he said, "have pity on your father, if I still deserve to be called your father. Do not deliver me up to the scorn of men. Think of your mother and your brothers. Have compassion on your child that cannot live without you. Lay aside your courage and resolve—for we cannot bear the thought of your suffering."

Then he knelt at her feet, kissed her hands and sobbed, say-ing, "My lady, please relent."

Perpetua bit her lip and fought back tears. "Father, do not grieve," she said. "Nothing will happen, but what pleases God. Know that we are not placed in our own power, but in God's."

Sighing and bowing his head, he left her.

The next day, guards led Perpetua and her four friends to the town hall, crowded with gawking spectators. The Christian prisoners stood before the provincial governor. First, he questioned the three men, and each one boldly professed Jesus Christ. While the governor was examining the men, Perpetua's father appeared, holding her son. Pulling her aside, he whispered, "Perpetua, please consider the misery that you will bring on this innocent child."

As Perpetua gently refused her father's request, the governor overheard their conversation. "What!" he bellowed. "Will neither the gray hairs of a father whom you are going to make miserable, nor the tender innocence of a child which your death will leave an orphan, move you?"

Stretching an opened hand toward her, the governor said, "Just make a sacrifice to the emperor and you shall be freed."

Perpetua looked him in the eyes and said, "I will not do it."

"Are you a Christian then?" he asked.

"I am a Christian," Perpetua answered. The governor ordered a soldier to strike her face for her obstinacy. The blow knocked her back, but she would not deny Christ nor offer incense to the emperor.

Sweeping his gaze over the Christian prisoners, the governor said, "Then you shall all be condemned to die by wild beasts." Their execution would be part of the games in the arena for the entertainment of the crowds.

Guards brought them back to prison. For several days, they were chained with their hands and feet in stocks. "The Holy Spirit inspired me to pray for nothing but patience under bodily pains,"

Perpetua said. But then the chief jailer, seeing how the Christians bore their torments with such courage and grace, took pity on them. He removed them from the stocks and allowed them to have visitors. Perpetua's father—looking haggard and exhausted—came to see her. Throwing himself on the ground, he begged her to recant her faith to save her life. "I cannot," she told him, "I am a Christian." After he left the prison, tears streamed down her cheeks and she said, "I was ready to die with sorrow to see my father in such deplorable condition."

One of the prisoners condemned to die with Perpetua was a young woman named Felicitas who was in her eighth month of pregnancy. As the day of their execution approached, Felicitas and Perpetua and the other Christian prisoners gathered together to pray that God would deliver her of her child. They had scarcely finished their prayer when Felicitas went into labor. When she shrieked from the pain of the contractions, one of the guards chided her, "If you cry out in pain during childbirth, what will you do when you are thrown to the wild beasts?"

"Now it is I who suffers," Felicitas said, "but then there will be Another in me that will suffer for me because I suffer for Him."

Moments later her baby daughter was born. Felicitas put her in the care of a Christian woman who raised her as her own. By this time, even the chief jailer himself had turned to Christ through the example of Perpetua and her friends. He secretly did all that he could for them. "I found the Lord's kindnesses to be very great," Perpetua said.

In the days leading up to the games, their cell block was full of people—prisoners and visitors—curious to see these Christians who would rather die than give up their faith. "If you do not trust in Christ for the forgiveness of your sins," Saturus told them, "you will one day face the judgment of God. Although we face death in the arena, we are happy for we are in the hands of God."

As more people came to gape at the Christian prisoners, Saturus smiled at them and said, "Tomorrow you will clap your hands at our death and applaud our murderers. But look carefully at our faces that you may recognize them on that terrible day when all men shall be judged."

The onlookers left them, astonished by their courage. Later, several of these people put their trust in Jesus Christ too.

When the day of execution arrived, guards led the Christian prisoners to the arena. An eyewitness reported, "Joy sparkled in their eyes and appeared in all their gestures and words." Perpetua calmly walked with her eyes to the ground. When they reached the gate of the arena, guards tried to force them to wear the clothing of pagan priests and priestesses. Perpetua pushed the pagan garb aside saying, "We came here on our own accord and we will not be forced to do anything contrary to our religion."

The guards relented. Perpetua sang a psalm of praise as they entered the arena. When they walked past the governor's box, one of the Christian men said to him, "You judge us in this world, but God will judge you in the next."

"Scourge them!" the enraged crowd shouted. The governor ordered soldiers to lash each of the Christian prisoners with a whip. After they had received the bloody blows, they huddled together and gave thanks to God that they were counted worthy to suffer in the same way that Christ had suffered before Pilate.

The men died first at the snapping jaws of a bear, a leopard and a wild boar. Then Perpetua and Felicitas faced a raging bull. It hooked Perpetua in its horns and threw her on her back. Perpetua arose and gathered her torn clothes around her. She ran to the aid of Felicitas who had been badly gored. Perpetua helped her to her feet, and they stood together arm-in-arm, expecting another charge of the bull. But guards led the women to a side gate for a time while gladiators entered the arena to fight. A Christian friend brought Perpetua's brother to her. "Stand firm in the faith and love one another," she told him. "Don't be discouraged by my sufferings."

As the games drew to a close, the spectators shouted for the blood of Perpetua and Felicitas. Guards dragged them to the center of the arena again where they died by a gladiator's sword.

Perpetua and Saturus wrote personal accounts of their persecution while in prison, and eyewitnesses wrote descriptions of their martyrdoms. These accounts spread the news of the steadfast faith and the courageous death of Perpetua and her friends, strengthening the resolve of the Christians of North Africa and beyond.

2 CRISPINA
A Clear Conscience for Christ, c. 274–304

The last great wave of Roman persecution against Christians began in 303 under Emperor Diocletian. Diocletian thought that the empire would only survive through a return to Roman traditions and the old pagan religion. So he ordered the destruction of church buildings, the arrest of Christian ministers and the rounding up and burning of all Bibles and Christian books. Finally, as a sign of loyalty to the state, the emperor demanded that Christians offer sacrifices to the Roman gods.

From one end of the empire to the other, tens of thousands of Christians were arrested. Many abandoned their faith under the threat of death, but others remained true to Christ in the face of terrible cruelties. In December 304, Crispina, a beautiful young mother from a prominent family in North Africa, was arrested for refusing to offer pagan sacrifices. Soldiers hauled her before the Roman governor named Anullinus. "You have spurned the laws of our lord the emperor," Anullinus said. "You are required to offer sacrifice to our gods for the welfare of the emperor in accordance with the law."

"I have never sacrificed," Crispina answered, "and I shall not do so—except to the one true God and to our Lord Jesus Christ, his Son, who was born and died."

"Leave your superstitions and submit to the sacred rites of the gods of Rome," the governor said.

"I know of no other gods besides my God, the Almighty One, whom I worship daily."

"You are a stubborn and defiant woman," Anullinus said. "You will soon feel the force of our laws against your will."

Crispina stood unbowed and said, "Whatever happens to me, I shall gladly suffer it for the faith which I hold steadfastly."

"You are insane!" Anullinus shouted, veins bulging in his neck and forehead. "Away with your superstitions—worship the Roman gods."

"Every day I worship," Crispina answered, "but I only worship my Lord, the living and true God, and no other besides Him."

"The emperor's edict must be obeyed!" demanded the governor.

"I will obey the edict," she said, "but the edict that I obey is the one given to me by my Lord Jesus Christ."

"If you do not sacrifice to our gods, if you do not obey the emperor's edict, I shall order your head cut off. You shall be forced to submit. You know very well that the entire province of Africa has offered sacrifice."

"They shall never find it easy to make me offer sacrifice to demons," Crispina said. "I only sacrifice to the Lord who has made heaven and earth and sea and everything in them."

"You blaspheme! You think that our pagan gods are not worthy of you!" the governor sneered. "You shall be forced to honor them if you wish to stay alive to offer any worship at all."

"A religion is worthless which forces people to practice it against their will," Crispina replied.

"Guards," the red-faced governor shouted, "take her, cut off her hair and shave her head. Turn her beauty into shame." The guards pulled her away, did as the governor ordered and brought her back to the council chambers. "Now will you sacrifice to our gods?" he asked.

"I will not," Crispina answered. "I have told you over and over, I am ready to suffer any tortures that you lay upon me rather than dirty my soul with idols which are merely the creation of men."

"If you will not worship our venerable gods," he said, "your head shall be cut off."

"I should be very happy to lose my head for the sake of my God," she said, "for I will not sacrifice to your silly deaf and dumb idols. My God, who lives forever, ordained me to be born. He gave me salvation through the saving waters of baptism. He is at my side, helping me and giving me strength so that I will not commit sacrilege."

"Why must we endure this irreligious Christian woman any longer?" Anullinus said. Then he wrote out his sentence and read it aloud: "Since Crispina has clung to her infamous super- stition and will not offer sacrifice to our gods according to the sacred decrees of the emperor, she shall be put to death with the sword."

The governor ordered that the sentence be carried out at once. As the executioner stepped forward, Crispina said, "I bless God who has chosen to free me from your hands. Thanks be to God!"

Soon after her death, Christians wrote down the account of her martyrdom, and it circulated widely, encouraging believers to hold fast to Christ until the end.

3 MARCELLA OF ROME
Full of Christ, 325–410

Around the year 345, a rich and powerful leader in Rome came courting a young widow named Marcella. Marcella hailed from a wealthy and prominent family—counting Roman senators and consuls among her ancestors. She had married young, but her aristocratic husband died seven months later. "If you will marry me," the Roman ruler said, "I will leave you all my money."

"If I wished to marry," she told him, "I would look for a husband and not an inheritance."

From her earliest days, Marcella trusted in Christ as her Lord and Savior. When the great church leader, Athanasius, came to Rome, he spent time with Marcella's family. He gave her a copy of a book he had written entitled: *The Life of St. Anthony.* Anthony had been a wealthy Roman citizen living in Egypt. His life changed when he read Christ's command in the gospel, "Go, sell all that you have and give to the poor, and you will have treasure in heaven; and come, follow Me."

Anthony sold his estates and gave away all his money to the poor. He retired to the desert to live a solitary life of self-denial and prayer. Although Anthony led a hard life, he lived it rejoicing. "Strangers knew him," Athanasius wrote, "by the joy on his face." Over time, other men gathered around Anthony to learn from him and serve God together.

Inspired by Anthony's example, Marcella decided not to re-marry. She traded her colorful, silk gowns and gold jewelry for a plain brown robe—the clothing of slave women, not the high-born. "Forsaking both wealth and rank," a Christian friend said of Marcella, "she sought the true nobility of poverty and lowliness."

She turned her mansion into a place of prayer and a haven for outcasts. Soon other widows and young unmarried women joined her, forming a community of Christian women dedicated to prayer, Scripture study and service to the poor—one of the first of its kind in the empire. Before long, Marcella had given away all her fortune. "She preferred to store her money in the stomachs of the needy," a friend said, "rather than hide it in a purse."

Marcella knew the Bible well and had mastered Greek—the language of the New Testament. "Her delight in the divine Scriptures was incredible," her minister observed. "She was always singing from Psalm 119, 'Your words have I hidden in my heart that I might not sin against You.'"

Knowing that Christians are called to strive, by the grace of God, to obey the Scriptures, Marcella trained her companions to know God's Word and to seek to obey it. She made it a point to live each hour in light of eternity, teaching her followers to daily present themselves as living sacrifices to God. "She lived always," one observer said, "in the thought that she must die."

In 382, Jerome, the famous theologian and Bible scholar, came to Rome to begin work on a new translation of the Scriptures into Latin. Marcella asked Jerome to teach her the Word of God. At first he refused, but her persistence, like waves lapping on the seashore, won him over. For three years in Rome, Jerome translated several books of the Bible and met, almost daily, with Marcella. "She never came without asking something about Scripture," Jerome said, "nor did she immediately accept my explanation as satisfactory, but she proposed questions from the opposite viewpoint—not for argument's sake—but to learn answers to objections that she perceived could be raised."

She made rapid progress in her understanding of the Scriptures under his instruction. Jerome marveled at how quickly she learned. "What had been for me the fruit of long study and meditation," he said, "she learned and made her own."

Jerome praised Marcella to others, calling her "a student of the Scriptures—a woman of virtue, ability and holiness."

Jerome was well known for his sharp tongue that lashed out at his critics. Marcella gently exposed his sinful temper and lack of charity. In one letter to her, he harshly criticized those who disagreed with him. "I know that as you read these words," he wrote, "you will knit your brows and worry that my freedom of speech is sowing the seeds of fresh quarrels. If you could, you would gladly put your finger on my mouth to prevent me from even speaking."

After Jerome left Rome to continue his translation work in Syria and Palestine, some preachers began to spread heresies among the Roman Christians. Marcella took the lead in shining the light of God's Word on their dark, unscriptural teaching. She called the false teachers to account and rallied church leaders to defend the faith. Jerome followed the conflict with great interest from afar. When the heretics were vanquished, he wrote, "This glorious victory began with Marcella—she was the source and cause of this great blessing."

In the later years of Marcella's life, the Roman Empire began to collapse as marauding tribes chipped away at the frontiers. Then in 410, the Visigoths, a Germanic tribe, overran Rome and ransacked the city. Visigoth warriors broke into Marcella's home, demanding she give them her jewels and treasure. "They have long since been sold to aid the poor," she told them. Tugging on her coarse dress, she said, "This is the extent of my earthly treasure now."

The intruders pulled Marcella away from her young disciple Principia. They whipped Marcella and beat her bloody with clubs, threatening to do the same to Principia if she did not reveal the whereabouts of her valuables. She fell at the soldiers' feet and begged them not to harm Principia. All the while she prayed for God to soften their hearts. Then suddenly the men stopped beating Marcella and hauled her and Principia away to a church for safety. With tears of joy, she prayed, "O Lord, I give you thanks for protecting Principia and answering my prayers."

In the wake of the Visigoth raid, famine stalked the land like a ravenous wolf. Marcella and her friends were homeless—without food or supplies. Although severely wounded, Marcella thanked God for His mercy. "By heaven's grace," she said, "the invasion has found me a poor woman, not made me one."

Marcella's injuries broke her health. She quickly lost strength, but she never stopped smiling. Her sisters in Christ kept vigil over her. Shortly before she died, Marcella told her friends, "Now I go without daily bread, but I shall not feel hunger since I am full of Christ."

4 MONICA
The Mother of These Tears, c. 335–390

I n 370 in North Africa, a Christian mother knelt, weeping in prayer for her son. As Monica's streaming tears wet the ground, she cried out to God. "Heavenly Father, preserve Augustine's heart for great waves of temptation threaten to destroy him. O Lord, that he might live before your eyes."

A few weeks earlier, she had acquiesced to her husband Patrick's plan to send their sixteen-year-old son Augustine to school in Carthage, the largest city in the province. "Our small town is no place to educate a boy of these talents," he had said. "He must become cultured to do great things."

Monica's pagan husband could not understand her concerns for her son's faith as he encountered a sinful city far from home. Monica alone raised Augustine to love and serve Christ. While sitting on her lap he had heard the good news of Jesus Christ and learned the songs of praise that she sang to the Savior of her soul. Through all her instruction and prayer for him, she held fast to the promise of God's Word: "Train up a child in the way he should go and when he is old he will not depart from it" (Prov. 22:6).

As Augustine packed for Carthage, Monica urged him to cling to Christ and live a holy life. But once away from home in an exciting city of the Roman Empire, the temptations to sin swept him away like a leaf in a raging river. Though he dearly loved his mother, he leapt into the wicked ways of his new friends. "I despised my mother's advice and went headlong on my way," Augustine later admitted.

When not studying, he filled his days with stealing, carousing, watching evil entertainments and sins of every kind. "I plunged into the filth and wallowed in it," Augustine said. "I even used to pretend that I had committed sins which I had not done in order to impress my friends."

Rejecting Christianity, Augustine embraced the popular philosophies of the day and grew proud. "I will make a great name for myself," he said.

Seized with fear at such news, Monica warned him, "My son, I fear the crooked path you are walking, for that way is walked by those who turn their backs toward God and not their faces."

Seeking out her bishop for help, Monica pleaded, "Will you please speak to Augustine? Show him the errors of his ways, and teach him what is good."

The bishop shook his head for he knew well Augustine's heart and mind at the time. "He is not yet ready to be taught," the bishop told her. "He is full of self-conceit with the novelty of these new ideas. But leave him alone for a while. Only pray to the Lord for him; he himself will find out by his reading what his mistake is and how great is its sinfulness."

Monica, unwilling to take no for an answer, wept, gripped the bishop's hand like a starving beggar and implored him to speak with Augustine. "No," he said firmly. "Now go away and leave me. It cannot be that the son of these tears should perish."

The bishop's words, "It cannot be that the son of these tears should perish," sounded to her as if they had come from heaven. Monica wept and prayed for Augustine, never losing hope that God would save his soul. "Augustine," she often told him, "the son of these tears shall not perish."

Her wayward son was not the only challenge that Monica faced in her family. Patrick, although generally kind, had a quick and violent temper. At times he lashed out at his wife, children and servants with cruel words. He walked in the ways of his pagan religion and failed in countless ways to be a faithful husband to Monica. But she bore it with patience and grace, seeking to point him to the living God. "She tried to win him to you," Augustine later wrote in a prayer, "speaking to him of you by her virtues through which you made her beautiful, so that her husband loved, respected and admired her."

Monica prayed as fervently for her husband's salvation as she did for her son's. And God granted her request. Over time, Patrick became willing to hear his wife tell him about Jesus Christ and the eternal life that he promises to all who come to him. To her great joy and thanksgiving, Patrick finally put his trust in Christ, repented of his sins, made a public profession of his faith and was baptized. And this came in the nick of time because a short time later he died suddenly.

Once, in the midst of Monica's deep grief over the state of her son's soul, she had a dream. In the dream, Monica was weeping and standing on a large wooden ruler, when a shining youth, smiling and joyful, approached her. "What is the matter?" the shining one asked. Monica told him that she was bewailing her son's rebellion against God and his headlong rush to hell. "Rest contented," he told her, "where you are, there your son is also." Then Monica looked up and saw Augustine standing near her on the wooden ruler. She awoke from her dream with renewed confidence that God would rescue her son from his rebellion.

The years passed and Augustine became a respected teacher, but he continued to reject the Lord. At age thirty, he moved from North Africa to Milan in Italy to become one of the head instructors of the city, bringing his widowed mother with him. At that time, the great preacher Ambrose was the Bishop of Milan. Augustine went to hear his sermons, not because he wanted to know Jesus, but to listen to his eloquent words. Augustine told Ambrose that he did not believe in Christ. To Augustine's surprise, Ambrose accepted him in love. "That man welcomed me as a father," Augustine said. "I began to love him first not as a teacher of the truth but simply as a man who was kind and generous to me."

Gradually, Augustine began to hear the truth of God in Ambrose's sermons, and he started to read the Bible himself. A friend gave him a book on the life of St. Anthony, and Augustine saw how the grace of God could transform a person. Through it all, Monica prayed for his salvation and urged him to trust in Christ.

As Augustine's doubts about the truth of Christianity faded, fears rushed in to take their place—fears that his many sins could never be forgiven. One day, overcome with guilt, he went into the garden to pour his heart out to God. Suddenly, a storm rose up within his heart, bringing with it a downpour of tears. To avoid embarrassment, he ran alone to the far end of the garden, flung himself down under a fig tree and cried out to God. "How long,

O Lord? Will You be angry with me forever? O Lord, do not remember my many sins."

While Augustine wept and prayed he heard the voice of a child singing the words, "Pick up and read. Pick up and read." He had never heard a children's song with those words before. Taking it as a message from God to read the Scriptures, he grabbed his Bible, opened it at random and read the first verses he saw: "Let us walk properly as in the daytime, not in orgies and drunkenness, not in sexual immorality and sensuality, not in quarreling and jealousy. But put on the Lord Jesus Christ, and make no provision for the flesh, to gratify its desires" (Rom. 13:13 and 14).

At once God opened Augustine's eyes to see that only Christ's goodness could cover his sins. He did not read any further; he did not need to. The Lord had changed his heart. He praised God for the forgiveness of his sins and the gift of faith. "When I read the verse," Augustine said, "it was as though my heart was filled with a light of confidence in Christ and all the shadows of my doubt were swept away."

He rushed inside and told Monica. Overjoyed, she threw her arms around her son saying, "This is what I have prayed for all these years." With eyes brimming with tears, she lifted her hands to heaven and prayed, "Praise to you, O Lord; for you are able to do far more than we can even imagine. You have turned my mourning into joy."

From that day an overpowering hunger gripped Augustine to know the Bible and worship God. "I can't have enough of the sweetness of meditating upon the depth of Your Word," he prayed. "What tears I shed in your hymns and how I am moved by your sweet singing church!"

Dressed in a white robe, Augustine was baptized by Ambrose along with many other converts in a candle-lit, Easter-eve service. He resigned his teaching job in Milan to serve God back in North Africa. One evening as they were preparing to leave, Monica and Augustine talked late into the night. "The greatest delights on earth," Monica said with a broad smile, "cannot be compared with the joys of heaven."

"As we talked of God and eternal life with the saints," Augustine later wrote, "our hearts thirsted for the heavenly streams—it was as if we had lightly touched the first fruits of the Spirit in heaven."

"My son," Monica said looking long into his eyes, "I don't know why I am still here on this earth. The only reason I wanted to stay a little longer in this life was to see you become a Christian before I died. Now God has granted me this beyond my hopes; for I see that you despise the pleasures of this world and have become God's servant."

A few days later, she fell deathly ill. "You may lay this body of mine anywhere," she told Augustine and the others holding vigil at her bed. "Do not worry at all about that."

"Aren't you afraid to die and be buried so far from home?" someone asked her.

Lifting her head she answered in a weak voice, "Nothing is far from God."

Augustine knelt by her bedside, his head bowed and his eyes welling with tears. He held her hand and prayed until her spirit slipped away to be with God. "I closed her eyes," Augustine said, "and a great flood of sorrow swept into my heart."

After burying his mother, Augustine returned to North Africa and eventually became the most important leader of the church in that region. Using the Word of God as his sword, he fought many battles against false teachers in the church.

For the last forty years of his life, Augustine taught, preached, organized charities for the poor and wrote books in defense of Christianity. His book, *The Confessions*, tells the story of his life, the influence of his mother and the saving love of Jesus Christ. The entire book is a prayer to God, making it clear that he owed his salvation to the grace and mercy of God alone. "O Lord," he wrote, "You have made us for Yourself and our hearts are restless until they rest in You."

Throughout his long life, Augustine never stopped showing people the way to Christ, and he always thanked the Lord for his mother. "God of my heart," he said, "I joyfully thank you for all those good deeds of my mother—for they were your gift to me to save and guide me. For in her body I was born into the light of time, and in her heart I was born into the light of eternity."

5 NONNA AND ANTHUSA
"What Remarkable Women are Found Among the Christians!" c. 330–374 and c. 347–407

After the first few centuries of Christianity's spread across the Roman world, the greatest growth in the church came from the nurture of the children in her midst. As always, the day-to-day task of bringing children their first impressions of faith in Christ has fallen primarily to Christian mothers. In the fourth century, Anthusa raised her son John and Nonna raised her son Gregory to become great leaders in the church. They, in turn, drew thousands to the Savior.

NONNA

Nonna rejoiced and thanked the Lord. Her husband Gregory had just told her that he believed in Jesus Christ. God had used the sweet persuasion and godly character of his wife to lead him to Christ. Now Nonna had a Christian spouse to help her raise their children in the Lord. Gregory became an officer in his local church, and then he was ordained a minister. Eventually, he was consecrated Bishop of Nazianzus, a city in the Roman province of Cappadocia. He held this position for nearly fifty years.

When Nonna was pregnant with their son—named Gregory after his father—she asked God to protect and consecrate the baby in her womb for His service. Shortly after Gregory was born, Nonna took his tiny hands, placed them on the Bible and prayed like Hannah prayed regarding her son Samuel. "O Lord, I give him to you. For his whole life he will be given over to the Lord."

Nonna toiled like a farmer in a field to plant and water the seeds of faith in her children, instructing them in the Scriptures, singing psalms and praying earnestly for their hearts and minds. She strove to draw her children to Christ and rested on God's promise: "I will be a God to you and to your children after you." "Her highest joy for her children," Gregory said, "was that they should be acknowledged and named by Christ."

Her husband joined her in the work. "My parents were lovers of their children and of Christ," their son Gregory said. "What is most extraordinary, they were far greater lovers of Christ than of their children. They sowed in us the seeds of piety."

Although she was a busy mother raising her children and managing her household, Nonna tried to live minute by minute in the presence of the Lord. "She applied herself to God and divine things," Gregory said, "as closely as if absolutely released from household care."

In a world where women of her class spent great sums of money on clothes, jewelry and cosmetics, Nonna sought loveliness in other things. "She acknowledged but one kind of beauty," her son said, "the beauty of the soul."

Young Gregory followed in his father's footsteps and became the Bishop of Nazianzus. His fame as a preacher and theologian spread far and wide. At that time, the church was fighting in a great battle over the deity and humanity of Christ. Gregory boldly proclaimed the Scripture truth that Christ is fully God and fully man. Through his preaching and writing, he helped to anchor the church on the rock of God's Word and became one of the most important church leaders of his day. Incredibly, all three of Nonna's children were later proclaimed saints by the church.

For the rest of his life, Gregory never stopped praising his mother and thanking God for her. "What a woman she was!" he said. "Not even the Atlantic Ocean could contain her great and boundless love and generosity."

ANTHUSA

Around the year 367 in Antioch, Anthusa clung to her baby and wept. Her husband had just died—shortly after the birth of their son John. Anthusa was not destitute because she came from a family of means and her husband had left an inheritance for her and their son. As an attractive, well-to-do, twenty-year-old widow, Anthusa had many men vying for her hand in marriage. At that time, it was expected that young widows would remarry to enjoy the protection of a husband. Her parents pleaded with her to accept a marriage proposal, but she refused. Anthusa wanted to devote herself completely to the Christian nurture of her son. "I have braved the storm and remained firm amidst all the opposition I have met with," she said.

It wasn't easy managing a household and raising a boy as a single parent. "How great is a mother's responsibility for her son," she said. "Not a day passes, but she trembles for him." Anthusa wanted her son's bright mind to be trained by the finest teachers, but first and foremost she wanted him to know the Scriptures. She read the Word of God to him daily and taught him to sing psalms of praise. Antioch in Syria, a large and prosperous city, had some of the finest teachers in the Roman Empire. Anthusa arranged for John to study rhetoric under Libanius, one of the greatest orators of the age.

John became Libanius's most accomplished student and went on to start a career in law, impressing everyone in court with his quick wit and eloquence. John was on the fast track to fame and fortune, but his conscience—shaped by his mother's teaching through the Holy Spirit—recoiled from the corruption of the courts. Longing to serve God full time, he quit practicing law. Anthusa was delighted that John had given up a law career because she had long prayed that he would devote his talents to the Christian church.

When one of John's friends became a monk, he persuaded John to follow him. So John decided to live in the wilderness as a hermit to study the Scriptures and pray. But Anthusa could not bear the thought of losing the company of her son. She begged him with tears not to leave her. "Thanks to the help of God," she told him, "I have spared nothing in my power to smooth the rugged path of life for you. The only gratitude I ask of you is not to reopen the wound of grief from the loss of your father. Don't leave me until you have closed my eyes in death and have laid my remains by the side of those of your father."

John honored his mother's request and remained with her until she died a short time later. With an unwavering commitment to the Scriptures and holy living, John became a monk and then a preacher and then Bishop of Constantinople. His Christ-centered, biblical sermons made him the most popular preacher in the empire. "By the cross," he preached, "we know the gravity of sin and the greatness of God's love toward us." His eloquence in the pulpit earned him the nickname *Chrysostom* which means "Golden Mouth."

Although John never married, he taught his congregation the great importance of the Christian family and the nurture of children—especially training them in the Word of God as Anthusa had done for him. "Your child will naturally sing the songs of Satan," John preached, "but teach him to sing those psalms which are so full of the love of wisdom. When in these you have led him on from childhood, little by little, you will lead him forward even to the higher things."

"From the very first," John told his flock, "bring your son up in the nurture and admonition of the Lord. Never think it an unnecessary thing that he should be a diligent hearer of the Holy Scriptures. Never say, 'This is the business of monks.' Make him a Christian! It is absurd to send children out to trades and to school and to do all you can for these objectives, and yet, not make them from the earliest age apply themselves to the reading of the Scriptures."

His old teacher Libanius, an outspoken pagan, mourned the fact that John used his great speaking skills to preach Christ. When Libanius was asked on his deathbed who ought to succeed him, he said, "John would have been my first choice had not the Christians stolen him from us."

Although Libanius despised Christians, Anthusa's devotion to God and to her son made such an impression on him that he was heard to say, "Good heavens! What remarkable women are found among the Christians!"

6   BRIGID
Pillar of the Irish, c. 451–c. 523

B y the middle of the fifth century, the good news of Jesus Christ spread rapidly across Ireland. Patrick and his disciples planted churches and monasteries throughout the island. Among those who turned to Christ was Tubtach, a Celtic chieftain from the kingdom of Leinster in central Ireland. Although his whole family became Christians and were baptized, the Holy Spirit moved most powerfully in the heart of his daughter Brigid. Overflowing with gratitude for Christ's love for her, a wretched sinner, Brigid sympathized with the sick and the poor. She readily gave away milk, butter and bread to the needy—much to the irritation of her father who thought she was overly generous with the family's food supplies. When she gave Tubtach's prize sword to a beggar, he hauled his daughter before the king of Leinster to have him straighten her out. "Why do you give away so much to the poor?" the king asked Brigid.

"Jesus Christ knows," she answered, "that if I had your power and the control of all your wealth, I would give it all away for the Lord's sake."

When Brigid was about eighteen years old, Tubtach arranged to have her marry a well-to-do nobleman of the clan. But Brigid refused, saying that she wanted to serve God as a nun. Her parents and brothers cajoled, argued and threatened her, but try as they might, they could not talk her out of it. "I have chosen Christ to be my spouse," she insisted. Eventually, she left home to live a life set apart for God. At that time in Ireland, Patrick had only established monasteries for men—there were no religious communities for women.

So Brigid left Leinster and struck out on her own. Soon seven like-minded young women joined her in a life of prayer and Christian service. They sought out a bishop to consecrate them for the work. After vowing to serve the Lord and pledging their union to Christ alone, they received the veil at the hands of the bishop as a symbol of their submission to Christ. A white veil covered Brigid's golden hair for the rest of her life. The women donned white robes and set out to show the love and compassion of Jesus Christ to all, especially to the sick and the poor.

Before long, the people of Leinster, impressed by their good work, urged the women to live among them. The chieftains invited Brigid to choose a spot for an abbey. She selected a plot of ground in a fertile plain where a large oak tree stood. The women built small huts out of twigs and clay. Each hut—or cell as they were called—housed one woman. Brigid built her cell under the green canopy of the oak tree. People started calling their little community Kildare which means "the cell of the oak." They planted a garden and, with the gift of some livestock, began raising cows, sheep and pigs in the lush pastures that surrounded them.

Kildare became a refuge for the poor. "Christ lives in the person of the poor who has faith," Brigid said. They shared what little they had with those who came in need. No one was turned away empty-handed. If the sick and poor were unable to come to Kildare, then Brigid went out to them, bringing firewood, food and a helping hand.

Once, the bishop invited Brigid and her seven companions to a banquet. As the food was being served, Brigid said to the bishop, "Father, please refresh our minds with spiritual food before we partake of this earthly meal."

The bishop spoke on the eight beatitudes from Christ's Sermon on the Mount. When he finished, Brigid said to her nuns, "My dearly beloved sisters in Christ, we are eight in number and eight virtues are proposed to us for our sanctification. Let each one of us select a particular beatitude for special devotion."

Her friends liked the idea, and one of them turned to Brigid and asked, "Sister, would you please be the first to choose one of the virtues to seek?"

"Mercy," Brigid said, "because without mercy all of the other virtues are of little account."

After each of the nuns had chosen a beatitude to pursue, the bishop offered thanks to God, and they all enjoyed the feast. From that day forward, Brigid and her sisters never ate a meal until they had first nourished their souls from the Scriptures.

Over time, many pious women—highborn ladies and peasant girls—joined them. Brigid loved the sisters like members of her own family. They called her "mother." She was a natural leader who corrected their faults with gentle words in private. "She never spoke ill of anyone," the sisters reported.

Brigid strove to keep her mind on her Savior throughout each day. "O Christ," she prayed, "we implore you by the memory of your holy and bitter anguish on the cross, make us fear you, make us love you." She was constantly speaking of the love of Christ and thinking of him as she worked the gardens, herded the sheep or offered hospitality to the needy. "Sisters," she said, "let us live so as to make a feast for Jesus in our hearts."

Brigid kept the purpose of the abbey simple. "I would like Jesus to be present," she said, "and cheerfulness to preside over all."

At Kildare, the poor found a friend in their distress. "I would like the poor to be gathered around us," Brigid told the sisters. She gave away food and clothing so often to the needy that she made her nuns worried. "O Mother," they said, "through your generosity, we quickly lose whatever God gives us through charitable Christians or our own labors. You often leave us nothing."

"Give earthly things to God's children," Brigid said, "and he will return you earthly and heavenly favors."

Once, Brigid and her sisters prepared to host a great feast at the abbey. They invited many guests from near and far. But before the guests had arrived, hungry beggars came to the gate. Brigid gave them all the food intended for the banquet. "Mother," one sister asked, "why did you do this? How will we feed all the people coming to the feast?"

"God will provide," Brigid answered. Then she led the sisters in prayer, asking the Lord to meet their needs. It so happened that a rich farmer who lived a short distance from the abbey had loaded several wagons with food to bring to the king. Having lost his way, he found himself at the gate of the abbey. Brigid greeted the man who was dumbfounded that he had gotten lost so close to his home. "It was in God's providence," the farmer said, "that

I strayed out of my way and to your house even though I'm well acquainted with the countryside. I believe that God meant this food for the abbey." He led his horse-drawn wagons into the abbey courtyard, and the grinning sisters unloaded the supplies.

"I will return home and prepare other provisions for the king," he said. When the king heard about what had happened, he sent another wagon load of food to the abbey. And so the sisters had far more than they needed for the feast.

One time, Brigid was riding on the road in the abbey's wagon pulled by two horses. She passed a poor man and his wife and children toiling along with heavy burdens on their backs. Brigid stopped and promptly gave the man her horses and wagon. She walked back to Kildare rejoicing.

Brigid's abbey was no place for idleness and self-indulgence. The women prayed and worked hard. They tended gardens, herded livestock, milked cows, churned butter, made cheese, cut firewood and cared for the sick. They spun wool and sewed clothes for themselves and the poor. They taught the neighborhood children to read and write. Brigid's nuns hand copied the Scriptures and Christian books. They developed great skill in the Celtic art of illuminating manuscripts—adding elaborate and colorful illustrations to the text.

The works of mercy and kindness performed by the sisters of Kildare shone like sunbeams in a dark and cruel age. In those days, Ireland was divided into many little kingdoms that warred against one another constantly. The frequent battles led to the enslavement of defeated men, women and children. Brigid often interceded with chieftains to get hostages and slaves released—sometimes paying the ransom from gifts given to the abbey. She won the respect of the violent clansmen who were used to settling arguments with the sword. At times, Brigid skillfully played the role of a peacemaker between warring clans.

Kings and bishops across Ireland asked her to start abbeys in their districts. Through the years she founded more than thirty houses for women where the white-robed sisters served the poor and shed the light of Christ in their communities. Brigid followed the pattern set by Patrick by establishing schools in each abbey. Countless boys and girls received instruction in the Christian faith and arts and letters. The foundation laid by Patrick's brothers and Brigid's sisters led to Ireland's reputation as "The Island of Saints and Scholars."

Of all the saints of God who served Christ in Ireland through the centuries, Patrick and Brigid have remained the closest to the people's hearts. Together they are known as "The Pillars of Ireland."

MIDDLE AGES

THRONE ROOMS AND CLOISTERS

During the Middle Ages (c. 500–1500) God used Christian queens sitting on barbarian thrones to lead whole nations to Christ. Clotilda's role in the conversion of the Franks tread a path that her great granddaughter Bertha and many other godly queens followed, adorning the gospel to their pagan husbands and people.

Women like Leoba who forsook marriage to serve as nuns were instrumental in the conversion of unbelievers. Then they taught the new Christians and their children the Scriptures. Their abbeys became centers of comfort for the sick and care for the poor.

Far more important for the growth of the church than queens and nuns were countless unsung Christian mothers. Sometimes they had the help of their husbands to bring their children to living faith in Christ and sometimes they toiled alone. They did their work in an age when the medieval church grew in numbers but became entangled in false traditions and unbiblical practices.

CLOTILDA, QUEEN OF THE FRANKS
A Servant of God, c.474–545

I n 493, nineteen-year-old Queen Clotilda cradled her lifeless infant son in her arms, weeping and praying. Just hours after he was baptized, the baby suddenly died while still wearing the white baptismal robe. Her husband Clovis, the pagan king of the Franks, had agreed to Clotilda's request that their first-born child be baptized. Then Clovis came to her, his eyes red and his teeth clenched. Pointing at his wife he said, "Your God is the cause of our son's death. If he had been consecrated to my gods, he would still be alive."

"I give thanks to Almighty God," Clotilda said through her tears, "that He has not considered me unworthy to be the mother of a child admitted into His heavenly kingdom. He will rejoice in the presence of God through all eternity."

A year later, she gave birth to their second son. Reluctantly, Clovis allowed him to be baptized. But a few days after his baptism, he fell gravely ill. As the baby grew weaker and weaker, Clovis told his wife, "Can we expect any other fate for this child than that of his brother? He was baptized in the name of *your* Christ, he is certain therefore to die."

Clotilda did not answer her husband, but bowed her head in prayer, begging God to spare the child's life. Not long afterward—to the relief of both parents—the baby recovered. Clotilda thanked the Lord, and Clovis stopped criticizing his wife's faith. This was the first step on the road to the conversion of the Franks.

Clotilda, the daughter of a Burgundian king, was raised by her mother, Caretena, to love and fear the Lord. Caretena taught Clotilda and her siblings to read the Scriptures, pray, fast and do works of mercy. When her husband died, Queen Caretena brought Clotilda and her sister to the court of her relative, the King of Geneva. He became the guardian of the two princesses. Caretena and her daughters became well known for their kindness and generosity to the poor of Geneva.

Envoys from King Clovis often came to the court of Geneva. They brought back to the young king glowing reports of Clotilda's beauty and her sterling character. Soon Clovis asked for Clotilda's hand in marriage. It must have been flattering to the young princess to receive an offer of marriage from the most powerful king in Western Europe. But Clovis was a pagan—could Clotilda in good conscience marry someone who was not a follower of Christ? The King of Geneva told her to marry Clovis as an important political alliance. She and her mother sought out their bishop for counsel. He advised her to accept the proposal under the condition that she have the freedom to practice her Christian faith and raise their children to be Christians. He challenged her to consider what great things might come if she could lead her husband to faith in Christ. "The unbelieving husband is sanctified by the believing wife," he said, quoting the Apostle Paul.

In 492, they were married in a lavish ceremony at Clovis's court in Soissons. Later, he made Paris his capital. A deep affection quickly grew between them. Clotilda's cheerful spirit and tact won her husband's admiration. Gently and patiently, she told him of the love of Jesus Christ for sinners. "I beseech you above all things," she said, "to adore God Almighty who is in heaven."

"You ask that I should forsake my gods and adore yours," he told her, "that is a difficult thing to do."

After four years of marriage, Clovis still clung to his idols, but Clotilda kept speaking to him and praying to God for his salvation. Then King Clovis led his troops in battle against the Allemanni, a fierce Germanic tribe living on the banks of the Rhine River. Clovis wielded his sword at the head of his men as the two great armies clashed. Soon, the Allemanni gained the upper hand and forced the Franks to pull back. Many Franks fell. Some began to run from the field. Clovis knew that if his army suffered defeat his whole kingdom would fall. Then, when all seemed lost, Clovis remembered his wife's God, Jesus Christ the victor over sin and death. In his despair he cried out, "Jesus Christ, You who are, according to Clotilda, the Son of the living God, I call on You. Help me in my distress. I desire to believe in You. Rescue me from my enemies."

Moments later, fresh courage reinvigorated his men. Clovis regrouped his troops and charged. In the desperate fighting that followed, they killed the Allemanni king. Seeing their leader dead on the field, the Allemanni soldiers broke ranks and ran. Those who did not surrender, the Franks cut down. Clovis's stunning victory was complete.

When he returned triumphant from the battlefield, Clovis told Clotilda what had happened. She rejoiced more in her husband's budding faith than in the victory. Seizing the moment, she sent for Bishop Remi to instruct the king in the Christian faith. Meeting in secret, Remi taught the king the fundamentals of Christianity. "Stop worshiping idols," he said, "repent and turn to the living and true God, creator of all things and to Jesus Christ His Son."

"I'm ready to listen to you," Clovis said, "but my followers will not forsake their gods."

He was concerned that, should he leave the gods of his people, his faithful bodyguard—the cream of his army and the core of his support—would fall away. Clovis was bound to these brave men by blood oaths of loyalty taken in the names of their gods. He feared that if he declared his allegiance to Christ, his men would abandon him and he would lose the throne. "I must speak to them about this," he told the bishop.

Clovis called a meeting of his closest advisors and his leading warriors. He told them of his battlefield prayer to Clotilda's God. "I am considering forsaking the gods of our fathers and following Christ," he said. "What do you think?"

To his surprise, most of his men declared that they were ready to follow him in the new faith. Bishop Remi arranged for Christian ministers to teach these men and their families. On Christmas Day 496, Clovis and three thousand Franks marched in procession through the streets of Reims to the cathedral. Clotilda, her face beaming, walked beside her husband. Every house along the route displayed ornate banners. Embroidered linens stretched across the street, creating a colorful canopy for the marchers. Dignitaries, whom Clovis invited from across his realm, witnessed his baptism in the crowded cathedral. The sanctuary glowed with the light from thousands of candles and the aroma of incense filled the air. As a hymn sung by a great choir echoed through the church, Clovis turned to Bishop Remi and asked, "Is this the kingdom of heaven that you promised me?"

"No," answered the bishop, "but it is the beginning of the road that leads there."

Then he asked the king, "Do you renounce Satan and all his works and all his empty promises?"

"I do," Clovis answered.

"Do you believe in God, the Father Almighty, creator of heaven and earth?"

"I do."

"Do you believe in Jesus Christ, His only Son, our Lord, who was born of the Virgin Mary, was crucified, died, and was buried, rose from the dead, and is now seated at the right hand of the Father?"

"I do," Clovis replied.

"Do you believe in the Holy Spirit, the holy catholic church, the communion of saints, the forgiveness of sins, the resurrection of the body, and life everlasting?"

"I do."

"God, the all-powerful Father of our Lord Jesus Christ has given us a new birth by water and the Holy Spirit and forgiven all our sins," the bishop prayed. "May He also keep us faithful to our Lord Jesus Christ for ever and ever."

After Remi baptized Clovis in the name of the Father and the Son and the Holy Spirit, a cadre of Christian ministers came forward and baptized three thousand of the king's followers. The conversion of Clovis and his kingdom to Christianity proved to be a milestone in the life of the church. Now the greatest kingdom in Europe supported the work of Christian missionaries and ministers. Hundreds of churches and monasteries sprung up throughout the land—many founded by gifts from Clotilda and Clovis.

Despite Clovis's confession of faith in Christ, he remained an aggressive warrior-king who often attacked friendly, peaceful neighbors to expand his empire. On several occasions, he resorted to treachery against his own Frankish relatives to extend his rule over all of Gaul. In 511, King Clovis died, leaving his wife a widow before she reached the age of forty. Clotilda left Paris and made her home in Tours. After her husband's death, Clotilda suffered many great trials and disappointments. According to the custom of the Franks, the kingdom was divided among his three sons. They would eventually wage war against one another, and even put to death some of their own nephews—Clotilda's grandsons.

In her widowhood, Clotilda put aside her silk robes and donned plain clothes. She no longer attended royal banquets, but ate simple fare and shared her possessions with the poor. "Queen Clotilda conducted herself in a way to be honored by all," an early chronicler wrote. "She gave alms without ceasing and passed her nights in prayer. She appeared to be not a queen, but in very truth a servant of God."

"All of Christian Europe owes a debt of gratitude to Clotilda," one Christian historian wrote. "The conversion of the Franks planted the church in the very center of Europe and fixed its doctrines and traditions in the hearts of the people."

Some of Clotilda's descendants followed in her faithful footsteps. Her great granddaughter Bertha and her great-great-granddaughter Ethelburga both married pagan kings, and both won their husbands and their subjects for Christ.

8   BERTHA
England's First Christian Queen,
c. 550–c. 606

I n 596 in Burgundy, Francia, forty monks and their leader Augustine cowered in fear. Several months earlier, Gregory, the Bishop of Rome, sent them to bring the good news of Jesus Christ to the Angles and Saxons of Britain. But as the monks made their way across the Kingdom of the Franks, they heard frightening tales of the cruel, barbaric pagans of Britain. "They are a violent people," they said to one another. "As soon as we set foot on their shore we'll be killed! The prudent thing to do is to go back to Rome."

All the men agreed to stop their journey and send Augustine back to Gregory to request that he recall them from their dangerous mission. When Augustine arrived in Rome, Gregory challenged him to look to Christ and face his fears. "Carry on!" Gregory told him. "Trust yourselves to God and to His aid."

Gregory sent Augustine back with a letter to encourage his companions. "My very dear sons," Gregory wrote, "it is better never to undertake any high enterprise than to abandon it when once begun. So with the help of God you must carry out this holy task which you have begun. Do not be deterred by the troubles of the journey or by what men say. Be constant and zealous in carrying out this enterprise."

Strengthened in faith, Augustine and his brothers trekked across the Kingdom of the Franks to the Atlantic coast. As they went they heard more horror stories of the violent Anglo-Saxons, but they got one bit of good news—Ethelbert, the pagan king of Kent, a kingdom in southeast Britain, had a Christian wife.

Several years earlier, Ethelbert had visited the royal court in Paris and fallen in love with and proposed marriage to Bertha, a princess from the Frankish royal house. Bertha was renowned for two things: her beauty and her devotion to Jesus Christ. At first Bertha and her family rejected the match because Ethelbert was not a Christian. But Ethelbert would not take no for an answer, and he continued to press the King of the Franks for Bertha's hand. The king finally consented under the condition that Bertha—as Queen of Kent—would have complete freedom to openly profess her faith in Christ and attend Christian worship.

Bertha left Paris with her female attendants and Luidhard, her Christian minister. She prayed that God would use her to bring the message of Christ's love to the Anglo-Saxons. Bertha must have often thought of her great grandmother Clotilda, a Christian princess, who married Clovis, the great king of the Franks, and led him to faith in Christ.

During the three hundred years that Britain was a Roman province, Christianity had spread throughout the southern half of the island. But when Roman troops withdrew around A.D. 400, the land was attacked and overrun by Angles and Saxons, Germanic tribes from northern Europe. The invaders destroyed churches and tried to rid the land of any remnant of its Christian heritage. Some Christians fled west and carried on their faith in the mountains and gorges of Wales.

The Anglo-Saxons believed in gods of thunder and rain and waters. They held that the natural world teemed with elves, fairies and dragons. Their chief god, Woden, reigned over war and death. Before battle, Ethelbert and his warriors offered animal sacrifices to Woden.

It must have been a great challenge for Bertha—a well-educated Christian princess who read classical philosophers, poets and the Church Fathers in Greek and Latin—to be married to a pagan and superstitious king.

Before Bertha arrived, King Ethelbert ordered workmen to repair a little ruined Christian church on a hill not far from the royal palace in Canterbury for her use. Bertha named it in honor of St. Martin. For many years, she performed her duties as a loving wife to her husband and mother to their children. Her gentleness and wisdom won Ethelbert's heart as well as his admiration and respect. Several times a week she and her court would worship in St. Martin's, a small Christian spark in the midst of a dark land.

Then, in the spring of 597, Augustine and his monks sailed across the English Channel to Kent. They landed on a small island separated from the mainland by the mouth of a river. Augustine brought interpreters from France who sent word to King Ethelbert, "We have come from Rome bearing very happy news which gives to all who receive it eternal joy in heaven with the living and true God."

No doubt Bertha entreated her husband to welcome the Christian men. "These are holy men, bearing good news—listen to them, be generous and kind to them for my sake."

King Ethelbert ordered the missionaries to wait on the island, believing that the river would protect his land from their magical powers. After several days, Ethelbert arrived with a company of warriors. He commanded the monks to cross the river for an outdoor meeting. Augustine and his men, dressed in black robes with wide sleeves, approached the king carrying a silver cross and a painting of Jesus Christ. They knelt and offered prayer to God and sang a hymn praising their Lord for eternal life. Then the king, wearing a purple tunic and a silver crown, motioned to them to sit down and tell him their message.

Augustine, tall and thin, stood up first and spoke through an interpreter. "The Lord, the tenderhearted healer," he said, "redeemed by His own death the sinful dwellers on this earth and opened a way to the kingdom of heaven."

After listening patiently to their explanation of the Christian faith, Ethelbert said, "Your words and promises are fair indeed; but they are new and uncertain, and I cannot accept them and abandon the age-old beliefs that I have held together with the whole English nation. But since you have traveled far—and I can see you are sincere in your desire to give to us what you believe to be true and excellent—we will not harm you. We will receive you hospitably and take care to supply you with all that you need. We will not forbid you to preach and win any of my people you can to your religion."

The king invited them to live in Canterbury and to use St. Martin's Church for worship. He gave them land on which to build a monastery and church. The monks marched in procession to Canterbury, carrying the cross and the picture of Jesus

Christ and singing: "We pray O Lord, for Your mercy, that Your wrath and anger may be turned away from this city, for we are sinners. Alleluia."

Bertha, dressed in a red gown with a blue cape, warmly greeted the missionaries and spoke with them in Latin. She rejoiced to be part of a Christian community again. The sight of the smiling queen must have put the men at ease.

There was a ruined church on the land that the king had donated to the monks, and with Ethelbert's help they repaired it—the beginnings of what would become Canterbury Cathedral. Augustine and his men spent their time in prayer and work. They preached about Jesus to any Anglo-Saxon willing to hear. Before long, some of the people believed in Christ and were baptized.

After a few months, King Ethelbert put his trust in Christ and was baptized—to the great delight of his wife. Word spread quickly throughout the kingdom that Ethelbert had become a Christian. Then great numbers came to hear the strangers preach the way to God. Many gave up their pagan practices and joined the Christian church. Ethelbert did not force anyone to convert to Christianity. Through the advice of Bertha and Augustine, he knew that the people would have to accept Jesus freely and not under compulsion.

The preaching of the missionaries and the example of their king and queen led thousands of Anglo-Saxons to turn from Woden to Christ. On Christmas Day 597, from sunup to sundown, ten thousand people came two by two to the river's edge and were baptized by the missionaries in the name of the Father and the Son and the Holy Spirit.

When Pope Gregory in Rome received news of the great awakening of faith among the Anglo-Saxons, he rejoiced, and he wrote Queen Bertha a letter. "We are glad to know that you labor earnestly to serve your Creator," Gregory wrote. "For we have received word how your Majesty has given great help and charity to our most reverend brother Augustine. And we bless Almighty God who has been mercifully pleased to reserve the conversion of the nation of the Angles for your reward."

Gregory praised Bertha for her faith, zeal and learning. Then he urged her to keep pressing her husband forward in following Christ. "Strengthen the mind of your glorious husband by constantly encouraging his love of the Christian faith," Gregory advised. "Let your encouragement inspire in him greater love for God, and so kindle his heart even for the fullest conversion of the nation he rules."

Bertha needed no prodding to encourage her husband in the faith and in the conversion of the people. Ethelbert, influential beyond the borders of his kingdom, was elected *bretwalda*, the leader of the Anglo-Saxon kings. Ethelbert won the permission of neighboring kingdoms to allow the missionaries to preach to them. He was instrumental in the conversion to Christianity of his nephew King Saebert of Essex, and Ethelbert paid for the building of St. Paul's Church in London, his nephew's capital. A short time later, Redwald, the king of East Anglia, became a Christian while visiting Ethelbert's court. From Canterbury, Christianity spread throughout Anglo-Saxon Britain.

One hundred fifty years ago, an English woman who had carefully studied the life of Bertha wrote, "We should remember

Queen Bertha's name and her example, for she was the first who showed our Saxon forefathers what Christianity is. She was brought here by Divine Providence 'to make ready the way of the Lord.' As long as England is a nation, she should love and honor the memory of her first Christian queen."

9 LEOBA
Fired by the Love of Christ, c. 710 –782

"Thor will strike you dead, you fool," a Hessian chief warned Boniface. Boniface, a missionary monk from Britain, had challenged the Hessians to forsake their idols and turn to Christ. Now, he stood with a large ax in his hands before their sacred oak on top of Mt. Gudenberg—a gathering place for pagan feasts and the worship of Thor. The Hessians held the tree in deepest awe, believing it to be sacred to Thor, their god of thunder and war. "Who does this babbler think he is?" one warrior asked. "When Thor wields his mighty hammer, he'll feel the lightning of his wrath!"

As Boniface firmly gripped the ax handle and prepared to strike, the people cried out, "Stand back!" fearful of being struck by Thor's lightning bolts. With faces white with terror, the people gaped as Boniface struck the tree with all his might. They looked expectantly to the heavens, but no lightning bolts flashed. Time and again the iron ax head hit its mark and soon the huge oak cracked and leaned. The tribesmen scattered as it crashed to earth with a thundering blast and splintered into four pieces.

The people stood bewildered and silent. Then a pagan chief stepped forward and with trembling voice declared, "Our fathers and grandfathers came here to win the favor of the gods and so have we. But if our gods are powerless to protect their own holy places then they are nothing."

He pointed to Boniface, "Tell us, holy man, about your God."

Motioning with his arms for the people to draw near, Boniface said, "We speak to you as messengers of the Lord who cannot be appeased by sacrifices or gifts of money. We believe that the Son of God took our sin upon His own body when He died on the cross. If you are to be saved, you must believe in Him and follow Him only."

Seizing the moment, Boniface ordered that a Christian church be built using the timber of the fallen tree. As the Hessians became open to Christianity, Boniface wrote to Christians back in Anglo-Saxon England, his homeland. He asked for men and women who had a reputation for holiness and hard work to join him in spreading the good news of Jesus Christ in Germany. "Let us give our lives for the Word of God," he told them. "Let us preach the whole counsel of God to the high and to the low, to the rich and to the poor, to every rank and age, as far as God gives us strength."

One of the Anglo-Saxon Christians who responded to Boniface's appeal was Leoba, a distant cousin of Boniface who had dedicated her life to Christian service as a nun. Leoba's parents brought her to the abbey at Wimborne in southern England when she was a young girl. She took to the monastic life at once, especially the study of the Word of God.

She strove to follow the New Testament command to pray without ceasing. Besides the set times of prayer that were part of the daily routine of the abbey, she tried to pray while doing manual labor, eating meals or reading the Bible.

Leoba carefully observed the older nuns and imitated their good qualities, modeling herself on the patience of one sister and the kindness of another, the cheerfulness of one and the meekness of another. She made it her aim to follow them as they followed Christ. "In this way," one observer said, "she so conducted herself that she was loved by all the sisters."

Boniface became the archbishop of Germany and started planting churches and monasteries and convents across the land. They served as centers of Christian education and mercy ministry to the poor and sick. He wrote the abbess of Wimborne asking her to send Leoba to Germany. "For her reputation," as one man reported, "for learning and holiness had spread far and wide and her praise was on everyone's lips."

When Leoba arrived in Germany in 748, Boniface put her in charge of a large community of nuns at a new convent on the Tauber River. Later, he made her the head of all the nuns in Germany. She taught them the discipline of monastic life. Although she took her duties seriously and held her subordinates to a high standard, she was friendly and kind. Her nuns reported that she was always cheerful. "We never heard a bad word from her," they said. She taught her sisters to always be hospitable—welcoming all who came in need.

In many convents the abbess imposed severe fasting and allowed the women very little sleep. Leoba taught her nuns a simple and disciplined life, but she knew that it was not in keeping with the Bible's teaching for Christians to practice excessive self-denial that weakened the body. Her sisters would have adequate food and rest so that they could concentrate on the study of the Scriptures, prayer and service to others.

From her earliest days, Leoba had been thoroughly trained in Latin and the classical philosophers and was well-versed in the writings of the Early Church Fathers. But first and foremost she excelled in the knowledge of the Bible. She was rarely seen without the Scriptures in her hands. As abbess, she not only directed the education of her nuns and novices, but also taught the daughters of noblemen who would spend their lives in manor houses and the royal court. Every part of their Christian education was rooted in Scripture and prayer. Many of her nuns went on to become abbesses of other convents.

Leoba—like all Christians in the Middle Ages—accepted some beliefs and practices taught by the church, but not found in the Bible. She believed in purgatory and prayer to saints, and she thought that objects blessed by holy men were used by God to help His people. But even so, she looked to Christ alone to save her soul and the Word of God to guide her steps.

Abbots and abbesses were important leaders to the communities surrounding their monasteries and convents. Leoba's godly character and wisdom led her neighbors to seek her guidance and aid. On one occasion, a fire broke out in the village near her convent. The flames spread rapidly—leaping from one thatched roof to another. Frightened villagers banged on the front gate of the convent and called for Leoba's help. Leoba calmed their fears and ordered them to bring a bucket of water from the stream that flowed nearby. She prayed over the water and sprinkled some salt into it—salt that had been blessed by Boniface. "Go pour it back into the river," she told them. "Then have all the people draw buckets of water from the stream and throw it on the fire."

As the villagers began to douse the flames, the fire died down quickly, saving many lives and homes.

At another time, a terrible thunderstorm broke upon the community and the convent. High winds uprooted trees, tore roofs from houses and collapsed buildings. Thick, black storm clouds turned day into night. Thunderbolts shook the ground. Terrified men, women and children crowded into the stone church, believing that the last judgment was at hand. They cried out in panic for Leoba. She came to them in the sanctuary, assuring them that they would be safe. "Be patient and trust God," she told them. "Pray with me for deliverance."

Then Leoba laid facedown in prayer in the front of the church while the storm raged on. As thunder rattled the church, the people pulled her up. "Protect us!" they cried. Leoba threw off her cloak and flung open the doors of the church. She lifted her hands toward heaven and three times prayed to Christ for mercy. Soon the thunder died away and beams of sunlight pierced through the dark clouds. The people counted it a miracle and praised God for His protection.

In those days, monasteries did not allow women inside their walls, and convents restricted access to men. However, at Boniface's monastery at Fulda an exception was made for Leoba because Boniface often asked her to come to talk with him and pray. In 754, Boniface, at the age of seventy-three, decided to leave Germany, sail down the Rhine with some companions to Fresia (Holland) and preach to the fierce pagan tribes there. Boniface believed he would be killed on the mission. As he packed a few belongings for the journey into a wooden chest, he included his white burial shroud. He asked Leoba to come to Fulda so that he might speak with her one last time. "Do not abandon this land when I am gone," he told her. "Do not grow weary of the difficult life you have undertaken for the Lord. Expand the good work you have begun." Boniface counseled her not to be discouraged by looking ahead to the many long years of service that lay before her. "For the years of this life are short," he said, "compared to eternity, and the sufferings of this world are nothing in comparison with the glory that will be revealed in the saints."

Turning to his monks, he directed them to always show Leoba respect. "When I am gone," he told them, "bury me in the monastery church, and later lay her remains beside me in my tomb." A few months later in Fresia, Boniface suffered a martyr's death.

Leoba pressed on in her work—training sisters and starting new convents. "May Christ our Creator and Redeemer grant that we shall meet again without shame on the Day of Judgment," she told her nuns.

Leoba's deep knowledge of the Scriptures led princes and church leaders to seek her advice. Charlemagne, the Christian king of the Franks, and his wife Queen Hildegard held her in high esteem. On many occasions, Charlemagne and his wife invited Leoba to talk to them about Christ. It was said that Hildegard "loved her as her own soul." Hildegard asked Leoba to live in the royal palace and serve as her spiritual guide. But Leoba hated the luxury of the court, believing that such a life of comfort was poison to her soul. And so she declined the offer and remained in the convent.

Through Boniface, Leoba and the Christian workers they trained, tens of thousands of Hessians and other German tribesmen came into the Christian church. By God's grace, they left behind a great legacy—firmly rooting Christianity in Germany and establishing a well-organized church with strong institutions of Christian education and service.

Several years after her death, a monk wrote Leoba's story. He concisely summed up her life when he wrote: "She was fired by the love of Christ."

10 QUEEN LUDMILA
A Shining Star of Bohemia, c. 850–921

In the middle of the ninth century, the Slavic peoples of central and eastern Europe worshiped the earth as the giver of life and followed the gods of thunder and lightning, of earthquakes and fire. The Slavs believed that their woodlands were alive with nymphs and fairies, making mischief and working magic. The people performed their rituals on hilltops or sacred groves—hoping that their sacrifices would appease the gods and bring good fortune. But that began to change when two Christian missionaries from Greece, Cyril and Methodius, told these people living in darkness about the light of Jesus Christ.

Cyril created an alphabet for the Slavs with special characters to match the sounds of the Slavic languages. He translated the Gospels and other portions of the Bible and taught the Slavs how to read them. First the Bulgarian Slavs trusted in Christ and then the Moravians believed. Around the year 871 in the Slavic kingdom of Bohemia, Methodius told King Borivoj and Queen Ludmila the good news of Christ's sacrifice on the cross for sinners. After hearing Christianity explained and considering it for a time, Borivoj and Ludmila decided to forsake their pagan gods and idols. Borivoj told Methodius, "I believe this to be true. Is there any reason why you shouldn't baptize me at once?"

"Nothing stops us," Methodius answered, "only be ready to believe with steadfast heart in God the Father Almighty and His Son Jesus Christ and the Holy Spirit for the salvation of body and soul, abiding with God forever."

So Methodius baptized Borivoj and Ludmila and many members of their court. Forsaking the pagan shrines, they destroyed their own golden-headed idol before which they used to prostrate themselves. The king and queen supported Christian ministers who preached throughout the land. Borivoj and Ludmila built Bohemia's first Christian church in the capital city, Prague. Thousands of their subjects turned to Christ, and churches sprang up across the kingdom. But many others did not want to abandon the gods of their fathers, and the pagan priests fiercely opposed Christianity.

Overwhelmed by Christ's love for her, Ludmila spent hours each day in prayer, worship and acts of charity. She trained her children to trust in Christ. Years later, Borivoj died and their son Vratislav became king. He followed the faith of his father and mother. Because Vratislav's wife Drahomira was a pagan, he asked Ludmila to teach his firstborn son, Wenceslas, the Christian faith. But Drahomira brought up their second son, Boleslav, to follow paganism.

Ludmila trained Wenceslas and devoted the rest of her time to worshiping her Savior, caring for the sick and visiting captives in prison. Wenceslas embraced his grandmother's teaching and example and put his trust in Jesus Christ. Ludmila rejoiced to see the first fruits of God's grace in her grandson's faith and godly character.

When Wenceslas was eight years old, his father King Vratislav died. Drahomira—with the help of her pagan supporters—seized power and reigned as regent in the name of the boy-king Wenceslas.

Ludmila left Prague and retired to her castle in Tetin. Drahomira dismissed her late husband's advisors and formed her own ruling council. Immediately, they set out to destroy Christianity in Bohemia—expelling Christian officials from the royal court and firing Christian magistrates in all the towns in the kingdom, replacing them with pagans. They ordered all churches closed and banned the practice of the Christian faith. Ministers and parents were forbidden to teach children about Christ and His commandments. When Christians protested, they were killed.

Drahomira—knowing that Ludmila was the most well-known Christian in the land and resenting her influence with Wenceslas—plotted to put her mother-in-law to death. Friends of Ludmila warned her of the danger, but she chose not to flee. Perhaps she thought that running away would dishonor Christ. Instead, Ludmila prepared for death by giving away her possessions and writing Wenceslas, urging him to hold fast to Jesus Christ. She told her priest that she would soon be killed and that she wanted to worship and receive communion one last time.

When Drahomira's assassins overran Ludmila's castle and broke open the locked doors of her chambers, they found her praying in her private chapel. As they dragged her from the spot Ludmila asked, "What are you doing? Have you forgotten what good I have done you?" Then they ripped the veil from her head and strangled her with it.

A few years later, Wenceslas was old enough to claim the throne and displace his mother. He restored Christianity as a legal religion in the realm and reopened the churches, but paganism remained strong in the land. Wenceslas followed in Ludmila's footsteps. He took time each day to meditate on Scripture and pray—often spending the whole night in prayer. Widows and orphans loved him for his generosity and kindness.

All the while, his brother Boleslav longed to be king, and pagan noblemen encouraged him to take action against Wenceslas. "He is better fit for a monastery than a throne," they told him. Boleslav finally decided his surest way to the crown was to murder Wenceslas. In order to get his brother out of the protection of the royal castle, he invited him to witness the baptism of Boleslav's newborn son. Wenceslas suspected treachery, but he went anyway. One night while visiting his brother's fortress, Wenceslas went to pray alone in the castle church. Boleslav followed him there and attacked. Wenceslas tried to escape, but Boleslav ran him through with a lance while he clung onto the iron ring of the church door.

Perhaps out of remorse for killing his brother, Boleslav did not launch a full-scale persecution of Christians as his mother had. Still his nickname has come down through history as Boleslav the Cruel. Ludmila's Christian faith lived on in the godly line of Christian princes and princesses who served Christ in the royal courts, churches, monasteries and convents of Bohemia. Boleslav's own son, Boleslav II, was a righteous king who used his office to extend Christianity throughout the realm.

One early chronicler praised Ludmila's godly influence on the nation—calling her "a shining star that illuminated all the land of Bohemia with the bright beams of her holy example."

11   QUEEN MARGARET OF SCOTLAND
A Pearl—Precious in Faith and Works, 1045–1093

In 1069, a ship from England dropped anchor in the mouth of the Forth River on the east coast of Scotland. Its passengers were Anglo-Saxon royalty who had fled England as William the Conqueror from Normandy consolidated his power and confiscated land. On board was Edgar, a prince of the House of Wessex who was proclaimed King of England in 1066, but was never crowned. The Anglo-Saxon nobles decided to back Harold's claim to the throne instead. When Harold was defeated at the Battle of Hastings in 1066, and the Anglo-Saxon nobles submitted to William as their new king, Edgar and his sisters, Margaret and Christina, sailed north to seek protection from Malcolm III, King of Scotland.

It was a windy and cold November day as they set foot on Scottish soil not far from Dunfermline—a land of densely wooded hills and heather-covered moors. They dispatched a messenger to Malcolm's court in Dunfermline Tower to request asylum. Malcolm warmly welcomed the refugees because, as a young man, he had fled Scotland after his father was assassinated by the wicked Macbeth and had found safety in London at the court of King Edward the Confessor, the great uncle of Edgar and his sisters. From the moment that Malcolm set eyes on the beautiful, twenty-four-year-old Princess Margaret, he was smitten.

Malcolm was a rugged, tall and broad-shouldered warrior who loved battle and the hunt. He could neither read nor write, but he reveled in ruling his dominion. Margaret, a thin, frail woman raised in the royal courts of England and Europe, had mastered Latin and French and was skilled in music and embroidery. From her earliest days, she learned the Scriptures and church doctrine. Out of love for Christ, Margaret planned to spend her life in prayer behind the walls of a convent.

Not long after they arrived, Malcolm asked Margaret's brother for her hand in marriage, but Edgar refused to grant it, telling him that she wanted to be a nun. But the king had made up his mind, and he persisted until Margaret and her brother accepted it as God's will. They were married a few months later. The king's low-lying castle was primitive and bare compared to the royal palace in London. No tapestries or curtains brightened the stone walls and no gold plates or goblets decorated the dining table.

Although Malcolm's castles in Dunfermline and Edinburgh were small and crude by the standards of London or Paris, they were magnificent compared to the poor hovels of his people. Most Scots lived in little huts with walls made of branches and twigs woven together and plastered with a mixture of mud and straw and roofs thatched with heather. They eked out a living on small plots of ground raising crops and livestock. Severe winters brought famine and sickness. Margaret could not rest content while the poor suffered.

Before sunrise each morning, Queen Margaret washed, dressed and fed several orphans whom she had brought to live in the castle, preparing their food and spoon feeding those too young or weak to feed themselves. It was one of her greatest joys to provide for helpless children. She had the cooks make breakfast for twenty-four poor people who were invited each day. She waited on their tables before eating her own breakfast. Every evening, she directed the chief steward to bring to the castle six needy people. In imitation of her Savior, Margaret got down on her knees and washed their feet and sent them home with a little money.

Her generosity to the poor drew them to her. Whenever Margaret went beyond the castle walls, widows, orphans and destitute folk crowded around her, begging alms. She always brought money to give away and when that was gone she gave articles of clothing and jewelry. "No one left her," one attendant reported, "without being comforted."

"She would have given to the poor all that she possessed," a friend said.

During Advent and Lent, Malcolm and Margaret brought three hundred poor people into the great hall each evening for dinner. The king and queen served them food and drinks alongside the other servants. In this way, thousands of needy subjects met their rulers.

Even though she was the king's wife and mistress of the royal court, Margaret lived a life of self-sacrifice for Christ. She woke before dawn each morning to pray. At midnight she arose and went to the chapel for an hour of prayer and worship. She often

spent the entire night in a vigil of prayer. Margaret loved to escape from the bustle of the court to pray—slipping out alone and
walking down the steep path into the valley to a small cave in the
rocks. There, she poured out her heart to God.

Her behavior aroused suspicions. "When you are gone,"
a nobleman told Malcolm, "the queen sneaks away from the
castle. She may be up to no good." The whispering planted
doubts in Malcolm's mind about his wife. So one day he told
Margaret that he was going hunting, but he hid in some nearby trees to watch her. When Margaret left the castle a short
time later, he followed her. She hiked to the valley and disappeared into the cave. Malcolm quietly crept to the entrance
and heard his wife's voice praying—asking God to bless her
husband and his people. The king, overcome with shame for
having doubted her, dropped to his knees. His sword clanked
on the stony ground. Margaret heard the noise and found her
husband kneeling with his head in his hands. Red-faced, he
confessed to her what had happened. She embraced him, and
they walked home arm in arm.

Wanting godly teaching and counsel, Margaret asked Turgot,
the abbot of Durham Abbey, to serve as the royal chaplain and
spiritual advisor. He was amazed to see the depth of her devotion to Christ. She loved the Scriptures and studied them
daily—memorizing large portions, especially in the Psalms.
"She always acted under the guidance of the Holy Scriptures,"
Turgot said. "In fact, every word which she uttered, every act
which she performed, showed that she was meditating upon
the things of heaven."

The king often sat beside Margaret as she read the Bible or Christian books. "Even though he could not read," one observer said, "he loved to hold and even kiss the pages of her most treasured books." He had his craftsmen make ornamental covers with precious metals and gems for her books.

Her faithful Christian life inspired Malcolm. "From her," Turgot said, "the king learned how to keep the vigils of the night in constant prayer. She instructed him by her exhortation and example how to pray to God with groanings from the heart and abundance of tears."

Margaret chose a group of young women as her ladies-in-waiting. She modeled for them a life of Bible study and prayer. She taught them the art of embroidery, often singing Psalms as they worked. Before long, they were providing ornate wall hangings for churches and vestments for the priests. The bare walls of the castle were covered with beautiful tapestries, and the women of the court began wearing colorful and elegant clothing that they had made.

Malcolm and Margaret had eight children—six sons and two daughters. Margaret worked hard at instilling a love for God in them. "She frequently called her children to her," Turgot said, "and carefully instructed them about Christ."

"My dear ones," she said, "fear the Lord; for they who fear Him shall lack nothing, and if you love Him, He will give you prosperity in this life, and everlasting happiness with all the saints."

Queen Margaret was concerned to discover some bad practices in the Scottish church. With Malcolm's help—he acted as her interpreter since she couldn't speak Gaelic—she spoke to the leading clergymen about them. "Why don't you take the Lord's Supper on Easter Sunday like the rest of the Christian church?" she asked.

"Because," they answered, "Paul warns that 'He that eats and drinks unworthily eats and drinks judgment to himself.' As we are sinners, we fear to approach the sacred sacrament on that day lest we bring down God's judgment upon us."

"But we are all sinners," Margaret said, "even the infant who has lived only one day. If none of us, being sinners, ought to receive the sacrament, then why did our Lord say that 'Unless you eat the flesh and drink the blood of the Son of Man, you shall have no life in you?'"

Margaret explained that Paul's warning was not meant to keep Christians from the Lord's Supper, but to keep away unrepentant sinners. "But we who confess our sins and turn from them," she said, "may approach in faith the Lord's Table on the day of His resurrection and receive the body and blood of Jesus Christ—not to judgment, but to the forgiveness of our sins, and as a health-giving preparation for eternal happiness."

It also disappointed her that the Scottish people did not keep the Lord's Day holy, but after going to church in the morning, they went about their usual business the rest of the day. Margaret was always careful not to do her usual work on that day, but made it a day of worship, rest and love. When Margaret asked the clergy why they did not obey God's commandment to honor the Sabbath day, they couldn't give her any biblical reasons. "For everything that she proposed," Turgot said, "she supported so strongly by the testimony of the sacred Scriptures and the teaching of the holy Fathers, that no one on the opposite side could say one word against them."

Margaret's humility and gentleness made the clergymen willing to listen. Her sound arguments led them to change some of their practices.

The Roman church of that day taught several unbiblical practices that Margaret accepted without question. She believed that venerating relics and making pilgrimages to shrines of saints would bring God's blessing. Her most prized possession was the Black Rood, an ornate crucifix she brought from England said to contain a piece of Christ's cross. In order to make it easier for people to get to the shrine of St. Andrews, she paid for a ferry to shuttle pilgrims across the Forth River free of charge and had a hostel built on the river bank where weary travelers could rest. The spot is called Queensferry to this day.

For many years, King Malcolm had battled the English over control of the borderlands between the two kingdoms. Several times, he invaded northern England, killing many and driving hundreds of men, women and children back to Scotland as slaves. English noblemen who were taken captive were ransomed by their families, but the rest were doomed to a life of slavery. It broke Margaret's heart to know that her husband and his warriors enslaved these poor folks, and she did what she could to help them. She sent agents throughout Scotland to pay the ransom and set free slaves suffering under the worst conditions. She spent large sums of money every year freeing captives.

In the fall of 1093, Malcolm brought his warriors, including his sons Edward and Edgar, into northern England to fight the forces of the King of England. King Malcolm and Edward were killed on the battlefield. Young Edgar returned to Edinburgh Castle with the remnants of the Scottish army. It fell to Edgar to bring his mother the sad news. He was shocked to hear that Margaret was very sick—near the point of death. Not wanting to weaken her further, he decided to wait to tell her of their deaths. When he entered her bedchamber, Margaret was clutching the Black Rood in her hands. She greeted him in a faint voice and asked, "How are your father and brother?"

Edgar knelt at her bedside. "They are well," he answered.

With labored breath, Margaret laid her thin hand gently on her son's shoulder and said, "I know it, my boy, I know it. But by this holy cross and by the bond of our blood, I command you to tell the truth. How fares it with the king and my Edward?"

"The King and Edward are both slain," he said weeping. Then he told her the details of the battle and how they died. Margaret sighed, closed her eyes and prayed silently for several minutes. Then she said aloud, "I give praise and thanks to You, Almighty God, for You have been pleased that I should endure such deep sorrow at my departing. I trust that by means of this suffering, it is Your will that I should be cleansed from the stains of my sins."

Margaret looked at her son and the others in the room. She weakly lifted her hand and prayed, "Lord Jesus Christ, who has by Your death given life to the world, deliver me."

As her words echoed in the bedchamber, she died. Several years later, Turgot wrote an account of her life. The name Margaret means pearl, and he wrote this about her, "She was called Margaret and in the sight of God she showed herself to be a pearl—precious in faith and works."

Margaret's children grew up to be faithful believers in Christ who used their gifts to serve the Lord. Three of her sons became in turn kings of Scotland. Historians considered them among Scotland's best and most just rulers. Her daughter Matilda married Henry I, King of England. She followed her mother's example in Christian devotion and care for the poor.

12   CLARE OF ASSISI
A Marvelous Lover of God, 1194–1253

The changes in Francis Bernardone astonished all the citizens of Assisi. Forsaking all worldly comforts, Francis started preaching and helping the poor. "Repent, my brothers and sisters, and look to our blessed Savior," he said. "Know that he who comes to Christ will have all his sins forgiven. Take heart, repent and find your joy in the Lord."

Walking barefoot and wearing a coarse brown robe, Francis lived among the lepers, begging alms for them, washing their wounds and easing their pain. He saw them as children of the King of Kings and treated them with kindness and respect. They loved him for it. However, many people in Assisi—including his own family—did not like the change in Francis. They thought him a dirty madman. When he first walked through town in his humble clothes, they ridiculed him. "Get out of here you fool," they shouted. They pelted him with dirt, rocks and insults.

Clare Favarone, a teenage girl from a wealthy family, did not see Francis that way. His love for Christ and the poor stoked a fire in her heart. She went to hear him preach and sought out his counsel. "Look to heaven and forsake the world," he said. Clare began to quietly bring food to the needy and spend long hours in prayer. Others were inspired too, and before long a number of men joined Francis in his work.

"We shall follow our Lord's example by preaching to the poor and caring for the sick," Francis said. The men who joined his order wore peasant robes and shaved the crowns of their heads as a sign of humble submission to God.

Although, as a woman, Clare could not join Francis's order, she began to follow in his steps. She visited the sick and poor and worked to relieve their wants. With a cheerful smile, she washed feet, dressed wounds and cleaned dirty linen. She continued to dress in the rich clothing of her station, but underneath she wore a hair shirt. It chafed her skin, reminding her not to grow comfortable with the world since Christ had called her to take up her cross and follow Him.

When Clare was about eighteen years old, her family arranged for her to marry a wealthy young man of a prominent house, but she wanted to dedicate her life to God as a nun. In the midst of Clare's dilemma she turned to Francis, telling him her heart's desire to serve Christ as a single woman. For some time, Francis had wanted to start an order of women who could serve poor girls and women in ways that the brothers could not. When he saw Clare's determination to reject marriage and commit herself to Christian service, Francis made a plan. "On Palm Sunday," he told Clare, "go to church in town as usual, but at nightfall come to the Church of St. Mary ready to dedicate your life to God."

Palm Sunday night, accompanied by a few trusted companions, Clare fled out her home's back gate. When she arrived at St. Mary's churchyard she found Francis and the brothers holding torches and singing hymns. They greeted her and escorted her into the church. Clare knelt in prayer and made vows of singleness and service to Christ. Francis cut her golden hair, and she exchanged her gown for a gray robe. Then the brothers led her to a nearby convent to stay for a time.

When her family discovered what she had done, they rushed to the convent. They found her at the front of the chapel wearing a hooded robe. "You are highborn—don't throw away your life," they pleaded. "Come home!" But Clare would not be moved. They threatened to carry her away by force, so Clare clung to the altar and removed her hood, uncovering her shorn head. "No one shall separate me from God—I am consecrated to Christ," she said. Seeing her resolve, her family left. Not long after, Francis arranged for Clare to lodge at St. Damian's, a ruined church and guesthouse beyond the city walls which Francis and his friends had restored.

Francis and his brothers wandered about preaching, ministering to the poor and begging for food. Clare's life took place behind the walls of St. Damian's. She sold her clothes and other possessions and gave all the money away to the poor. When she wasn't caring for the sick women whom Francis's men brought to her, she prayed.

Soon many other women came to St. Damian's to join Clare. "Heed these words from the Holy Gospel," Clare told them, 'Go, sell all that you have and give to the poor.'" Hundreds of women—most from the upper classes—did just that. They embraced what Francis and Clare called "holy poverty." They owned nothing, not even a pair of shoes, only a peasant's robe and a belt of rope. "As Christ was content to be wrapped in humble swaddling clothes and laid in a manger," Clare told them, "so you, my sisters, are always to wear lowly garments."

Francis named the group "The Order of Poor Ladies." Clare saw Christ in the poor and took to heart the words of her Savior: "Truly, I say to you, as you did it to one of the least of these my brothers, you did it to me." She taught the sisters to bow to the sick and needy as a sign of respect. "By serving the stranger, we worship Christ," Clare said.

Although the sisters had little to give, no one coming to them in need departed empty-handed, and no one seeking shelter was turned away. As the number of Poor Ladies increased, the abbey was enlarged. Adjacent land was donated, and workers built dormitories and extended the stone walls to enclose several acres of gardens and woodland. Clare and the sisters had little and worked hard, yet thanksgiving and joy marked their lives. Each day, they gathered several times in the chapel for worship, and they set aside time for private prayer and Scripture meditation. Once a week, Clare and the sisters confessed their sins to one another and sought mutual forgiveness. She arranged for preachers to bring the Word of God frequently to the abbey. "She knew how to get profit for her soul," a friend said of Clare, "from the sermon of any speaker."

Word spread about the charity and kindness of Clare and her sisters. Other houses of Poor Ladies were started throughout Europe.

The Poor Ladies placed their trust in God to daily meet their needs—living off the vegetables they grew in the garden, gifts brought to the abbey and the bread that Francis and his brothers begged on their behalf. Although Clare was the leader, she insisted on doing the most menial tasks—dressing the wounds of the sick or cleaning the latrines.

Like Francis, Clare followed a strict regimen of fasting and self-denial. She slept on the hard floor, using a block of wood for a pillow. Her diet was sparse, and three days a week she ate nothing at all. Despite the severity of her abstinence she remained cheerful. Although Clare denied herself a blanket for her bed, on cold nights she made the rounds of the sleeping quarters, pulling up covers and placing more blankets over the sleeping sisters.

Over time, Clare so mistreated her body that it broke down in pain and illness. Finally, she grew so weak that Francis intervened. He commanded her to eat at least one meal everyday and to sleep on a bed stuffed with straw.

Later in life, Clare realized that her severe fasting had destroyed her health, and she urged others not to follow her excess. "Our bodies are not made of stone," she counseled a younger sister, "use discretion, do not overdo abstinence as I have done so that you may live in Christ and offer Him your service." But the damage to her body was done. Clare was bedridden for many years.

Once, Muslim raiders invaded central Italy, attacked Assisi, and surrounded the abbey. The hearts of the sisters melted like wax as they heard the commotion and saw the raiders jumping over the wall. The women rushed to Clare's room weeping and wailing, "Mother, protect us—what shall we do?" Clare, ill and unable to walk, asked the sisters to help her to the abbey's front door. Lying facedown, she prayed. "Does it please You, O my God, to deliver Your defenseless children into the hands of these beasts? Protect them good Lord, I beseech You."

Then Clare stood up and looked at her sisters. "Fear not, little daughters; have confidence in Jesus!" No sooner had Clare finished her prayer, than the raiders broke off their attack and retreated back over the walls.

On her deathbed Clare prepared her heart to meet the Lord while the sisters stood around the room weeping and praying. "Go forth, Christian soul," Clare said, "go forth without fear for He that created you has sanctified you. He has protected you always, and He loves you with the love of a mother."

"Who are you talking to Mother?" one of the sisters asked Clare. "I am talking to my own soul," she answered. A few minutes later, Clare's face brightened. She turned to one of the women and said, "Can you see the King of Glory whom I see?" And then she passed away. "She was a marvelous lover of God," one of them said.

Clare's life of service to the needy serves as an example to all Christians, but some of her beliefs and practices do not. She accepted the teachings of the church in her day which encouraged the adoration of Mary, prayer to saints and other things not found in the Bible. The church taught that it was more holy and pleasing to God to be a monk or nun, rather than a husband or wife, father or mother. People revered those who harshly mistreated their bodies as a form of penance. Although Clare's ways are not our ways, the spirit in which she served the Lord by putting others before herself challenges us to do the same.

13 ELIZABETH OF HUNGARY
Servant of the Poor, 1207–1231

Famine gripped the German states of Thuringia and Hesse in the summer of 1226. The famished poor wandered in the fields and forests, searching for wild nuts and berries, clawing at the earth for roots, stripping the bark from trees and devouring every kind of dead animal encountered in their desperate search for food. Many starved to death, covering the roads with corpses. The ruler of the region, Duke Louis, and most of the fighting men were away on a military campaign in Italy. When desperate crowds hiked the steep road to Wartburg Castle and clamored at the gates for food, nineteen-year-old Duchess Elizabeth, wife of Louis and daughter of the King of Hungary, heard their pleas.

The beautiful, olive-skinned duchess threw her energies by day and by night into relieving the suffering of her people. The duke's advisors, fearing an uprising, cautioned the duchess to keep a tight rein on finances and a strong guard at the royal granaries. Instead, Elizabeth emptied the royal treasury, giving the money to the poor, and depleted the granaries to feed the hungry. She instructed the castle's kitchen staff to bake bread and cook soup from sunrise to sundown, and she even served the people with her own hands.

Coordinating her efforts with the monks, nuns and priests, she organized food distribution across the land with money gained from the sale of most of her jewels and other property. "Stop it," the advisors warned. "You'll bankrupt the royal house!"

But Elizabeth pressed on, grateful for God's call to help the needy. "O Lord," she prayed, "how can I sufficiently thank You for having given me the opportunity to serve these poor ones who are Your dearest friends."

She fed nine hundred people who came to the castle each day. To those too weak or ill to ascend the mountain to the castle, she carried food herself. Elizabeth began a hospital and two houses for the poor in Eisenach, the town nestled below the massive, gray-stoned castle. Laying aside her royal robes, she twice daily donned a peasant's cloak and walked down to Eisenach to make beds and comfort the sick. She gave new clothes and shoes to able-bodied men and women and set them to work in the fields, preparing the ground and planting seeds in the hopes of raising a small crop by harvest time. When her money failed, she gave the poor her veils, silk scarves and other articles of clothing saying, "Sell these to satisfy your wants and work as your strength allows, for the Bible says, 'He who does not work does not eat.'"

When word of the famine reached Duke Louis in Italy, he hastily returned home. As he drew near to Wartburg, his officials went out to meet him. They denounced Elizabeth's reckless spending and the emptying of the granaries. "We warned her," they protested, "but she wouldn't listen."

The duke stopped their complaining and said, "Let my good little Elizabeth give to the poor as much as she pleases, so long as she leaves me Wartburg and Naumburg, alms will never ruin us."

When Louis arrived home, Elizabeth threw herself in his arms and showered him with kisses. As he held her in his arms he asked, "Dear sister, what has become of your poor people during this terrible year?"

With a gentle voice and broad smile she answered, "I gave God what was His, and God has kept for us what was yours and mine."

In her youth, Elizabeth's father told her about Francis of Assisi. His decision to honor Christ by turning away from riches and loving the poor inspired her to follow in his steps. She often met the lepers, kissed them, eased their pain and prayed for them. She bathed them, cutting up castle curtains and linens for towels to dry them. "O, how happy we are," she told a fellow worker, "to be able by this work to cleanse and clothe our Lord."

Once when her husband was away, she discovered a poor leper whose body was so diseased that no one would help him. She took him into the castle, bathed him, rubbed medicine on his sores and laid him in her own bed, much to the consternation of her mother-in-law and the royal officials. When the duke returned, his mother ran to him and said, "Come with me, dear Son, and I will show you what your Elizabeth does. You will see one she loves much better than you."

Taking Louis by the hand, she led him to his bed chamber saying, "See—your wife puts lepers in your bed and I can't stop her. You can see for yourself that she wants to give you leprosy."

Louis did not rebuke his wife, but praised her for her loving kindness and built at her request a home for lepers on the castle road.

When affairs of state called Louis from the castle, Elizabeth wore plain, dark clothes and spent her time in works of mercy, prayer and fasting. But when Louis came home, she dressed in her finest jewelry and her most colorful gowns. "It is not vanity or pride that leads me to dress this way," Elizabeth told her maidens, "for I would not give my husband any occasions of discontent or sin by having anything in me to displease him."

God blessed Louis and Elizabeth with four children. A few days after her first child, Herman, was born, she wrapped herself in a gray robe, took her new-born son in her arms and slipped secretly out of the castle. She walked barefoot to the town church and laid the baby on the altar saying, "My God and my Lord, with all my heart I give my child to You as You have given him to me. Please receive this child, all bathed in my tears, into the number of Your servants and friends, and bless him."

In autumn 1227, Louis packed his armor and sailed off for a crusade to the Holy Land, leaving Elizabeth and the children in the care of Henry, his brother. But this trip would bring great sadness. Not long after he left, Louis contracted a disease from which he finally died. In the meantime, court officials who despised Elizabeth's religious zeal and her use of the royal treasury to help the poor turned Henry against her. To strengthen his own claims to the throne, Henry ordered the expulsion of Elizabeth and her children from Wartburg Castle and from all royal lands. A court official declared to her, "You ruined the country, wasted the treasury and dishonored your husband. By order of Duke Henry, you must leave the castle immediately."

Astonished by the sudden, cruel demand, Elizabeth asked if she might have some time to prepare her departure. "No," he answered firmly, "leave this place at once!"

It was a late winter afternoon and a bitterly cold wind whipped across the mountainside when guards pushed Elizabeth and her children and two companions outside the castle walls, slamming the great metal gates behind them. She carried her baby daughter in her arms, and the other children wept as they trod the narrow path to Eisenach. By the light of the moon, she walked the streets seeking shelter, but Duke Henry forbade the citizens to help Elizabeth in any way, and the cowardly people of Eisenach obeyed him. After her years of selfless devotion to them, no one opened his home to her. "They have taken from me all that I had," she said weeping, "now I can only pray to God."

Finally, an innkeeper let her stay the night in a backyard shack where he kept his pigs. At midnight, her children fast asleep, Elizabeth heard the bell ringing for matins at the Franciscan convent which she and Louis had founded. She arose and worshiped with the gray-robed friars. She asked them to sing a hymn of thanks to God for the tribulations He had sent her. Then she prayed aloud, "O Lord, may Your will be done. My children are born of royal race, and behold them hungry, and without a bed to lie on. Yesterday, I was a duchess in strong castles and rich domains; today I am a beggar and no one takes me in."

For many nights they slept in the church. "This is God's house," Elizabeth said, "at least from here no one can drive me away."

To feed her children, she resorted to begging and later earned her livelihood by spinning wool. In her poverty, she reserved a portion of food from every meal to share with the needy. Remembering the sufferings of Christ, she did not complain, but accepted her lot with thanksgiving. "O, yes Lord," she prayed, "if

You will be with me, I will be with You, and I wish never to be parted from You."

Later, outraged knights, friends of the late duke, forced Henry to give Elizabeth part of the estate. She used these resources to build a hospital and care for the poor. Later, she gave away all her money to the poor and took a vow of poverty. She spun wool and ministered to outcasts.

When her father, the King of Hungary, heard that his daughter was living in poverty, he dispatched an ambassador at once to bring her to him. When the finely dressed and jeweled ambassador found Elizabeth spinning wool in a dark hovel, he burst into tears and cried out, "Did anyone ever before see a king's daughter spinning wool?"

He pleaded on bended knee with her to return to Hungary where she would be treated as a royal princess. "I am a poor sinner," she said, "who never obeyed the law of God as I ought to have done."

"Who has driven you to this state of misery?" he asked.

"No one," she answered, "but the infinitely rich Son of my Heavenly Father, who has taught me by example to despise riches."

"Come, noble Queen," he said, his arms outstretched to the frail Elizabeth, "come with me to your dear father, come, possess your kingdom and your inheritance."

"I hope indeed," she replied, "that I already possess my Father's inheritance—the eternal mercy of our Lord Jesus Christ."

As the ambassador left she arose from her spinning wheel and gently took his hand saying, "Tell my dearest father, that I am happier in my life than he is in his regal pomp, and that far from sorrowing over me, he ought to rejoice that he has a child in the service of the King of Heaven."

A short time later, Elizabeth was bedridden with a high fever. For two weeks she suffered, wracked with pain, but she remained joyful and prayerful. In her last words to friends, she said, "Let us speak of Jesus who came to redeem the world; He will redeem me also."

Three hundred years later, Wartburg Castle, the home of King Louis and Queen Elizabeth, became the hideaway of Martin Luther, where he translated the New Testament into German and wrote pamphlets in defense of the Protestant Reformation.

"Elizabeth of Hungary: Servant of the Poor" is excerpted from Richard M. Hannula's *Trial and Triumph: Stories from Church History* (Moscow ID: Canon Press, 1999).

14   ANNE OF BOHEMIA
Good Queen Anne, Nursing Mother of the Reformation, 1367–1394

In 1382, John Wycliffe, a minister and the master of Balliol College in Oxford, came under fierce attack. The bishops hated his criticism of the church's unbiblical teachings and his efforts to get the Bible in English into the hands of the people. But he was loved by many of the people, and two influential women protected him from harm. Four years earlier, the Bishop of London—with prodding from the pope—had summoned Wycliffe to St. Paul's Cathedral to stand trial for heresy. During the trial, a great crowd of Wycliffe's supporters surrounded St. Paul's, striking fear into the hearts of those who sat in judgment over him.

In the middle of the trial, Joan of Kent, the Queen Mother, a follower and defender of Wycliffe, sent a representative to speak on her behalf, warning the tribunal not to condemn Wycliffe or his teaching. "Master Wycliffe is not the detestable heretic which the pope represents him to be," the Queen Mother said, "and if I can prevent it, he shall not be arrested and imprisoned."

However, Pope Gregory XI had demanded that leaders of church and state in England suppress Wycliffe's teaching and his followers. Joan's courageous stand for Wycliffe, and the support of the London crowds, convinced the tribunal to release him.

But they warned him not to spread teaching contrary to the doctrines of the church.

Pope Gregory erupted when he learned of the trial's outcome. He sent sealed documents declaring Wycliffe a heretic to King Richard of England, the Archbishop of Canterbury and the Chancellor of Oxford University. "John Wycliffe," he wrote, "is vomiting out of the filthy dungeon of his heart most wicked and damnable heresies. He hopes to deceive the faithful and lead them to the edge of destruction. He wants to overthrow the church and bring ruin to the land. Arrest Wycliffe immediately and hold him until a church court can be convened to pass a final sentence."

John Wycliffe's teachings came out of his study of the Bible. The pope called them heresies because they went against some of the doctrines of the church. Wycliffe taught that Christ is the head of the church not the pope. Indulgences, masses and pilgrimages do not add to salvation—only faith in Christ saves. The bread and wine are symbols of Christ's body and blood, not the physical body and blood of Jesus. The Bible alone is sufficient to guide the church, not the teachings of popes, councils or kings that are contrary to Scripture. Wycliffe believed that the Bible was for everyone. "Jesus taught the people simply and in their own language," he said. "At Pentecost, the Holy Spirit gave the apostles the gift of tongues so that everyone could hear the good news in his own language."

So Wycliffe and his followers translated the Bible into English. "Press on in this work," he told his helpers, "for if the people of England will read the Scriptures for themselves it will be the surest road for them to follow Christ and come to heaven."

This violated the laws of the church which forbade the reading of the Bible by anyone except priests, and the translating of the Bible into the language of the people. The pope hoped to stop John Wycliffe and his ideas once and for all by condemning his writings and putting him to death. "The pope has no more power to judge than any other minister," Wycliffe said, "his words should be followed only so far as he follows the words of Christ. I am under obligation to obey the law of Christ."

Pope Gregory died before he could silence Wycliffe. Then a forty-year struggle ensued over who should be his successor. The church was split with two rival popes claiming to be the head of the church. This struggle enabled Wycliffe to continue teaching, writing, translating and training young men to go out and preach the Word of God. "Live a prayerful, holy, and honest life," he told them. "Let your deeds be so righteous that no man may be able to find fault with you. For the example of a good life stirs men more than true preaching alone."

Hundreds of young men, dressed in simple robes with handwritten copies of the English Bible, traveled across Britain reading from the Scriptures and proclaiming forgiveness in Christ. The Lollards—the name given to Wycliffe's followers—led thousands of people to believe in Jesus Christ. Students came to Oxford from all over Europe. Many returned to their homelands to translate the Bible and preach Christ to their countrymen in their own language.

But the Archbishop of Canterbury, desperate to silence Wycliffe, condemned Wycliffe's teachings as heretical and banned his writings. Church officials hauled Lollards into court and burned their copies of the Scripture in English. Remarkably, Wycliffe himself was not arrested. Joan, the Queen Mother, spoke again on his behalf. And he had a new defender, Anne of Bohemia, the wife of Richard II, King of England.

Anne of Bohemia was the eldest daughter of Charles IV, the Holy Roman Emperor—the most powerful monarch in Europe. She was raised in the imperial court in Prague, Bohemia and received a strong classical education, learning to speak several languages. From her earliest days, she had a warm faith in Christ, and she studied the Scriptures daily. During her childhood, reformers in Prague preached the good news of Christ and spoke out against false teaching in the Roman church. Her father had supported the reformers' views.

Anne married King Richard II of England in 1382 when they were both teenagers. She agreed to marry Richard, in part, because she had heard of the revival of faith in England through the work of John Wycliffe. King Richard, a stubborn and proud ruler who did not share his wife's zeal for the Christian faith, loved and admired Anne. And she genuinely loved him. "It is my bounded duty," Queen Anne said, "to do all that the king desires of me, for I have vowed before God and man to cherish and to obey him."

In 1381, a few months before Richard and Anne got married, the Peasants' Revolt broke out in England. Protesting high taxes, thousands of peasants took up arms, but they were brutally crushed by the king's troops. Harsh penalties were meted out on the leaders of the revolt. Many were executed. The sentence of death hung over the heads of thousands who had taken part in the rebellion. Anne urged Richard to pardon them. He agreed and issued a royal amnesty to everyone except the ringleaders. "We grant this pardon," Richard said, "from the fear of God and the special request of the most serene lady, the Lady Anne."

Shortly thereafter, Richard and Anne were married in a lavish ceremony in Westminster Abbey. Anne set up her royal household with a number of friends from Bohemia—including some reform-minded ministers. From the start, she served the poor, and Richard happily worked with his wife in offering charity to the needy. Soon, several thousand poor people received food from the royal palace each day. Officials complained that too much money was being wasted on the poor.

Anne frequently urged her husband to pardon people who had fallen foul of the authorities. Her sympathetic intervention often curbed King Richard's temper. The common people took note of her generosity and kindness and called her "Good Queen Anne."

She did not hide her evangelical faith. Once, she showed the Archbishop of York her English translation of the gospels—despite his opposition to the English Scriptures. Even he admired her faith. "I was very surprised," the archbishop said, "on finding that the queen—although a foreigner—daily studied the gospels in English. It appears to me a marvelous instance of godliness that so illustrious a princess devoted herself to study these excellent words. Never before did I have the happiness of knowing such an extraordinary lady."

Through the encouragement of Joan of Kent, her mother-in-law, Anne studied Wycliffe's writings. She found his arguments from Scripture convincing. In her own gentle way she tried to make Richard more accepting of Wycliffe's ideas. She often read to him from Bible passages that supported Wycliffe's teachings and discussed them with him. Anne interceded with the king often when church leaders wanted to have Wycliffe or his supporters arrested. During his reign, King Richard did not allow Lollards to be executed. Church leaders and members of Parliament complained that the queen's court was full of Lollards.

Wycliffe rejoiced to learn of Anne's faith and her devotion to the Scriptures. In one of his papers defending the use of the Bible in English, he used Anne as an example. "Our noble Queen of England," he wrote, "has the gospels written in three languages, Bohemian, German, and Latin. Now, to brand her with heresy on that account would be satanic folly."

In 1391, King Richard had overspent his treasury. He demanded that London magistrates loan him a thousand pounds, but the city officials refused. The furious king threw city leaders into prison until they paid a large fine. He revoked London's royal charter which deprived the city of much needed revenue.

London officials paid their fines, collected a gift for the king of ten thousand pounds and asked Richard to reinstate the royal charter. He took the gift, but refused the request. The Lord Mayor went to the queen to seek her help. "Illustrious daughter of imperial parents whose name means grace in Hebrew," the mayor said, "intercede for us to the king."

"Leave it to me," Anne replied. The next day, she went to the king's throne room and found him seated, scepter in hand, with the officials of London standing before him. She knelt in front of

Richard. As he took her arm and lifted her up, he asked, "What do you want me to do? Speak and your request shall be granted."

"My sweet," she replied, "my king, my spouse, my light, my life. Be pleased to govern your citizens as a gracious lord. Like us, they are mortal and frail. Cast their offenses far from your memory, my king, my sweet love. Be pleased to restore these worthy and penitent people to their ancient charters and liberties."

"Be satisfied, dearest wife," King Richard answered, "I am loath to deny you any reasonable request." Turning to the leaders of London he said, "We will restore to you our royal favor as in former days. We pardon you at the earnest entreaty of our dearly beloved queen."

In 1394, Anne died of the plague at the age of twenty-seven. Richard wept for days. All the citizens of London mourned. The Bohemian members of her court returned home, bringing with them Wycliffe's writings. His ideas moved many ministers to press for further reforms of the church in Bohemia. John Huss, the Bohemian reformer, said that John Wycliffe was his greatest inspiration apart from Scripture. Later, the writings of Wycliffe and Huss inspired Martin Luther and other reformers. Wycliffe became known as the Morning Star of the Reformation. So Queen Anne played an important role in the spread of ideas that gave rise to the Protestant Reformation.

As one historian wrote long ago, "To Anne of Bohemia is attributed the honor of being the first of that illustrious band of princesses who were the nursing-mothers of the Reformation."

REFORMATION
AND BEYOND
STANDING FOR THE GOSPEL

Since the dawn of the Christian church, Christian mothers—confident in God's promise to be "Your God and the God of your children after you"—nurtured their children to love and fear the Lord. In the 1500s, a great spiritual revival known as the Reformation swept across Europe. As reformers rediscovered the central truth of the gospel—sinners are justified only by the righteousness of Christ—brave men and women risked their lives to proclaim that truth to their children and to others.

In the two centuries that followed the Reformation, persecution and blessings abounded. Enemies of the truth labored to stamp out biblical Christianity, and the Holy Spirit awakened countless people to faith in Jesus Christ.

Some died in the flames at the stake, such as Mrs. Smith of Coventry, who suffered martyrdom for teaching her children the

Lord's Prayer in English. Others endured the loss of husband and home for their loyalty to Christ and His Word. Some dwelt in humble cottages and others sat on regal thrones, but they shared a common gratitude for the saving grace of Jesus Christ and a willingness to stand for Him in a hostile world.

15 MRS. SMITH OF COVENTRY
Mother and Martyr, c. 1485–1519

One evening in 1519, Mrs. Smith, a widowed mother, sat with her children around the hearth of their cottage in Coventry, England.* She was reading to them from the Gospel of Luke and teaching them to recite the Lord's Prayer in English. They worshiped secretly with a small group of Lollards who read the Bible in English and followed the teachings of John Wycliffe. About 150 years earlier, Wycliffe, a professor at Oxford University, studied the Word of God in Latin and discovered a welcoming Savior, not an aloof judge. He came to find that many of the teachings of the Roman church—purgatory, prayers to saints, indulgences and many others—were contrary to the teaching of the Scriptures.

Wycliffe began to teach his students that the church's unbiblical doctrines hid the good news of Jesus Christ. "Church Law has no force," Wycliffe wrote, "when it is opposed to the Word of God."

At that time, the Latin Vulgate was the only Bible translation allowed by the church, but only the educated elite understood Latin. Wycliffe longed for the people to hear and read the Scriptures in their own language. So, with the help of his

---

*The Coventry authorities in 1519 did not record Mrs. Smith's first name. In the 1560s when the reformer John Foxe was writing his book on the Christian martyrs, he did not include her first name either.

students, he translated the Bible into English. He sent out his helpers to preach and distribute hand-written portions of the Scriptures. The Lollards, as they were called, won thousands of Englishmen to Christ, but the bishops convinced the king to crush them. Hunted and hounded for decades, scores of Lollards were burned at the stake. They went underground, worshiping behind closed doors and secretly passing out hand-copied passages of the Bible.

In reaction to Wycliffe's efforts, the authorities enforced severe punishments for translating the Bible into English or reading the Scriptures in English. But persecution by the Church and the Crown could not fully extinguish Wycliffe's Bible or the Lollards.

One hundred thirty years after Wycliffe's death, when Martin Luther in Germany began using the Scriptures to boldly challenge the teachings of the Roman church, leaders in England feared that their island kingdom might be infected by the German Reformation. They had good reason for concern. The English had long resented papal taxation and the unrestricted powers of church courts where a dungeon cell awaited those who dared bring complaints against the clergy. Immoral and greedy priests made a mockery of Christ's commands.

"What a trade is that of the priests!" William Tyndale, the English reformer, wrote, "They want money for everything: money for baptism, for weddings, for buryings, for images, penances, and soul-masses. Poor sheep! The parson shears, the vicar shaves, the parish priest polls, the friar scrapes, the indulgence seller pares. We lack but a butcher to pull off the skin."

As Luther's writings rolled off the printing presses in Germany, they were smuggled into England and then spread throughout the kingdom by merchants and booksellers—many of them Lollards. The Bishop of London warned, "There have been found certain children of iniquity who are endeavoring to bring into our land the old and accursed Wycliffite heresy and along with it the Lutheran heresy."

Young King Henry VIII, enraged by Luther's criticism of the Roman church, called the German reformer "a serpent, a cunning viper." He said that Luther's writings "sprung from the depths of hell." Henry ordered them publicly burned in London, and made it clear that English supporters of these ideas would face persecution. A crackdown on Lollards soon followed.

In the spring of 1519, the Bishop of Coventry received word that certain families were teaching their children the Lord's Prayer and the Ten Commandments in English. The bishop ordered the arrest of Mr. Hatchets, Mr. Archer, Mr. Hawkins, Mr. Bond, Mr. Wrigsham, Mr. Landsdale and Mrs. Smith. While they were held at an abbey outside of town, their children were brought to Greyfriar's Monastery in Coventry. The boys and girls were made to stand before Friar Stafford, the abbot. One by one, Stafford interrogated the children about their parents' beliefs. "Now then," he told them, "I charge you in the name of God to tell me the whole truth—you shall suffer severely for any lies you tell or secrets you conceal."

"What do you believe about the church and the way to heaven?" he asked them. "Do you go to the services of the parish church? Do you read the Scriptures in English? Do you memorize the Lord's Prayer or other Scriptures in English?"

After getting from the children's own lips the information he needed to convict their parents, he warned them. "Your parents are heretics!" he bellowed. "They have led you away from the teachings of the church. You are never to meddle again with the Lord's Prayer or the Ten Commandments or any other Scriptures in English. And if you do—rest assured you will burn at the stake for it!"

The next day, the six fathers and Mrs. Smith stood before a panel of judges that included the bishop and Friar Stafford. After presenting the evidence against them—and because the men had been warned before by the bishop not to persist in their Lollard ways—the men were condemned to death by burning. But since this was Mrs. Smith's first offense, the court dismissed her with a warning not to teach her children the Scriptures in English any-more under pain of death.

It was late in the evening when the court dismissed, so the bishop's assistant decided to see Mrs. Smith home in the dark. As they walked out into the night, he took her arm to lead her across the street. Hearing the rattling of papers within her sleeve, he stopped and said, "Well, what do you have here?" He grabbed her arm, reached into the sleeve and pulled out a little scroll. Under the light of a lantern, he read it and found that it contained handwritten in English the Lord's Prayer, the Ten Commandments and the Apostle's Creed. "Well, well," he said with a sneer. "Come now, this is as good a time as any!"

He dragged her back again to the bishop. The panel quickly sentenced her to be burned with the six condemned men and sent her off to prison to await her fate.

A few days later, guards led Mrs. Smith and the Lollard men to an open space in the center of Coventry known as Little Park. They tied them to a stake and burned them to death for the crime of teaching their children the Word of God in English.

16 MARGARET, QUEEN OF NAVARRE
Protector of the Persecuted, 1492–1549

I n Paris on January 21, 1535, Francis I, King of France, led a great procession from the Louvre to the Cathedral of Notre Dame. Bareheaded and holding a lighted torch, Francis walked along with hundreds of others. All the high officials of the royal court, university professors, members of parliament, cardinals, bishops, priests and monks marched in line, carrying relics from all the churches of the French capital. The Bishop of Paris carried a consecrated host protected under a crimson canopy held aloft by the king's three sons and a duke.

When they reached Notre Dame, they celebrated high mass. After the service, the king addressed the assembly. With tears in his eyes, he told the immense crowd that he would resist the Protestant reformers whom he called "enemies of God." "And if my own right arm," he said, "were infected with the radical pestilence, I would cut it off and cast it from me. And if one of my children were so miserable as to favor it, I would with my own hand deliver him up to the just fate of a heretic and blasphemer." Applause erupted from the congregation, as they looked forward to the main event—the burning of several people who had accepted the Reformation teaching that sinners are justified by faith in Christ alone.

The procession and the king's speech had been prompted by the placing of placards on church doors across Paris. The posters condemned the Roman church's teaching that the bread of the Eucharist was the physical body of Christ. Placards were even affixed to the front gates of the king's palace. Church leaders and government officials had long complained that King Francis was too lenient with his subjects who accepted the ideas of Luther and other reformers. "The detestable doctrines of Luther are everywhere finding fresh adherents," one bishop lamented to the king. "Condemn them to be burned alive."

The "Affair of the Placards" was just the excuse they needed to get the king to act.

Shortly after Francis's speech, six French Protestants were burned slowly at the stake in front of a large gathering of leaders of church and state. One was a school teacher who ate meat on Friday, a day set aside by the Roman church for abstaining from meat.

The executioner suspended them above the fire with an iron chain and drew them in and out of the flames to prolong their agony. In the crackdown against French Protestants that followed, thousands were killed and thousands more fled the country.

Conspicuously absent from the procession and the executions was the king's sister, Margaret, Queen of Navarre. Raised in a royal house that embraced the Renaissance, Margaret received a classical education. The tall, blond-haired princess mastered Italian, Spanish and Latin, and she learned a little Greek and Hebrew. Her diligent study of literature, philosophy and theology made her one of the best educated women in Europe.

As a young adult, Margaret embraced many of the ideas of the Protestant reformers. She loved to read the Scriptures in French from the translation by Jacques Lefevre. Although the doctors of the Sorbonne in Paris, the world's oldest university, condemned Lefevre's writings, Margaret hailed him as a bright light for the Christian faith. Lefevre won many disciples, including William Farel, Gerard Roussel and John Calvin. In 1522, the bishops asked the French assembly to condemn Lefevre as a heretic. Margaret urged her brother the king to use his power to halt the proceedings, and he did. With the enthusiastic support of Margaret, Francis established the College of France to expand the Renaissance and create an alternative to the Sorbonne. The king endowed professorships in Greek and Hebrew. "To study Greek and to meddle with Hebrew is one of the greatest heresies of the world," a Sorbonne professor said.

Margaret was very close to her brother. Her love and loyalty for him often clouded her judgment. "The king is more than ever inclined to aid the reform of the church," she once wrote to Lefevre. But she didn't understand that King Francis would never accept the reformation of the church. To do so, Francis told an advisor, "would prejudice my estate."

With openness and generosity, Queen Margaret and her husband King Henry ruled the Kingdom of Navarre, a small principality closely allied with France located between Spain and France. They founded hospitals and orphanages throughout the kingdom. Margaret made it her practice to visit the sick and the poor. She walked through the streets of the capital, Nerac, in plain clothing, talking with the people and striving to relieve their needs. Margaret and her husband spent most of their income helping orphans and the elderly. "No one," Margaret said, "should leave sad or disappointed from the presence of a prince, for kings are the ministers of the poor—not their masters."

"To see her you would never have thought she was a queen," said one observer, "for she went about like an ordinary woman."

In the early years of Francis's reign—through the encouragement of Margaret—he tolerated the reformers and defended them against the religious establishment, especially if he thought he could use it to his advantage. But after the Affair of the Placards, he turned against the Protestants. Francis unleashed a widespread persecution. When reformers were accused of heresy and fled from France, many came to Navarre for Margaret's protection. "The truth of God is no heresy," Margaret said. Jacques Lefevre, Clement Marot, who translated the Psalms into French, the reformers John Calvin and Gerard Roussel, and others found sanctuary and support there.

Margaret appointed Roussel to be a royal chaplain. In the palace at Nerac they celebrated mass in French rather than Latin as ordered by Rome. Worshipers received the bread and the wine during communion, and no mention was made of the Virgin Mary or the saints during the service. Those who attended such services in France, Spain or Italy could face the death penalty. French bishops complained that Navarre was throwing off the true faith of the holy Church of Rome. A high official told Francis, "If your majesty really wishes to exterminate the heretics of his kingdom, he ought to begin with his nearest relative, her highness Queen of Navarre."

"Do not speak of her," Francis replied, "she loves me too much. She will never believe anything save what I believe, and will never embrace a religion harmful to my rule."

When King Francis increased the pressure on Margaret to stop sheltering heretics, she sent the reformers to other safe havens. She helped John Calvin make his way to Geneva. Margaret sent money to Protestant refugees in Switzerland and Germany, and she supported Reformed scholars studying in exile. Margaret considered herself a loyal member of the Church of Rome, but she wanted corrupt and unbiblical practices ended. And she wanted the Bible available to the people in their own language.

Margaret was an accomplished poet and writer of short stories. In her writings, she exposed the corruption and immorality of church officials. She pointed her readers to the Word of God for their spiritual guidance. "If you ask me what keeps me so joyous and so healthy in my age," she wrote in one of her stories, "it is that as soon as I arise in the morning I take the Holy Scriptures and read. I see and contemplate the will of God who sent His Son for our sake into the world to announce glad tidings. He promises remission from our sins and the full discharge of our debts by the gift of His love and martyrdom. The thought of this so fills me with delight that I take up my Psalter and sing the beautiful canticles and songs which the Spirit of God composed in the heart of David and other writers."

Her enemies at the Sorbonne carefully examined her writings for heresy. In one of her devotional poems, they discovered that she did not mention purgatory or prayers to Mary and the saints. They placed the poem on the list of banned books. King

Francis, enraged at the attack on his sister, sent a bishop to defend the poem and demanded punishment for those responsible. Margaret urged him to forgive them. Not long after, some students at the Sorbonne staged a play that mocked Queen Margaret—showing an evil spirit handing her a copy of the Gospels in French. When Francis ordered the arrest of all those involved in the play, Margaret intervened again and asked her brother to pardon them. One prominent Franciscan monk criticized Margaret publicly: "If this patron of heretics had her just deserts," he said, "she would be tied up in a sack and drowned in the River Seine."

As time passed, the persecution of Protestants in France grew, and Margaret's influence on her brother waned. Although brokenhearted at the suffering of the French Protestants, she did what she could to protect them. Many years after her death, a French historian wrote: "Let us always remember this tender Queen of Navarre, in whose arms our people, fleeing from prison or the pyre, found safety, honor and friendship."

17 KATHERINE VON BORA
Wife of Martin Luther, 1499–1552

I n the spring of 1523, an old fishmonger led his horse-drawn cart through the city gate and onto the cobblestone streets of Wittenberg, Germany. He carried a full load, but it wasn't his usual cargo of pickled herring or salted trout. No, this day, he was hauling a cartload of nuns who had just left their convent in a nearby town. These women—like thousands of monks and nuns across Germany—had trusted in the work of Christ on the cross alone for their salvation and not their own good works. They had come to this faith through the writings of the German reformer, Martin Luther, and by reading his German translation of the New Testament.

Luther had also written a paper criticizing the Roman church's promise that the surest way to heaven was to live behind clois-tered walls—telling young men and women that the single life of a monk or nun was holier than the married life of a husband or wife.

The nine women in the fish wagon had recently asked for Martin Luther's help in leaving the convent to start a new life. Luther had arranged with the fish seller to bring them to Wittenberg. They arrived at Luther's home—a defunct monas-tery that was taken over by Wittenberg University. Luther, a doctor of theology and university professor, lived there with a number of his students. Luther's heart went out to these women who arrived with nothing more than the clothes on their backs, like castaways set adrift on the ocean of the world. "They need our compassion," he said, "in helping them we are serving Christ."

Luther wrote to the women's parents, imploring them to take their daughters home. Some parents welcomed them back into their family. For those who remained in Wittenberg, Luther found them jobs in the homes of the wealthy. And he started to search for suitable husbands for them. When someone suggested that Luther marry, he said, "Good heavens! They won't give me a wife."

Believing that marriage was the God-ordained path for most people, Luther taught that God promised that his favor would rest upon faithful Christian wives and husbands. "The greatest blessing that God can confer on man," Luther wrote, "is the possession of a good and pious wife. We sing the praises of marriage!"

But he did not think marriage was for him. "Although God can change a heart at any moment," he wrote, "for now my mind is set—I shall not take a wife because I am expecting any day to be killed as a heretic."

Before long, all of the nuns who came to Wittenberg had returned home to their parents or were married—except one—Katherine von Bora. At one point, it looked like she might marry a young nobleman, but when that didn't work out, Luther tried to arrange a marriage to one of his friends, but Katherine refused to accept him. "I am not unreasonable," she told Luther. "I should be happy to accept a marriage proposal from Herr Amsdorf or from you, Dr. Luther."

At first, Luther did not seriously consider marrying Katherine, but when he told his parents what Katherine had suggested, his father urged him to marry. "I want grandchildren to carry on the Luther name," he said.

Not long after, Luther asked Katherine to be his wife. "While I was thinking of other things," Luther wrote a friend, "God has suddenly brought me to marriage. I'm going to get married! God likes to work miracles! You must come to the wedding."

Luther's enemies in the Roman church heaped scorn upon him for getting married and called it "wicked" and "from the devil." Even some friends of the Reformation thought it was a big mistake. "Should he marry," one said, "the whole world will burst into shouts of laughter, and he himself will destroy what he has been building up."

Their marriage was a happy one from the start. "Katie, my dear rib, salutes you," Luther wrote a friend during their first year of marriage. "She is, by the blessing of God, gentle, kind, and obedient in all things, far above my hopes—thanks be to God!"

Katherine leapt into married life with diligence and devotion. It was easy for her to respect her husband because she admired his brilliant mind, solid faith and great courage. While under the threat of death from the pope and from Emperor Charles V, Luther worked tirelessly. He taught at the university, preparing young men for the ministry. He wrote commentaries on books of the Bible, religious treatises and a catechism for children. He preached, developed a new worship service liturgy, wrote hymns and corresponded with kings, churchmen, and dignitaries from across Europe. And he completed his translation of the whole Bible into German. A great awakening of faith in Christ was sweeping the continent, and Martin Luther was at the heart of it. Katherine knew that God was doing a mighty work through him.

She relieved him of the care of running the household—a household that included a steady stream of guests and a pack of student boarders. These students lined their table for meals, eating their fill and taking notes on every word that Martin Luther uttered. "Before I was married," Luther said, "I would not make my bed for a whole year and it would become foul with sweat. But I worked so hard and was so weary I just tumbled in without noticing it."

Katherine changed all that. His bed was made and linens and clothes were regularly washed and aired. She cooked balanced meals and saw to it that he got his rest. Luther's poor health improved.

Before Katherine arrived in the home, Luther's personal finances were a mess. She brought them under control. Luther's income as a university professor was small, and he never took a penny from the sale of his books. He often gave away more of his money to the needy than seemed prudent. Martin didn't give much thought about his mounting debts—but Katherine did. It was her constant challenge to balance the family's income and expenses. "I do not worry about debts," Luther said, "because when Katie pays one, another comes."

Katherine planted a vegetable garden and worked a fruit orchard they rented on the edge of town. She raised pigs, chickens, ducks and fish from a pond she had dug in the garden. "My Katie is in all things so obliging and pleasing to me," Luther wrote a friend, "that I would not exchange my poverty for the riches of Croesus."

Katherine was as hospitable as her husband, and she cheerfully made up beds for the needy who arrived at their door. Many of these came—as she had—from monasteries and convents. She often nursed sick people in a wing of their home that became a makeshift hospital.

In the convent, Katherine had learned very little of the Bible, but life in the Luther home revolved around the Scriptures. They read the Bible together in the morning and evening, and the Word of God was often discussed at meals. Martin encouraged her to memorize Scripture passages. Psalm 31 was one of the first she committed to memory, and it served as a life-long anchor of peace and encouragement for her. "I attentively listen to the reading and preaching of the Word," Katherine told a friend, "and I read portions of it every day; so that I am able to repeat from memory many passages from it."

Once at the dinner table when Martin and his guests were discussing God's command to Abraham to sacrifice his son Isaac, Katherine interrupted saying, "I cannot believe that God would require anyone to kill his son."

Luther looked his wife in the eyes and said, "Dear Katherine, can you believe then that God delivered up to death for us His only begotten Son, our Lord and Savior Jesus Christ?"

But it wasn't always Martin reminding Katherine of Scripture truth; she also pointed him to the Word of God. Luther would occasionally fall prey to bouts of discouragement and gloomy moods. Once, when a depression lasted longer than usual, he left home to visit friends for a few days, hoping that a change of scene might help. It didn't, and he wrote Katherine that he was coming home. When he arrived, he found her sitting in a chair dressed from head to toe in black with a dark veil covering her face. She was sighing and holding a wet handkerchief to her eyes. Luther rushed to her side and asked, "Katherine, what is the matter?"

"Only think, my dear doctor," she said, "the Lord in heaven is dead! This is the cause of my grief."

Luther stepped back and smiled. "It is true, dear Kate," Martin said with a laugh, "I am acting as if there is no God in heaven." His depression left him at once. "Katie now understands the Bible better than any papists did twenty years ago," Luther told a friend.

Over the years, Martin and Katherine were blessed with six children of their own, and they also raised eight orphaned children of relatives.

"I love my Katie," Luther said. "I love her more than I do myself, for I would die rather than that any harm should happen to her or to her children." At times, Luther worried that he might be making an idol of his wife. "I give more credit to Katherine than to Christ who has done so much more for me," he said.

When their daughter Magdalena was fourteen years old, she got very sick. "O God," Luther prayed, "I love her so, but Your will be done." He and Katherine spent several days by her bedside as her strength slipped away. With his eyes welling with tears, Martin said to her, "My little girl, you would like to stay with your father here—and would you be glad to go to your Father in heaven?"

"Yes, dear father," she answered, "as God wills." Katie stood at the edge of the room sobbing. Luther held Magdalena in his arms until she passed away. "Well," he sighed, "whether we live or die we are the Lord's." When Martin and Katherine laid her in the grave, Luther turned to his weeping wife and said, "Katie, remember where our Magdalena came from."

After Martin Luther died, Katherine's life became very difficult. Her finances dried up, and she still had children to care for. Emperor Charles V waged war against the Protestants, and his forces overran Wittenberg. Katherine fled with the children for their lives. She lived in poverty for the remainder of her life, taking in boarders to make ends meet. Toward the end, she prayed, "Lord, my Savior, I desire to depart and be with You. Let my children be committed to Your mercy. Lord, look down with mercy upon Your church. May the pure doctrine which God has sent through my husband be handed down to succeeding generations. Good Lord, I thank You for all the trials through which You lead me, and by which You prepared me to behold Your glory. You have always caused Your face to shine upon me. I will cling to You for evermore."

The joyful match between Katherine von Bora and Martin Luther proved to be a boon for the Protestant Reformation. For centuries, the Roman church had forbidden priests to marry, so there was no example of married clergymen. The Christian family established by Martin and Katherine Luther became a model for Protestant ministers to follow throughout Western Europe.

18 KATHERINE PARR

*Queen of England and
a Real Follower of Christ, 1512–1548*

I n 1543 in the royal court in London, the aging and ailing
King Henry VIII saw a petite and beautiful woman named
Katherine. Henry took a fancy to the thirty-year-old Katherine
at once and set his sights on making her his sixth wife. Twelve
months earlier, Henry had ordered his fifth wife beheaded. Before
that, he had a previous wife executed and had divorced two others. When Henry asked an Italian duchess to be his wife, she replied, "Your highness, I have only one head, if I had two, then I
would be willing that one of them should be at your service."

Katherine was well aware of the danger that she faced if she
married him. She also knew that refusing the tyrant could prove
fatal too. After prayerful consideration she agreed to marry the
king, believing that it was God's will for her to do so. Friends
of the Protestant Reformation rejoiced because Katherine was a
strong supporter of the reformers.

"I have no hope or confidence in any creature," she said, "but
in Christ, my only Savior. He came into the world to save sinners."

As queen, Katherine carefully studied two things: her Bible
and the moods of the king. Henry suffered from several painful
ailments that made him short tempered and impatient. Katherine
quickly learned how to please Henry in word and deed. She

greeted him with smiles and warm affection and tried to ease his pains. He delighted in her and controlled his behavior around her in ways that he did for no other.

At receptions in the royal palace, Katherine dressed in robes of crimson velvet and gold satin and wore a necklace and tiara of rich diamonds. But the pomp and splendor of the royal court were not where she found her joy—that came from Scripture reading and prayer. She often used a prayer book for devotions. Her favorite prayer included these lines: "Lord Jesus, I pray You give me the grace to rest in You above all things, and to make me prefer You above all creatures, above all glory and honor, above all dignity and power, above all health and beauty, above all riches and treasure, above all joy and pleasure, above all fame and praise."

Queen Katherine invited the leading Protestant ministers to preach to her court. She held Bible studies in her chambers with her ladies-in-waiting, and together they studied the books of the reformers. Although some of these activities were against the law of the land, the king left the queen alone to pursue her faith as she saw fit.

Katherine developed close relationships with Henry's three children—Mary, Elizabeth and Edward—each child of a different mother. Katherine knew Greek, Latin, French and Italian. She had intently studied the Scriptures and theology and knew well the arguments of the Roman Catholic theologians and the Protestant reformers. She encouraged Henry's children in their studies and urged them to embrace the Reformed faith. From her own resources she paid for the translation of Erasmus's Latin Paraphrase of the New Testament into English. She arranged to have Princess Mary—a staunch supporter of the Roman faith—translate the Gospel of John from Latin into English. She gave similar assignments in the Scriptures to Elizabeth and Edward, the heir to the throne.

Katherine wanted all the people to be able to read the Bible in English for themselves. She opposed Bishop Gardiner and other anti-Protestant officials in Henry's court who wanted to restrict the use of the Scriptures to the clergy and the ruling class. They argued that if common people read the Bible it would make them arrogant and disloyal. "These men," Katherine said, "slander God and blame the Scriptures for man's sin."

Not long after they married, Henry went off to France to lead his last military campaign. In the months that he was away, he appointed Katherine as his regent. She worked closely with the King's Privy Council and Thomas Cranmer, the Archbishop of Canterbury who was a Protestant reformer. Her wise and diligent oversight earned Henry's gratitude and respect.

The king's fruitless wars depleted the royal treasury so he had to call Parliament into session to raise funds. The House of Commons voted the king a large sum, and they placed all the property of the colleges at the king's disposal. The University of Cambridge feared that the king would strip them of their wealth and bankrupt their institutions—several of the Cambridge colleges were centers for teaching the doctrines of the Reformation. One of the college masters wrote Queen Katherine, asking her to intercede for them with the king. She did, and Henry agreed to waive his right to appropriate their resources. When Katherine informed the college masters of Henry's decision, she challenged them to not simply teach secular knowledge to their students. "Set forth," she wrote, "Christ's reverent and most sacred doctrines."

As Katherine got to know the king, she took every opportunity to urge him to reform the Church of England which he had half-heartedly begun. Henry wanted independence from the pope in Rome, but he did not want the English church thoroughly reformed according to the Scriptures. Katherine defended the primary doctrines of the Reformation that salvation is a gift of God's grace and not of man's work, and that sinners are justified only by faith in Christ. "My lord," she told him, "we all must seek forgiveness only through the merits of Christ." Katherine knew how far to press her points before she tried the king's patience. Bishop Gardiner and Lord Chancellor Wriothesley—two of the king's closest advisors—overheard these talks with dismay. Gardiner and the Lord Chancellor hoped to bring the Church of England back under the pope in Rome, and they worried that Katherine's influence would block their plans, but they saw little opportunity to get rid of her.

Then one day when the king was suffering terribly from leg pain, Katherine talked to him again about the church. Bishop Gardiner noticed the king's face growing tense as Katherine pressed her arguments from Scripture in favor of reform. Henry cut the conversation short, and dismissed his wife with a smile saying, "Farewell, sweet heart." When Queen Katherine left the room, the king turned to Gardiner and grumbled, "Must I in my old age be taught by my wife!"

"Sire," Gardiner said with a bow, "it grieved me to hear the queen take it upon herself to instruct your majesty—especially when my Lord is renowned for his great learning in matters of religion."

As he spoke, Bishop Gardiner closely watched the king for any sign of displeasure with him. Seeing the king nodding in agreement, Gardiner continued. "Sire, it is a dangerous matter for a king to suffer such insolent words at the hands of his subjects. If they are so bold to contradict the sovereign in words, will it not one day lead them to seek to overthrow him in deeds? And the religion that the queen so stiffly maintains teaches the people to disregard princes and will lead to great calamity for his majesty's reign."

Then bowing low Gardiner added, "In all humility and reverence my Lord, the words she spoke and the religion she defends do by law deserve death."

Gardiner assured Henry that he could prove that Katherine and her ladies were treasonous. "It is perilous," he told the king, "to cherish a serpent within your own bosom." His words filled Henry's naturally distrustful mind with grave doubts about his wife. The king signed a warrant, granting Gardiner and the Lord Chancellor the power to investigate the queen and her court. "I will not spare her," Henry said, "if she has violated the statutes of the realm." Gardiner left with the intention of swiftly building a case for the queen's execution.

Bishop Gardiner and Lord Chancellor Wriothesley gathered evidence of the queen's Bible studies and the Reformed ministers that preached to her court. Queen Katherine knew nothing of the plot against her, and she continued to press the king to reform the church and expand the use of the Scriptures in the kingdom. Then it happened that a friend of the queen found a list of the charges against her that the bishop and Lord Chancellor had drawn up. He went to Katherine in secret and told her of the trap that they were laying for her. When Katherine heard the news and realized that she might be the king's next victim, she fainted. When she revived, she found her stomach twisted in knots and her head throbbing—she went straight to bed.

When Henry heard that his wife was ill, he went to her chambers to see her. "Sire," she said, "I fear that I have displeased your majesty by my words. I hope my lord will be patient and not utterly forsake me."

"O sweet heart," Henry said, "it is not so. You rest and let your mind be at peace—be assured of my love."

As Katherine regained her composure, she told her ladies to remove from the palace any Christian books that were against the law, and she asked them to pray for her relationship with the king. The next evening she went to see the king in his chambers. He invited her to sit and talk about religion. "Your majesty," she said, "knows that I am ignorant of many things. I am weak and subject to your majesty as my head. Since therefore God has appointed a natural difference between man and woman, and your majesty is excellent in gifts and wisdom, and I am just a poor woman—how then does it come to pass that your majesty should inquire of my judgment on religion? I refer to your majesty's wisdom as my head under God on earth."

"Not so," said the king. "Kate, you are well versed in theology and may instruct us, as we take it, and not be instructed by us."

"If your majesty thinks that," she replied, "then your majesty has very much mistaken me. I would never take upon myself the role of an instructor to my lord and husband. When I have—with your majesty's permission—been bold to speak, it was to take your majesty's mind off his painful infirmities for a time with heavenly talk and that I might profit from my husband's learning."

"Is it so sweet heart?" Henry said with a smile. "Then we are perfect friends again!" He rose and kissed his wife saying, "Kate, hearing these words from you has done me more good than if I had received a gift of a hundred thousand pounds! I will never mistake you again."

The next day, while the king and queen talked together in the garden, the Lord Chancellor entered with forty armed guards to arrest the queen and imprison her in the Tower of London. When Henry saw him and understood his intent, he stepped away from the queen and pulled the chancellor aside. "No, you knave!" the king told him. The Lord Chancellor, on bended knee, pleaded with the king about the queen's treachery. Henry's face glowed red, and he clenched his fists. "You beast," the king said, "you fool, drop this matter and get out of our presence at once!" He left humiliated and worried that his head might be next on the block.

When Henry rejoined Katherine, she said, "Your majesty, I could not hear your conversation, but I perceived the king's displeasure with the Lord Chancellor. I hope your majesty will show him mercy."

"Ah, poor soul," Henry said, "you do not know how little of your grace he deserves. Trust me, my sweet heart, he has been an arrant knave toward you—so let him go."

King Henry removed the Lord Chancellor and Bishop Gardiner from the list of men who would oversee the regency of his son Edward at his death. This helped to pave the way for the great progress of the Reformation during the reign of Edward VI.

Sadly, not everyone close to Katherine escaped punishment. Her friend, Anne Askew, was arrested and thrown in the Tower of London. Despite Katherine's pleas to her husband for mercy, Askew was burned at the stake as a heretic for her Protestant beliefs.

Henry VIII died a short time later, and Katherine left the royal palace. She rejoiced to see the rapid reformation of the Church of England under King Edward's rule. An English minister who carefully studied her life wrote, "Katherine Parr was a main instrument in protecting and advancing the English Reformation at a most critical period. She was a real follower of Christ."

19 ANNE ASKEW
The Lord's Bold Witness, 1521–1546

Late in the reign of King Henry VIII when the Church of England still clung to many false beliefs, an enraged husband burst into his home shouting for his young wife, Anne. A priest had just taunted him saying, "Your wife is a heretic! She openly renounces the teachings of the church." Anne Askew ran to her husband's side.

Grabbing her by the arm, he dragged her to the front door and violently threw her out of the house. "Get out and never return," he cried. Banished from her home and uncertain where to turn, Anne went to live near her brother in London. Her brother, a soldier in King Henry VIII's bodyguard, introduced her to Queen Katherine Parr and several devout Christian ladies of the court. Katherine was Henry's sixth wife. Henry divorced two of his previous wives and had two others beheaded.

Before long, Anne and several Christian ladies met daily in the queen's private rooms to hear a sermon, pray and study the Bible. Although the king had decreed all such religious meetings illegal, he did nothing to stop his wife.

These were difficult days for the Protestants of England. Even though Henry VIII had separated the churches in England from the Church of Rome, he did so not because he embraced the ideas of the Protestant Reformation, but because he wanted a divorce which the pope refused to grant. Henry and his supporters in the Church of England clung to the doctrines of the Church of Rome, many of which were against the clear teachings of the Bible.

The churchmen who hated the Reformation decided to make an example of Anne Askew. By attacking her, they hoped to scare the queen and others of the royal court away from the Protestant reformers. Anne's outspokenness about her faith made her an easy target. Once she said, "I would rather read five lines in the Bible than hear five masses in the church."

She openly declared that the bread and wine of the Lord's Supper were not changed by the priest into the physical body and blood of Jesus as the Roman church taught. For these beliefs the authorities arrested Anne and threw her into prison. The Lord Mayor of London and a judge questioned her at length. "Why did you say that you would rather read five lines in the Bible than hear five masses?" the judge asked.

"Because the one helps me greatly," Anne answered, "and the other does nothing at all."

"Have you the Spirit of God in you?" he asked.

"If I don't," Anne replied, "I am unsaved and without hope."

"Do you think private masses help the souls of those who have died?" he asked.

"It is great idolatry to believe them to be of more value than the death that Christ died for us," she said.

Looking down his nose at Anne, the Lord Mayor said, "You foolish woman, in the mass after the priest says the words of consecration over the bread, does it not become the Lord's body?"

"No," she answered, "it is but consecrated or sacramental bread."

"What if a mouse should eat it after the priest's consecration?" the mayor asked her. "What do you say, foolish woman, will become of the mouse?"

"What do you say will become of it, my Lord?" Anne asked.

"I say the mouse is damned," the Lord Mayor answered.

Anne smiled and said, "Ah, poor mouse!"

Next, Edmund Bonner, Bishop of London, visited Anne in prison, determined to drag a recantation out of her. Beforehand, he had drawn up a list of beliefs of the Roman church. Thrusting the list into her hands, he ordered her to sign it. She carefully read it and then wrote at the bottom of the page, "I believe everything written here which agrees with the Holy Scripture."

As Bishop Bonner read the statement his cheeks flamed red. Snatching the pen from her hand, he scratched out her sentence and pushed the paper and pen back demanding, "Sign this document!"

She wrote, "I, Anne Askew, do believe many things contained in the faith of the Catholic Church."

Enraged at Anne's refusal to comply, he hurried out of her cell saying, "She is a woman and I am not deceived by her."

Three months later, the bishop hauled Anne before a church court which declared her a heretic and sentenced her to death by burning.

"I have searched all the Scriptures," she said to the court, "yet I have never found that either Christ or His apostles put anyone to death."

The court sent her to the Tower of London to be tortured in hopes that she would give them evidence against the ladies of the royal court. Soldiers shackled her wrists and ankles with chains, threw her on the rack, and turned two wooden cranks, pulling her arms in one direction and her legs in another. Anne grimaced in pain as her ligaments and tendons stretched to the breaking point. "Tell us who else defies the king and the church. Renounce your faith and you will be pardoned," they demanded.

"I will sooner die than break my faith," she answered.

Seeing that she would not break, guards returned her to her dungeon cell where, falling to her knees, she prayed, "O Lord, I have more enemies now than hairs on my head; yet, Lord, let them never overcome me with vain words, but fight Lord, in my place, for on You I cast my care."

On the July 16, 1546, a huge crowd gathered to view the execution of Anne Askew and three other prisoners in front of St. Bartholomew's Church in Smithfield, London. Because of the torture, she was unable to walk and had to be carried to the stake. Before the burning, the bishop delivered a sermon during which Anne pointed out statements contrary to the Bible by saying, "He errs, and speaks without the Book."

As soldiers chained her to the stake and made ready the bonfire, a messenger arrived offering the king's pardon if she would recant. "I did not come here," Anne said, "to deny my Lord and Master."

Then she died for Christ in the flames.

A year later, Henry VIII died, and the Protestant Reformation moved forward quickly. The beliefs that Anne Askew died for became the teachings of the Church of England. Her bravery in the face of death still shines as a beautiful example of the faithfulness of God to uphold His children in the midst of great trials.

"Anne Askew: The Lord's Bold Witness" is excerpted from Richard M. Hannula's *Trial and Triumph: Stories from Church History* (Moscow ID: Canon Press, 1999).

20 KATHARINE HAMILTON
Reformation Sister, c. 1506–c. 1560

P atrick Hamilton sat with his sister Katharine in front of
the fireplace in the great hall of their manor at Linlithgow,
Scotland. Katharine Hamilton and her brothers, Patrick
and James, were children of noble blood. Their deceased father
came from a line of the greatest dukes and earls of the kingdom, and their mother was closely related to the royal family of
Scotland. As the firstborn, Patrick inherited the family estate and
could have served on the Privy Council, ruling Scotland alongside his nephew, the king.

But a few years earlier, Patrick began reading the Greek New
Testament and the writings of Martin Luther, the German reformer who taught that sinners are saved by faith in Christ alone and
not by their own good works. He turned to Jesus Christ and felt
freed from the burden of his sins like a liberated captive unshack-
led from his iron chains. He couldn't keep the good news to himself. Patrick began proclaiming forgiveness in Jesus throughout
the region. Soon church leaders regarded him as a heretic and
made plans to arrest him. So he fled Scotland for Germany to
study the Scriptures and the writings of the German reformers.
There, he befriended William Tyndale, the English reformer and
Bible translator. But—in spite of the danger—he longed to return
to Scotland to preach Christ's love to his lost countrymen.

In 1527, he slipped back into Scotland and went straight to his family estate to tell his sister all about the Savior. As they sat looking at the glowing embers of the fire, they talked long into the night. "But can it be that simple?" Katharine asked. "All I need to do is trust in Jesus, and all my sins are forgiven and I inherit heaven?"

"As I have been showing you from Scripture," Patrick said, lifting up his English New Testament, "we sinners can find peace with God only by believing in Christ. He that lacks faith cannot please God."

"But the priests and friars have always taught us," she said, "that the way to heaven is through obedience to the church and good works."

"Whoever believes or thinks that he can be saved by his own works," he told her, "denies that Christ is his Savior and that Christ died for him. For how is He your Savior if you can save yourself by your own works?"

"Are you saying that all my acts of penance and alms for the poor and pilgrimages to holy shrines—that none of that wins God's favor?"

"Faith in Christ alone makes a sinner right with God," he answered. "Look to Jesus who did it all for you on the cross. Forsake your trust in religious acts and come to Christ."

"But, Patrick, isn't this the heresy of Luther that the bishops so vehemently warn us against."

"This is no heresy," Patrick said, shaking his head, "nor did it begin with Martin Luther—it is the good news that the evangels wrote about in the Scriptures. Katharine, come to Christ. Christ is our Savior. Christ bore our sins on His back. Christ was the price that was given for us and for our sins. Christ is ours!"

The testimony of Scripture and Patrick's changed life convinced Katharine of the truth—she opened her heart to receive Jesus Christ by faith, forsaking her own good works as filthy rags. Soon their brother James put his trust in Christ also.

Patrick started preaching salvation through faith in Christ in the manors and churches of his home county. His straightforward preaching proclaimed the Scriptures in clear terms. He urged everyone to believe in Jesus Christ. "It is not sufficient to believe that Christ is a Savior and Redeemer," Hamilton said, "but that He is *your* Savior and *your* Redeemer."

He demonstrated that the teachings of the Roman church about purgatory, penance, prayers to saints and the like were contrary to the Word of God. The leaders of the Church of Rome in Scotland—especially Archbishop Beaton of St. Andrews—did not want this message spread in the land. Beaton feared the Reformation would sweep through Scotland like a plague as it had done in Germany. He banned Martin Luther's writings and got the Scottish Parliament to pass a law condemning the ideas of the reformers, making it a crime punishable by death to speak about them or own their books. Church officials did not want the people reading the Scriptures for themselves, so when Tyndale's New Testament in English began to filter into the country in 1526, they banned it as well. But Reformation ideas kept spreading.

And now, Patrick Hamilton, an articulate nobleman from an influential family, was back in Scotland openly preaching faith in

Christ alone—the message of the Protestant Reformation. "If he isn't stopped," Beaton said, "all will be lost."

But getting his hands on Hamilton would not be easy. Patrick preached in the homes and churches of the area controlled by his clan. If Beaton sent men to arrest him, they would face resistance. So the archbishop resorted to deception, sending Patrick a letter inviting him to St. Andrews. "Come," he wrote, "and we will discuss the state of the church in Scotland and the steps that might be taken to reform her."

Patrick was not deceived by the archbishop's invitation, but he wanted to speak for Christ in St. Andrews, the center of the Scottish church and home to Scotland's most important university. "Don't go!" Katharine implored him, "It is a trap!"

"I must," he told her, "but I do not think I have long to live."

In January 1528, Patrick arrived in St. Andrews. At first, Beaton permitted him to publicly proclaim his views so that later there would be no question of his guilt. For nearly a month, Patrick taught justification through faith in Christ alone and debated churchmen openly in the university about the unbiblical doctrines of the Roman church. The college students had never heard teaching like this before. Hamilton defended his ideas exclusively from the Scripture—not from church theologians as their professors did. Many people came to him privately for spiritual counsel. He urged them to look to Christ alone for their salvation. "We have a good and gentle Lord," he said, "let us follow His footsteps."

As Beaton built his case against Hamilton, Katharine and Patrick's friends urged him to flee before the archbishop arrested him. "I came here," he said, "to strengthen the faith of believers by my death as a martyr to the truth—if I turn back now, I would lay a stumbling block in their path and might cause some of them to fall."

When the time was ripe, Beaton sent a band of armed guards to seize Patrick at night. Early the next morning, he stood trial in St. Andrews Cathedral. The archbishop and a panel of bishops and friars condemned Hamilton as a heretic and ordered death by burning—to be carried out that very day. Armed guards marched Patrick through the rain to a stake. "You may save your life," a churchman called out, "if you recant your errors that you professed this morning in the cathedral."

"I will not deny my testimony," Patrick said. "I am content that my body burn in this fire for my faith in Christ, than my soul should burn in the fire of hell for denying it. I trust in the mercy of God."

The wet wood and straw smoldered. Patrick suffered for six hours. Through the pain, he spoke to the people, imploring them to look to Christ.

The crowd, watching the terrible scene marveled that Patrick never grew impatient or angry. As word of his execution spread throughout the kingdom, people asked, "Why was Master Patrick Hamilton burned?" His dignity and patience during his trial and execution had adorned the gospel he preached.

Despite their brother's cruel death, Katharine and James clung to their new faith in Christ and told others about the way of salvation. Not long after, Katharine got married, but her husband died a short time later. She used her home to spread

Reformation teaching and distribute the Scriptures in English. James, a well-known supporter of the Reformation, inherited the family estate and became the Sheriff of Linlithgow. After a few years, Archbishop Beaton summoned James Hamilton to stand trial for heresy. When James fled the country to avoid execution, the archbishop seized all his lands and property.

Then the archbishop ordered Katharine to appear before their tribunal at Holyrood Palace in Edinburgh. Katharine did not try to run away, but came determined to testify to her faith in Christ alone for salvation. Her nephew, the King of Scotland, sat in on the trial, although he had no power to rule over heresy cases. The king hated the Protestant Reformation and did what he could to stamp it out of his kingdom, but he did not like church officials harassing members of his extended family.

Katharine stood accused of heresy and of reading the Scriptures in English. When they questioned her about justification by works, she answered simply, "No person can be saved by their works."

Then the prosecutor launched into a long explanation of the many different kinds of works recognized by the church as helping to merit justification. After a while, Katharine grew weary of his convoluted jargon and said, "Work here, work there, what kind of working is all this? I know perfectly well that no kind of works can save me but the works of Christ my Savior."

As the cheeks of the archbishop flamed red, the king stepped in and broke the tension created by her bold reply. With a hearty laugh, he approached Katharine. Taking her by the arm to the corner of the room, he coaxed her into rephrasing her beliefs in such a way as to satisfy the court. She did, and they released her. If the king had not been present, Katharine would likely have suffered the same fate as Patrick.

As soon as Katharine reached home, she regretted her failure to stand firm before the church court. She determined to redouble her efforts to support the cause of the Reformation. A year later, fearing that Archbishop Beaton would soon arrest her, she fled to Berwick-upon-Tweed, an English city on the border with Scotland. She remained there for many years doing what she could to help her persecuted brothers and sisters in Scotland.

21 LADY JANE GREY
Nine-Day Queen, 1537–1553

Lady Jane Grey has been remembered for centuries by Christians not merely because she held the title of Queen of England for a few days or because she died a tragic death. She has been remembered and admired for her sturdy faith in Christ and firm convictions in the doctrines of the Reformation under the most difficult of circumstances. This is her story.

In 1553, Edward VI, the young king of England, was dying. With Edward's unwavering support, the Reformation had leapt forward. Through the efforts of Thomas Cranmer, the Archbishop of Canterbury, and other reformers, the gospel rang out across the kingdom. But next in line to the throne was Edward's half-sister Mary, a staunch Roman Catholic and enemy of the Reformation.

To avoid the crown falling into the hands of Princess Mary, the Duke of Northumberland, the king's chief advisor, convinced King Edward to draft a will. The will outlined a different order of succession from the one that Edward's father, King Henry VIII, had passed through Parliament. Northumberland persuaded Edward to name his cousin Jane Grey as his successor—bypassing his half-sisters, Princess Mary and Princess Elizabeth. Jane Grey's father was a close advisor to the king, and Northumberland was her father-in-law. They had hoped to have the new succession plan approved by Parliament, but Edward died before that could be done. Jane was unaware of the plan.

Jane Grey was closely related to the kings of England through both her mother's and her father's families. Her parents supported the Reformation, and Jane put her faith in Christ at an early age. "I am a sorrowful wretch," Jane said, "for whom Jesus Christ shed His precious blood on the cross." When she was ten years old, Jane went to live with Katherine Parr, who had been King Henry VIII's last wife. Katherine encouraged Jane in her studies of the Scriptures, the Reformed writers, and Latin, Greek and French. Jane became so familiar with Greek that she could speak it nearly as well as she could speak English. One Greek scholar considered Jane Grey the best educated woman in England.

Jane's bright mind and earnest faith caught the attention of Martin Bucer, the Strasbourg reformer who came to England to teach at Cambridge University. Bucer instructed Jane in the Christian faith. "He was the most learned and holy man," Jane said of him, "who by his excellent advice, encouraged my progress in all virtue, godliness and learning."

When King Edward died, Northumberland and the king's council kept his death a secret until they could make Jane Grey queen. Three days later, Northumberland, Jane's father and her husband met with her. "The king is dead," Northumberland said, "and it was the king's will that you, Lady Jane, should succeed him on the throne." Then the men dropped to their knees and swore their allegiance to Queen Jane. "We pledge our lives in defense of your Majesty," they said.

The shocking news filled Jane with dread. Falling to the floor and breaking down in tears, she sobbed, "How can this be? Is the honor rightfully and lawfully mine?"

"You are of true and direct lineage," Northumberland told her, "and the rightful heir to the throne."

"I cannot—I am not sufficient for the task!" Jane said.

With urgent pleadings, Northumberland and her father convinced Jane—against her better judgment—that it was her duty to follow the wishes of the late King Edward and take the crown. After some time, she consented. Then Jane knelt down. "O Lord," she prayed, "if what is given to me is rightly and lawfully mine grant me such grace and spirit that I might govern this realm to Your glory and service."

Northumberland had launched a dangerous scheme. If it failed, Jane and all those involved would be guilty of treason. Only the king's council and some key leaders in London knew of Edward's will and the plan to make Jane Grey the heir to the throne. Most members of Parliament were in the dark and so were most of the noblemen in the country. Northumberland was not beloved in the kingdom. His rule as Edward's regent had made him many enemies.

The next day, Northumberland proclaimed Jane Queen of England and led her through the streets of London in a grand procession. Confused crowds came out to see her, but they did not cheer. Assuming that Princess Mary would take the crown, most Englishmen saw Northumberland's effort to put his daughter-in-law on the throne as an ambitious politician's bald-faced attempt to seize power.

Northumberland's plan fell apart from the start. Mary had been warned about the conspiracy against her, and she had stayed away from London, rallying nobles to her side. Mary won the support of key Protestant leaders by promising not to change the Reformed faith of the Church of England. Seeing Northumberland and Jane as usurpers, Roman Catholic and Protestant nobles prepared to fight for Mary's cause.

Just nine days after Jane was declared queen, Mary took the crown and was hailed as Queen of England. Now Jane would reap the whirlwind for her father-in-law's ambition. Although the imprisoned Northumberland informed Queen Mary that Jane did not want the crown and that he had forced her to accept it, Mary ordered the arrest of Jane and her husband. Charged with high treason, they were jailed in the Tower of London in separate quarters and were never permitted to see one another again. Lady Jane pleaded guilty to the charges against her, and in November 1553, Jane and her husband were convicted of treason and sentenced to death.

In the meantime, Queen Mary abandoned her pledge to preserve the Protestant faith. She ordered the arrest of Archbishop Cranmer and other leading reformers—hundreds would soon be burned at the stake. Mary and her bishops hoped to damage the cause of the Reformation by persuading Lady Jane to reject her Protestant faith. Church officials visited Jane and promised her that if she accepted Roman Catholicism, she would be pardoned, freed, and restored to her family fortune. Jane clung to Christ alone as her Rock and steadfastly refused. "Should I forsake my faith for love of life?" Jane said. "No, God forbid! May God be merciful to us, for the Lord says, 'Whoever shall confess Me before men, him will I confess also before My Father in heaven.'"

After she was condemned to die, she sent a letter to her father. "Father, it has pleased God to hasten my death by you, by whom my life should rather have been lengthened; yet I can take it patiently—I yield to God. Although my death seems woeful to you, yet to me there is nothing that can be more welcome than to go from this vale of misery to that heavenly throne of all joy and pleasure with Christ our Savior."

She wrote a note on the last page of a Greek New Testament and sent it to her sister. "Good sister Catherine," she wrote, "delight yourself only in the Lord. Follow the steps of your Master, Christ, and take up your cross, lay your sins on His back, and always embrace Him. Fare you well, good sister, and put your trust only in God."

In her final days, she wrote a lengthy prayer which began with these words: "O merciful Savior, I come to You defiled with my sin, encumbered with affliction, disquieted with troubles, overwhelmed with miseries, vexed with temptations, and grievously tormented with long imprisonment. Be unto me a strong tower of defense. Suffer me not to be tempted above my power. Either deliver me out of this great misery, or else give me grace patiently to bear Your heavy hand and sharp correction."

In a final effort to change Lady Jane's faith, Queen Mary sent the abbot of Westminster Abbey to persuade her. "Madam," the abbot said, "I have been sent by the queen and her council to instruct you in the true doctrine of the right faith."

"I heartily thank the Queen's highness," she replied, "and I hope that you will do your duty truly and faithfully."

Then the abbot began to question Jane about her faith. "What is required of a Christian?" he asked.

"That he should believe in God the Father, God the Son and God the Holy Spirit—three persons in one God," Jane said.

"Is there nothing else required or looked for in a Christian, but to believe in Him?" he asked.

"Yes," Jane replied, "we must love Him with all our heart, soul and mind, and love our neighbor as ourselves."

"So then faith alone does not justify or save," he said.

"Faith alone saves," Jane said. "As the Apostle Paul says, 'Faith alone justifies.'"

"Why then does Paul say that if I have all faith, but do not have love it is nothing?" the abbot asked.

"True it is," Jane said, "faith and love go together. Love is comprehended in faith. For how can I love Him who I do not trust? Or how can I trust Him who I do not love?"

"Then it is necessary to do good works to be saved," he said, "and it is not sufficient to believe only."

"I deny that," Jane replied, "I affirm that faith alone saves, but it is right for a Christian to do good works as he seeks to follow in the steps of his Master, Christ. Yet Christians do not say that our good works save us. Faith only in Christ's blood saves us."

"You ground your faith on authors who disagree with one another and not the church," he said.

"No," Jane said, "I ground my faith upon God's Word and not upon the church. The faith of the church must be tried by God's Word and not God's Word tried by the church."

Throughout the long interview Jane ably defended her faith in Christ and the doctrine of justification by faith alone. The exasperated abbot rose to leave and said, "Madam, I am sorry for you—for I am sure that you and I shall never meet again."

"It is true," Jane said, "that we shall never meet again except God turn your heart. For I am assured that unless you repent and turn to God you are in a sad and desperate case. And I pray God, in His mercy, to send you His Holy Spirit to open the eyes of your heart to His truth."

On the appointed day, the axeman escorted Jane to the green in the Tower of London.

"Good people," she said to the small crowd permitted to witness the execution, "I am by law condemned, and I have come here to die. The act against the Queen's highness was unlawful and so was my consenting to it. But for my part, I never desired it, and I wash my hands in innocence before God. I pray you all, good Christian people, to bear me witness that I die a true Christian woman. I look to be saved only by the mercy of God and the merits of the blood of His only Son, Jesus Christ."

Then she recited Psalm 51. Just before the end, she repeated Christ's final prayer on the cross, "Lord, into Thy hands I commend my spirit."

22 JEANNE D'ALBRET
Reformation Queen, 1528–1572

During the Reformation, the kings of France, fearing that the Huguenots, the French Protestants, would divide their kingdom, persecuted them without mercy. Though burned at the stake, drowned in rivers and cut down by the sword, the number of Huguenots still grew. Many Huguenots, like John Calvin, fled the country for the safety of Switzerland. After Calvin became the chief minister in Geneva, the Genevan church became a haven and model for the Huguenots.

In most places in France, the Huguenots worshiped in secret, gathering in fields or barns to sing God's praises from the Genevan Psalm book, read from Scripture and hear a sermon. Huguenot ministers, many of them trained by Calvin in Geneva, disguised themselves and used false names to protect their identities. "Send us wood," Calvin told the Huguenots, "and we will send you back arrows." The arrows he referred to were well-trained preachers. These brave young men returned to France knowing they faced certain death.

On Christmas Day in 1560, a courageous and devout woman strengthened the Huguenot cause. Jeanne d'Albret, Queen of Navarre, publicly proclaimed, "I am a follower of the Reformed faith." With her husband Anthony, Jeanne ruled Navarre, a small kingdom allied with France, and located on the border with Spain.

Anthony was a French nobleman in the line of succession to the throne of France. For years they had brought Protestant ministers to their court and sent money to support those who fled to Geneva. Yet they feared to declare themselves Protestant since their tiny kingdom was surrounded by powerful Roman Catholic countries.

But finally Jeanne believed herself compelled to stand for the truth no matter the cost. "The Reformation of the Christian faith is so right and so necessary," she said, "that I would be disloyal and a coward before God and my people if I failed to join it."

Like other Protestants she embraced the Reformed faith because the Roman church had strayed far from God's Word. "I follow Calvin and the other Reformed preachers," she said, "only so far as they follow the Scriptures."

The kings of France and Spain, along with the pope, sprang into action to prevent Navarre from leaving the Roman church. They promised Anthony land and money if he declared himself and his kingdom loyal to the Roman faith. He agreed. Crushed by her husband's lack of spiritual courage, Jeanne said, "He planted a thorn in my heart."

Anthony brought Jeanne to Paris and made her a prisoner in her own quarters, threatening to divorce her unless she returned to the Roman church. She still refused. French officials urged her to follow the lead of her husband. "You may lose everything you have if you don't change your faith," they warned her.

"I would rather plunge my kingdom to the bottom of the ocean than do that," she said.

Jeanne fled Paris for Navarre and used her power to promote the Reformed faith in her kingdom. She purified the churches of images, called Genevan pastors to preach to her people and established Reformed seminaries. Jeanne herself wrote essays to defend and persuade others of the evangelical faith. Spending her personal funds and selling her own jewels, she supported Huguenot schools, paid pastors' expenses and printed Bibles. She had the Bible translated into Bearnnois, the language of Navarre, and encouraged her subjects to study God's Word for themselves.

But the situation for the French Huguenots grew more perilous. In Vassy, soldiers massacred hundreds of Huguenots gathered in a barn for worship, and they slaughtered three thousand at Toulouse. Finally, the Huguenots took up arms to defend themselves. Anthony led an army into battle against them, laying siege to a Huguenot city. Yet a musket ball fired from the wall ripped through his arm. He later died from the wound.

Jeanne, now ruling her kingdom alone, decreed that in Navarre both Roman Catholics and Huguenots were free to worship. The pope dispatched a French cardinal to persuade her to forbid Huguenot worship in her kingdom. "Your majesty," he told Jeanne, "You are being misled by evil men who want to plant a new religion in Navarre. If you go ahead with this, you will never succeed. Your subjects will not stand for it, and your enemies will stop you. You do not have an ocean to protect you like Queen Elizabeth of England."

He called the Huguenots murderers, rebels and heretics. "Madame," he said, "Don't let these people ruin your conscience, your goods and your grandeur. I implore you with tears to return to the true fold."

Jeanne leaned forward, looked the cardinal squarely in the eye and answered boldly, "Your feeble arguments do not dent my tough skull. I am serving God, and He knows how to protect His cause. Our ministers preach nothing but obedience, patience and humility. Keep your tears for yourself. I pray from the bottom of my heart that you may be brought back to the true fold and the true Shepherd."

Eventually the struggle between the Huguenots and the French Roman Catholics exploded into war. Thousands on both sides perished. At the battle of Jarnac, when the leading Huguenot general was killed, the troops wavered, uncertain if they could fight on. Jeanne raced to the field with her son Henry, an heir to the throne, and rallied the men to victory.

But Jeanne, hating the bloodshed, sent a letter to the king of France. "I am confident in your natural goodness and fatherly love for your people," she wrote. "I beg you to take to heart the misery which this war has caused. If you will let your subjects worship as Roman Catholics or as Reformed, your name will be celebrated by all nations."

At last, in 1571, both sides, exhausted from the war, signed a peace treaty. In order to strengthen the peace, the Queen Mother of France, Catherine de Medici, suggested that Jeanne's son, Henry of Navarre, marry her daughter, Margaret, hoping that if a Huguenot prince married a Catholic princess, peace would be secured. Jeanne d'Albret stood firmly against it. But Huguenot leaders throughout France pleaded with her to accept the marriage for the sake of peace. "Perhaps it will lead to greater religious freedom," they told her.

Reluctantly, Jeanne finally agreed but she warned her son to remain true to the Word of God no matter what his future wife might do. Jeanne traveled to Paris to make the wedding arrangements, but while there she fell gravely ill. Many believed she was poisoned. On her deathbed she asked to hear some chapters from the Gospel of John. She died with the words of Jesus sounding in her ears: "In this world you will have trouble. But take heart! I have overcome the world." (John 16:33)

Two months later, Henry of Navarre married Margaret in Paris. Huguenot leaders from all of France gathered for the royal wedding. But Catherine de Medici, scheming to destroy them once and for all, told her son, King Charles, that the Huguenots must be wiped out or he would never control France. Full of anger, Charles shouted, "By God's death! I want all the Huguenots of France killed. See to it immediately!"

A few days after the wedding, French troops received the order against the Huguenots. "Kill them all, the king commands it."

Archers, horsemen and foot soldiers fanned out across Paris to attack the ten thousand Huguenots visiting the city. The Paris rabble joined in when the king's soldiers shouted: "Kill them! Massacre the Huguenots!"

Mobs ran wild through the streets, breaking into houses, killing Huguenots—running them through with daggers or throwing them headlong from buildings. They knocked little children and old people senseless and cast them into the river to drown. Soldiers, trying to clear the streets of dead bodies, wheeled carts loaded with corpses to the river and dumped them in, turning the water red.

This happened on August 23, 1572, the Feast of St. Bartholomew, so the terrible day is remembered as the St. Bartholomew Day's Massacre. The killing of Huguenots continued across France for weeks. Tens of thousands of men, women and children were slaughtered.

The massacre sparked a renewal of war which continued for many years until Jeanne's son Henry was crowned King of France. Although Henry did not hold to the evangelical faith as his mother had, he gave the Huguenots freedom of worship by issuing the Edict of Nantes, which granted religious freedom to both Roman Catholics and Huguenots.

One of Jeanne's favorite passages of Scripture was Psalm 31. Just before she died, she had it read to her, and it beautifully expressed her own struggles and faith: "For I have heard the slander of many, Terror is on every side; ...They schemed to take away my life. But as for me, I trust in Thee, O Lord, I say, 'Thou art my God.' Make Thy face to shine upon Thy servant; save me in Thy loving-kindness."

"Jeanne D'Albret: Reformation Queen" is excerpted from Richard M. Hannula's *Trial and Triumph: Stories from Church History* (Moscow ID: Canon Press, 1999).

23   LADY ANNE HAMILTON
The Lioness of the Covenant, c. 1585–1647

I n 1629, Lady Anne Hamilton, a Scottish noblewoman, rode in her carriage with an entourage of ladies and servants. As the carriage rolled along the road to Edinburgh and passed through the little town of Shotts, it broke down. Lady Anne often traveled that road, and she knew the minister of the kirk, Mr. Home. When Pastor Home discovered that Lady Anne and her party were stranded in Shotts, he invited them to spend the night at his house. They gladly accepted and enjoyed the simple hospitality that the minister of a small parish could afford. Lady Anne noticed that the house needed major repairs. Not long after spending the night, she purchased a plot of ground in Shotts and arranged for a new and larger house to be built for the pastor.

Mr. Home, overwhelmed by her generosity, traveled to her estate to thank her. "Is there anything I can do for you to show my gratitude?" he asked.

"Well, there is one thing," Lady Anne told him. "I would be pleased if you would be kind enough to allow me to choose the ministers who will assist you at the celebration of the Lord's Supper."

Pastor Home bowed and smiled, "I would most happily, your ladyship."

At that time, Scottish churches held communion services just a few times each year. These became important occasions where people came from all the surrounding communities to participate in several days of preaching services before the Sunday Lord's Supper service. In June 1630, when the next communion season came around for the Kirk of Shotts, Lady Anne asked Pastor Home to have Robert Bruce, David Dixon and a few others assist him in the services. Bruce and Dixon were among the best known preachers in Scotland. When word spread that they would be preaching in Shotts, a crowd thronged the town to hear them.

For several days people heard fine sermons, urging them to ready their hearts to receive the Lord's Supper. Some groups of believers prepared by spending the whole night in prayer. On Sunday, they enjoyed a great celebration of communion. Hour by hour, one group after another came forward and sat around one of several tables and received the bread and wine from a minister.

That evening, Pastor Home and the other ministers decided to hold a Monday morning service of thanksgiving before everyone departed. They chose John Livingstone to preach the sermon on Monday. Livingstone, a young chaplain, felt unworthy among such a distinguished group of ministers, but they insisted that he should do it. Early Monday morning, Livingstone went alone into the fields to pray. The more he thought about it, the more inadequate he felt. Try as he might, he couldn't bring himself to do it. So he decided to quickly leave town. As he walked briskly down the road away from Shotts, he met a steady stream of people heading into town for the thanksgiving service. Overcome with guilt, Livingstone stopped in his tracks and prayed. After confessing to God his cowardice and lack of faith, he turned around and walked back. More than a thousand people had gathered on the grassy slope of the churchyard. Livingstone preached a sermon from Ezekiel chapter 36, a passage about God's promises to purify His people with clean water and give them new hearts. For an hour and a half, Livingstone explained the meaning of the passage, and he called all the unbelievers in the crowd to put their trust in Christ.

Then a light rain began to fall. As the people pulled up their coats and hoods to cover themselves, Livingstone said, "What a mercy it is that the Lord sends us rain and does not pour down upon us fire and brimstone as He did on Sodom and Gomorrah."

As Livingstone continued, he suddenly felt the Lord melting his heart, and he noticed a change in the people too. "I never experienced anything like it before," he said later. He preached on—warning his hearers to flee the wrath of God and look to Christ. Hundreds turned to Jesus Christ for the forgiveness of their sins. After the service, they sought out ministers and elders to counsel them and pray with them. When they returned home, they told their family members and friends—hundreds more put their faith in Christ. No one rejoiced more over the spiritual awakening of faith in Shotts than Lady Anne Hamilton.

Lady Anne came from a family that had long supported the Reformation in Scotland. In her youth she trusted Jesus Christ and embraced the Reformed faith and the Presbyterian government of the Church of Scotland. Presbyterians believed that the spiritual control of the church rests solely in the hands of the ruling elders and ministers who make up the church courts—not the king or his bishops. Lady Anne inherited from her father and grandfather a determination to defend the freedom of the church from the king's domination.

King James—who reigned over Scotland and England—believed that he ruled by divine right. He despised Presbyterian church government because he had no control over it. James wanted the Church of Scotland to be ruled like the Church of England. The Church of England declared that the king was the supreme governor of the church, and bishops ruled, not elders and ministers chosen by the people. "Presbyterianism agrees as well with monarchy as God and the devil," James said.

Using flattery and bribes or threats and imprisonment, James pressed Scottish nobles and church leaders to bring the Church of Scotland under his influence. One nobleman whom the king swayed was the Marquis of Hamilton, Lady Anne's husband. An unscrupulous and ambitious man, he did not share his wife's beliefs. He took the lead for King James in forcing the rule of bishops on the Church of Scotland. But in 1625, at the age of thirty-six, he died. Anne survived, and she used her wealth and influence to protect and advance the cause of Christ in the Church of Scotland. She helped pay the salaries for a number of gospel preachers. She encouraged and supported bright and pious young men as they trained for the ministry. After King James died and his son King Charles began to openly persecute Scottish Presbyterians, Lady Anne sent money and notes of encouragement to the suffering believers.

In 1637, when King Charles I tried to force the Scots to worship in the style of the Church of England, ministers and noblemen from across Scotland petitioned the king to let them worship as they believed the Bible directed them to. But Charles ignored their requests, demanded that the Scots bow to his will, and declared that all who resisted the new worship were rebels. Alarmed that the king's order stripped them of any legal recourse, the Scots rose up. They wrote a National Covenant that stated the primary beliefs of the Church of Scotland and the errors that they stood against. The tens of thousands of Scots who pledged to uphold the National Covenant were called Covenanters. One of the most stalwart Covenanters of them all was Lady Anne Hamilton.

King Charles decided to crush the Covenanters by force of arms. When the Covenanters discovered that Charles was gathering an army to invade Scotland, they quickly formed an army of their own. Lady Anne gave money to train and equip men for the Covenanter force. In these desperate times, the Covenanters needed every able-bodied Scot—man or woman—to defend the Church of Scotland against the king. However, Lady Anne's son James, who became the Marquis of Hamilton after the death of his father, sided with Charles against the Covenanters.

In 1639, James Hamilton sailed to England and brought a fleet of ships back to Scotland loaded with several thousand of the king's soldiers. They anchored off the port of Leith, preparing to invade. A strong Covenanter army came to stop them. Among them was Lady Anne on horseback, dressed for war with two pistols at her side, riding at the head of a troop of horsemen. "I will be the first to shoot the Marquis of Hamilton," she told her horsemen, "if he dares to land the king's men and attack the troops of the Covenant."

James Hamilton was waiting to link up with the king's army marching into Scotland from England. The Covenanters repulsed that army, and so James Hamilton never attacked the Covenanters at Leith. That summer Lady Anne rode in the Covenanter cavalry during the Battle of Berwick. This Covenanter victory forced King Charles to sign a truce which recognized the right of the Scots to run their own church affairs.

For Lady Anne Hamilton's brave defense of the cause of Christ and the Church of Scotland, Scots have called her "the Lioness of the Covenant."

24 JANE GORDON, VISCOUNTESS OF KENMURE
A Woman Beloved of the Lord, c. 1611–c.1672

In the winter of 1626, the chancellor of Edinburgh University fired Samuel Rutherford, a professor and ordained minister. The scandal that had led to his dismissal had left Rutherford's reputation in tatters, and he wondered if he had ruined his chances to be of service to Christ in the world. For months, he languished out of work with little hope of pursuing his calling in a university or a church. Then in 1627, Sir John Gordon and his young wife, Lady Jane Gordon, stepped in and called Rutherford to their parish church in Anwoth—a small congregation in the hills of Galloway in southwest Scotland.

Rutherford thanked God for the opportunity and threw himself into the work. Every day he hiked across his parish, visiting farms and cottages, never failing to be at the bedside of the sick or in the home of the grieving. He often made his way to the Gordon's castle to talk with them about the things of God, forming a strong bond of fellowship with Lady Jane. She came from the Campbells of Argyll, a distinguished family that had long supported the Reformation in Scotland. From her youth, Jane had trusted Christ and sought to obey His commandments. She believed it was the duty of noble families to support gospel preaching and to set an example of Christian love and service. Her heartfelt faith, humble spirit and bright mind impressed Rutherford.

The goal of all Rutherford's labors in Anwoth was to lead people to Jesus Christ. "Come to Christ and receive all things with Him," he preached. "What a Rose of light and love Christ is!"

A parishioner reported that when Rutherford preached about Jesus Christ, it looked like he would fly out of the pulpit for joy. No one rejoiced more in his preaching than did Lady Jane. Although her husband supported Rutherford's work, he was a proud man of the world with a great interest in titles and wealth. Jane knew her husband was double-minded, and it broke her heart. Rutherford saw it in John Gordon too. "I pity him because of his many temptations," he told Lady Jane. "Drop words in the ears of your husband continually of eternity, judgment, death, hell and heaven."

The power and status of John Gordon did not keep Rutherford from telling him the truth about his soul's condition. "Stoop, stoop!" Rutherford told him, "It is a low entry to go in at heaven's gate."

During Rutherford's first three years in Anwoth, his two young children died and then his wife died after a long and painful illness. The consolation of Lady Jane supported Rutherford during those dark days of mourning. He, in turn, comforted her when she suffered the loss of a child. When her daughter passed away, Rutherford encouraged her with the thought that she was in heaven. "She is like a star," he wrote Lady Jane, "which going out of our sight does not die and vanish, but still shines in another hemisphere."

Through the years, all three of Lady Jane's young children passed away. Rutherford urged her to see God at work even in her sorrows. "Consider what the Lord is doing in it," he advised. "God knows what is most helpful for your soul. Your tender-hearted Savior holds every cup of affliction with His own gracious hand."

Jane Gordon took her sin seriously. She often confessed her lack of repentance to Rutherford and bemoaned the sin that still plagued her. "You complain about yourself," he told her, "and it is good for a sinner to do so. The more sense of sin—the less sin."

All the while that Rutherford was caring for his flock, King Charles I was plotting to force the rule of bishops upon the Church of Scotland. Rutherford spoke out against the king's plans. "I dare not be silent," he said, "to see my Lord's house burning, and not cry 'Fire, fire!'"

In 1630, when Rutherford was brought to trial for his stand, Lady Jane intervened. She asked one of the judges who was a family friend to come to Rutherford's defense. He did—and Rutherford was released.

During those difficult times in Scotland, one of Samuel Rutherford's steadfast fellow defenders of the church was Lady Gordon, but sadly her husband was not. To win over Scottish nobles to his policies, King Charles bribed them with titles and lands. In 1633, he elevated John Gordon to the title of Viscount Kenmure, which greatly expanded his estates. And Charles's favors did their work. Later, when Gordon sat in Parliament in Edinburgh, he sacrificed his principles and refused to take a stand against the king's efforts to control the Church of Scotland. Afraid to offend the king, he pretended to be sick and left Parliament for his castle before a vote was taken on the king's plan. Lady Jane must have been disgusted by her husband's cowardice.

Although Jane now held the regal title of Viscountess Kenmure, the prestige and luxury of the world held no charm for her. She heartily agreed with Rutherford who sent her a note shortly after her husband's fake illness. "The Lord has taught you," he wrote, "that worldly glory is nothing but a vapor, a shadow, the foam on the water—even nothing."

A year later, John Gordon, at the age of thirty-five, lay on his deathbed. When Rutherford came to visit him, Gordon told him, "I never dreamed that death looked so terrible and gloomy. I dare not die—but I know I must die."

Over the course of several days, Rutherford called him to repent and trust Christ for the forgiveness of his sins. Wracked by a guilty conscience, Gordon confessed his cowardice. "I find the weight of the wrath of God pressing down on me for not giving testimony for the Lord my God when I had the opportunity once in my life at the last Parliament! I grieve at the thought of it."

"O, my lord, dig deeper," Rutherford implored him. "Believe in Him who died for you!"

A relative of John Gordon, irritated by Rutherford's boldness in speaking to Lord Gordon, asked, "Why did you bring Rutherford to Galloway in the first place?"

"God knows," Gordon answered, "that I rejoice that God did put it in my heart to do so; and now, the Lord has made me to find comfort to my soul in the end. If this man had not come, my soul would have been murdered."

In his last days, John Gordon confessed his sins and begged Christ to forgive and cleanse him. He thanked his wife for her holiness, goodness and kindness. "Please forgive me," he told her, "for everything I did that offended you. May the Lord be your comfort." Although Lady Jane mourned the loss of her husband, she gave thanks to God for rescuing him in the nick of time. Rutherford assured her that all of life's sufferings would be worth it in the end. "Traveling to heaven is a well-spent journey," he said, "even though seven deaths lay between."

By 1636 the king's men had had enough of Rutherford. He was put on trial in Edinburgh and declared an enemy of the king. The court forbade him to preach anywhere in Scotland and banished him to Aberdeen, a city hundreds of miles to the north. During his exile, Rutherford wrote letters—hundreds of letters—to believers across Scotland. Dozens of them went to Lady Jane Gordon, urging her to press on in the Lord. "Wrestle, fight, go forward, watch, believe, and pray," he wrote her.

Samuel Rutherford knew that Lady Jane was capable of taking in the deep spiritual truths that he wrote to her in his letters. He dedicated to her his book *Trial and Triumph of Faith*, a weighty theological work on Christ's death for sinners.

In 1638, ministers of the Scottish church and many noblemen rose up to break the king's domination over the church and the state. Within a few months, people throughout Scotland resisted the king's claim to be the head of the church. They signed a National Covenant, pledging to restore biblical worship and church government to the Church of Scotland. The supporters of the National Covenant became known as Covenanters and prominent among them was Lady Jane Gordon. Rutherford left Aberdeen and became one of the leaders of the Scottish church, helping to guide her through turbulent times.

Not long after Charles II became king in 1660, persecution against the Covenanters grew fierce. Lady Jane's brother, Archibald Campbell, the Marquis of Argyll, was the most fearless Covenanting nobleman. King Charles had him arrested and thrown into the Tower of London. To ease her worries for her brother, Rutherford wrote her a letter. "I am mindful of you. Be not afflicted for your brother. The love of God and His people are in him—it will be well. The Lord reigns, let the earth tremble, and let the earth rejoice. Let us watch and pray and live more by faith and we shall be more than conquerors. Wait upon the Lord; faint not. The Lord Jesus be with your spirit."

Archibald Campbell was sentenced to death. A few weeks before Campbell's execution, the king's men planned to put Rutherford to death also. They sent him a summons, ordering him to appear before Parliament to stand trial for high treason. Rutherford would willingly have died on the gallows for Christ, but when messengers delivered the summons, he was gravely ill and near death. Rutherford propped himself up in bed and said to the messengers, "Tell them that I have a summons already from a superior Judge, and I must answer my first summons; and, ere your day arrives, I will be where few kings and great folks come."

Not long after Rutherford died in 1661, King Charles II unleashed a wildfire of persecution that raged over Scotland for years. Thousands were executed for their faith and thousands went into hiding. Lady Jane distinguished herself by her generosity to the poor benighted Covenanters. She sheltered ministers who were on the run from the king's troops and sent money to families driven into hiding in the hills and to ministers forced into exile overseas. The persecution pushed Robert McWard, a minister and close friend of Rutherford, to escape to Holland. Lady Jane sent him support on several occasions. "I will always be grateful for your ladyship's undeserved kindness and bounty toward me in my difficult circumstances," he wrote her.

When McWard decided to publish a collection of Samuel Rutherford's letters, he wrote Lady Jane and asked her if she had kept any of Rutherford's letters. A short time later, McWard opened a package sent from Scotland. It contained forty-seven carefully preserved letters of Rutherford to Lady Jane Gordon. McWard gathered more than three hundred of Rutherford's letters and printed them in a book. Few Christian books have been so widely read and so greatly loved. For the last 350 years, Christians around the world have learned about Jane Gordon by reading *The Letters of Samuel Rutherford*. Perhaps the most fitting tribute to her came from Rutherford himself when he called her "a woman beloved of God."

25 MARGARET NISBET
Equal, True and Kind Yoke-fellow,
c. 1635–1683

One evening in 1666, Margaret Nisbet paced the stone floor of her farmhouse in southwest Scotland, her brow furled and her fingers gripped in prayer. She was pregnant with her fourth child and was soon to give birth. Having just put her young bairns to bed, the only sounds in the house were the rhythmic breathing of the children and the chill night wind blowing against the shutters. That morning, her husband John had joined a band of Covenanters who decided to stop the king's troops from ravaging the land. Several hours crept by and then came a gentle knocking at her door. She opened it to find her neighbor—out of breath, her cheeks flushed and tears in her eyes. "I've bad tidings, Margaret," she said. "There's been a terrible slaughter. The dragoons scattered our men—some ran away, some were captured, and many more were killed."

Taking Margaret's hand, she whispered, "I heard that your dear John is among the dead."

Margaret collapsed onto a wooden bench and cried. Then she turned to her Savior in prayer.

Meanwhile, about forty miles to the east, her husband awoke after lying unconscious for hours. As he tried to stand, he fell back under the pain of his wounds and groaned. Weakly raising his head, he glimpsed in the darkness the bodies of his slain comrades scattered around him. Earlier that day, Nisbet and a poorly armed band of Covenanters had fought the king's well-equipped troops on Rullion Green, a field in the Pentland Hills near Edinburgh, Scotland.

The royal dragoons slaughtered many Covenanters and took others prisoner. John suffered multiple wounds and passed out on the battlefield. His enemies, taking him for dead, stripped him of his sword and most of his clothes and left him to rot on the ground. But hours later, he came to, and under the cover of darkness he crawled away and escaped. It would be a long time before he reached home.

The next afternoon, while Margaret and her children mourned, they were startled by the sound of thundering hoofbeats that shook the ground. Hearing that John had fought in the battle, a troop of horsemen descended on the Nisbet farm known as Hardhill in search of him. They barged into the house, pulled Margaret aside and demanded to know where her husband was. "I don't know," she said. One of the soldiers drew his sword and held the point against her body. "I'll run you through," he threatened, "if you don't tell us where your husband is!"

With tears streaming down her cheeks, she said, "I have not seen him. For all I know he has been killed—or so I was told."

Pushing Mrs. Nisbet aside, the soldiers left the farmhouse, stealing what they could carry off.

But a few days later, when the soldiers learned that John Nisbet was still alive, they burst upon Hardhill like raging bulls. Kicking open the door, they pushed a sword tip to Margaret's chest and pointed a cocked pistol at her head. "Where is he?" the leader shouted. "You lied—we know he is alive. We'll kill you where you stand, if you don't tell us!"

"I don't know," she said, "I have not seen him."

Grabbing her by the arm, they dragged her through the house and the outbuildings, searching in every nook and cranny. Seeking to strike more terror in her, they beat one of the farmhands and threatened to do the same to her if she did not reveal her husband's whereabouts. "I can't!" she said, "I don't know."

They left, taking valuables, tools and supplies and driving all the family's livestock away with them.

For months, hardly a day or night passed without soldiers searching the Nisbet farm and harassing Margaret and her children. When the king's dragoons dropped the search and left the area, John returned home. It took a year of Margaret's constant care before his wounds fully healed and his strength returned. Then he and Margaret began the hard work of rebuilding their farm and livestock.

The Nisbets—like all Scottish Covenanters—pledged their support for the National Covenant which honored the king as the head of the state but not head of the church. Covenanters wanted biblical worship and preaching in their churches without interference from the Crown.

In the early years of their marriage, John and Margaret had lived and worshiped in peace. But not long after King Charles II came to the throne in 1660, he abolished all the laws supporting the independence of the Church of Scotland. Bishops appointed by the Crown took control of the churches and expelled hundreds of ministers who spoke out against it. Many Covenanters refused to go to their parish church after their pastors were expelled. "They cast out gospel-ministers," John said, "and fill their places with profane and false curates."

When "outed" ministers began preaching in the fields, the Nisbets went to hear them. Those attending illegal field meetings could be punished by death. Soldiers roamed the countryside trying to suppress the gatherings.

Over time, the fire of the king's persecution of the Covenanters blazed hotter. His troops arrested thousands—stole property, beat women and children and executed hundreds. "Margaret," John said to his wife, "my conscience won't allow me to sit idly by and do nothing when Christ's church and His people are under attack."

"Then you must not do it!" she answered.

"But if I act, it will lead to great danger not only for me but for you and the children."

"Be true to your conscience," Margaret said, "come what will for me and my bairns. God lives, we need not be afraid."

Then, taking her husband's hand and smiling, she added, "Once we are in heaven, God will richly make up for any sufferings we endured here below."

John Nisbet was an experienced soldier who had fought in Germany for several years to defend the Protestant Reformation. He felt duty bound to join those Covenanters who had decided to fight back. And that is what had led him to battle the king's men at Rullion Green.

For many years after that first battle, the Nisbets lived peacefully on their farm. Then in June 1679, not far from their home, a group of men, women and children had gathered to hear a sermon. They met in a field called Drumclog near Loudoun Hill. But a troop of the king's men had got word of the meeting and fell upon them. The Covenanters had brought weapons, and they rallied to resist the soldiers. With the help of John Nisbet, they killed many of the king's men, and the rest were forced to retreat. But the victory was short-lived. Just three weeks later, the king's troops crushed the Covenanters at Bothwell Bridge where John played a prominent role as a captain of a company of men. He suffered many wounds, but managed to escape into the hills. After the battle, soldiers scoured the countryside for him. A large reward was offered for his capture.

The next morning, troops overran Hardhill farm. Not finding John, they drove Margaret and her children from their home. Not long after, officials decreed that the Nisbet farm and all their goods were forfeit to the Crown. To magnify the cruelty, they declared that anyone who took in John Nisbet or his family or offered them so much as a cup of cold water would have their land and property seized for the king. Most of their friends and relatives wouldn't risk losing all to help them.

So the Nisbets wandered from place to place where they were not known—sometimes finding shelter in caves in the wilderness and sometimes lodging in the cottage of a welcoming Covenanter.

Most of this time, John lived away from his family because his presence exposed them to even greater risks. They cherished each moment when John dared join them for a day or two.

For years, the Nisbet family survived on the kindness of others. Although life was very hard, Margaret clung to Christ and believed in her husband and the Covenanter cause. Years later, her son James wrote about his mother. "She proved to be an equal, true and kind yoke-fellow to my father. Despite the many troubles she suffered at the hands of the king's cruel savages, she was never heard nor seen to show the least discontent with her lot. Her cheerful acceptance and sincere sympathy with him was a great comfort and encouragement to him."

In December 1683, after four years of wandering—while John was still hiding in the moors—Margaret and her children found shelter in a shepherd's hut. It stood on the back of a farm owned by a sympathetic family just outside the town of Stonehouse. While there, Margaret and her daughter and three sons came down with fevers. One week later, Margaret died. Her Covenanter hosts buried her at midnight in the Stonehouse churchyard, being careful to replace the dirt and sod so it would remain concealed. For government and church officials had decreed that "rebels" could not be buried in church graveyards. They were known to dig up and desecrate Covenanter bodies that had been buried in defiance of their dictates.

The news of his wife's death and his sick children did not reach John for several days. He rushed to the place. As he entered the hut, he discovered that his little daughter had passed away shortly before he arrived. He tried to speak with his sons who were shivering in the corner of the dark hut, but they were so delirious with fever that they didn't recognize him. As his friends prepared his daughter's body for burial, John leaned over, kissed her forehead and sighed, "Naked I came into this world and naked I must go out of it. The Lord is making my passage easy."

"Sir, I hope you know who has done this!" complained one mourner, remembering the cruelty of the king's men who had forced the Nisbet family from their home.

"Yes, I know who did this," John whispered. Lifting his head, he added, "I know that God has done it. He makes all things work together for the good of them who love Him and keep His way. This is my comfort."

Then, thinking of Margaret, he said, "It comforts me very much that my wife—whom you have already buried out of my sight—notwithstanding all the trouble she met with on my account, never asked me to do anything that might hurt my conscience. On the contrary, she encouraged me to do what I thought was right regardless of the consequences."

That night, Nisbet buried his daughter next to his wife in a hidden unmarked grave in the Stonehouse churchyard. "I bless God who gave me such a wife," John said, "and I bless Him who has taken her again."

Then he took his sons and fled.

The minister at Stonehouse—installed by the bishop against the people's wishes—hated the Covenanters. When he learned of the burial of Margaret and her daughter in the churchyard, he spewed, "This consecrated ground is not for treasonous rebels. By heavens, I'll have them dug up and burned or thrown to the dogs."

A local Covenanter—disregarding Christ's command to love those who persecute you—threatened the minister, sending an anonymous letter that evening: "If you so much as lay a finger on those graves or cause anyone else to," he wrote, "I'll burn your house down around you and yours."

The minister left the graves alone and did not inform the authorities about them.

Two years later, John Nisbet was captured and sentenced by the king's council in Edinburgh to death by hanging. An eyewitness of John Nisbet's execution said, "He went rejoicing and praising the Lord."

26 ERDMUTH VON ZINZENDORF
Holding Tightly to the Savior, 1700-1756

In the summer of 1722, Count Nicholas von Zinzendorf, his face beaming, stood holding the hand of twenty-one-year-old Erdmuth Reuss. The petite Erdmuth kept her eyes fixed to the floor. He had come to Ebersdorf, her family's palace in the German principality of Thuringia, to propose marriage. "I love you with all of my heart, to the depths of my soul," he said. "However, I love the Lord Jesus much more."

Nicholas told her that he wanted their relationship to be a marriage of Christian warriors. As a couple they would strive to serve Christ as His soldiers. A few months later, they were married in the palace chapel. The engravings on their wedding rings symbolized their determination to live together for Jesus Christ. On Erdmuth's ring, they had engraved the phrase, "Let us love Him," and on his ring the words, "because He first loved us."

A year earlier when Zinzendorf first visited Ebersdorf, he was as taken by the vibrant Christian community as he was by Erdmuth. Like-minded believers from the surrounding countryside worshiped in the palace chapel. Their motto was "to live completely in and with Jesus."

"In Ebersdorf," Nicholas said, "I was allowed to see the Savior's face!"

Zinzendorf wanted to make his new home and community to reflect a similar Christ-like character. He knew that Erdmuth could help him do it. Although she was a young woman, Erdmuth ran the Ebersdorf estate, overseeing its finances and managing the large staff of servants with efficiency and grace, earning the love and respect of guests and employees. She was an ideal partner for Nicholas von Zinzendorf. With his vision and zeal and her levelheaded administrative skills, they would do great things.

Although Nicholas and Erdmuth were born into the wealth and privilege of German nobility, they had been raised by their pietist parents to serve others sacrificially. Pietists sought a close and deeply emotional walk with Christ that engaged the heart as well as the mind. They wanted a real relationship with Jesus Christ, not merely the correct doctrine but cold faith that had overtaken much of European Protestantism. Pietists emphasized heart-felt prayer, personal Bible study, evangelism and care for others, especially the very needy.

After the wedding, they settled into the rundown manor house and large estate that Nicholas had recently purchased in Saxony with his inheritance. Soon Pietist refugees, fleeing religious persecution by the emperor in neighboring Moravia, requested permission to settle on Zinzendorf's extensive lands. With Nicholas's approval, they dug wells and built cabins. Month by month new refugees from Moravia and Bohemia arrived. The Zinzendorfs welcomed them all and called the budding community Herrnhut, which means "The Lord's watch."

From the start, Nicholas entrusted the management of their estate and Herrnhut to Erdmuth. She faced daunting challenges from the needs of the refugees and the demands of a home undergoing major renovation. Erdmuth confided to her mother that she felt inadequate for the task. Her mother wrote back, "I know you are so timid and fainthearted, even afraid. May God grant you a little more heart and well-placed courage."

The lands brought in a meager income, and Nicholas spent money they didn't have starting a Christian school and an orphanage. "Money and I are complete strangers," Nicholas admitted. "If I receive money it is soon gone."

Nicholas's mind sprouted new plans like a fountain. Some were sound and bore fruit, but many were impractical and swallowed money. Often, Erdmuth needed to curb his enthusiasm. "My dear," she told him when he came up with another extravagant plan, "I believe it will result in starting more new projects that will not be completed but will build castles in the air."

But their love for one another grew. "Under all these pressures we continue to grow fonder of each other and that makes everything tolerable," Erdmuth told a family member. "Thank God we live together very happily and we can endure bad and good together."

Meanwhile, Herrnhut had grown to several hundred residents—most of them refugees from religious persecution in the Holy Roman Empire. With the help of the Zinzendorfs they sought to make Herrnhut a beacon of Christ's light and grace in the heart of Europe. Trying to follow the pattern of the Early Church, they elected elders and deacons and appointed spiritually mature women to oversee the nurture of younger women and girls. Erdmuth led the women. She was a gifted spiritual leader who listened well and gave sound biblical advice that was easy for the hearer to receive. "I could speak with her best and very straightforwardly about all my spiritual and physical circumstances," one woman said about her, "and I can also accept her instructions with love."

Her kindness and ready smile drew the people of Herrnhut to her. "She has an ear for anyone who needs advice and comfort," one resident reported.

The believers at Herrnhut called themselves the "Unity of Brethren," but they were commonly called "Moravians" by outsiders. Nicholas, Erdmuth and others wrote hymns for the worship services of the Brethren. She wrote more than sixty hymns that were included in the Brethren hymnal—hymns of faith in Christ and a personal walk with Him.

The people of Herrnhut soon became self-sufficient by planting crops and starting businesses. Before long there was a prosperous lumber mill and brickworks as well as factories for building furniture and dyeing cloth. Visitors took note of their industry and their warm Christian fellowship. Erdmuth rejoiced in the growing Christian community's love for Christ. "They are filled with faith and an insatiable desire for God's Word," she reported. "It is very uplifting to talk with them."

The imperial court in Vienna resented that refugees fleeing persecution from its provinces in Moravia and Bohemia found sanctuary at Herrnhut, and it did not like Count von Zinzendorf's brand of Christianity or his growing influence. The emperor demanded that the prince of Saxony expel Zinzendorf. The prince, afraid to anger his powerful neighbor, banished Nicholas from Saxony. Nicholas left Erdmuth in charge of the ministries.

She felt the crushing weight of responsibility that fell to her, and she prayed earnestly for strength. "The Savior provided me the grace to remain calm before Him and just watch," she wrote in her diary. Despite increasing pressures, the work at Herrnhut thrived under Erdmuth's leadership. "Things are going quite well here," she wrote to Nicholas. "The time of suffering is a glorious time."

Nicholas considered Erdmuth's work essential to the success of Herrnhut. "She is like the key to the clock," he said.

While Nicholas was in exile, their son Christian passed away suddenly. His death was a devastating blow to Erdmuth who slipped for a time into a deep depression. "These are the trials we endure on our pilgrimage," she wrote to her brother. "Pray for me that the Savior might achieve His purposes in bringing me through this fire of cleansing."

She tried to comfort her grieving husband by letter. "There is light in the darkness," she wrote Nicholas.

Christian was not the first or the last of the Zinzendorf children to die before Erdmuth's eyes. Of the twelve children born to them, only four survived to adulthood. In the midst of her trials and responsibilities she turned to Christ. In 1742, she wrote in her journal: "I was able to talk with the Savior a great deal in my innermost being. I felt inwardly and outwardly unfit for the task. I thought about many things, especially how alone I was as a woman who had to take on so much. 'You know this, my Lamb, and You have helped me to breathe again.'"

After a time, the prince allowed Nicholas to return to Saxony, but in a few years he was banished again. By that time, Nicholas's writings on the Christian faith were widely read, and the witness of Herrnhut became known throughout Europe. People from many lands asked him to help them start communities of Brethren. Count von Zinzendorf traveled extensively and established Christian settlements in the Netherlands, Switzerland, Denmark, Russia, England and the American colonies. Sometimes Erdmuth joined him abroad, but she mostly remained behind to oversee Herrnhut and keep her eye on the finances of the ministry. "Brother of my heart," she wrote Nicholas, "please watch your spending as carefully as possible."

The Zinzendorfs and the Moravian Brethren sparked a revival of personal faith in Christ in many people across Europe. And Moravian missionaries went out from Herrnhut to preach the gospel overseas at a time when few Protestants thought foreign missions were important. Some went to the islands of the Caribbean to proclaim the good news of Jesus to the benighted African slaves there. Others went to the colonies in North and South America. Many died of tropical diseases as they labored to win souls for Christ. Their witness led thousands to the Savior, including the Anglican minister, John Wesley.

Between his exiles and his travels, Nicholas was away from Erdmuth more than he was with her. On their twenty-fifth wedding anniversary he wrote her a note of thanksgiving. "Who else would have managed my entire household for so many years as generously as circumstances allowed? Who else would have lived so frugally and yet so nobly? Who else would have allowed her husband to undertake such journeys and tests? Who else would have held her head so high under such oppressive circumstances and supported me?"

Later, Nicholas acknowledged that he had often left Erdmuth alone with heavy burdens and did not love and support her as he should have. "In many respects," he said, "I failed to do the things rightly expected of a man who attempts to model his marriage on Christ."

When Erdmuth reached her fifties, she stepped down as the administrator of Herrnhut, but she continued to encourage many through her spiritual counseling. "Hold tightly to the Savior," she constantly told herself and others.

Erdmuth walked closely with Christ to the end of her days. Not long before she died at the age of fifty-five, she told her son, "Jesus released my heart on the cross and enables me to sleep in His arms."

27   SARAH EDWARDS
An Uncommon Union of Love,
1710–1758

I n July 1727, Sarah Pierpont married Jonathan Edwards. The next Sunday, she took her seat on a pew in the front of the sanctuary facing the congregation of Northampton church. New England churches in that day had a strange custom of placing the pastor's family on a pew in full view of the congregation where every expression and fidget could be observed by all. For the next twenty-three years, Sarah's every move and those of her children would be observed and judged by the people of Northampton, Massachusetts.

It took the tall, gangly and socially awkward Jonathan Edwards four years to win the heart of Sarah Pierpont, a beautiful, well-educated brunette, skilled in the social graces and at ease in conversation. Although they differed greatly in personality, they shared a deep love for Jesus Christ, the Savior of their souls. Jonathan, who possessed one of the most brilliant minds of the age, appreciated and honored his wife's intellect and shared with her his deepest insights from God's Word and sought her help in his work as a minister.

Within a year of their marriage, God blessed them with the first of eleven children. By the grace of God, Sarah and Jonathan formed a close-knit and happy home. "Every Christian family ought to be a little church, consecrated to Christ and wholly influenced and governed by His rules," Jonathan taught. "And family education and order are some of the chief means of grace."

Jonathan led the family in morning and evening devotions, and he set aside an hour each day to talk with the children and help them with their studies. Jonathan and Sarah wanted their daughters educated as well as their sons, which was unusual for the time. Every evening, after the children had been put to bed, Sarah and Jonathan talked and prayed together. But most of Jonathan's time—thirteen hours each day—was spent in his study, pouring over the Scriptures, preparing his sermons and writing books on theology. So he counted on Sarah to run the household and nurture the children. "It was a happy circumstance," one friend wrote, "that he could trust everything to the care of Mrs. Edwards with undoubting confidence. She worked to make everything in the family agreeable and pleasant."

As her husband's writings became well known, their home was often filled with guests. Although it greatly added to her workload, she enjoyed making visitors feel at home, drawing them into joyful and lively conversation. "Sarah spared no pains to make guests welcome and to provide for their convenience and comfort," said an old family friend.

Her primary duty was raising her children in the Lord. Sarah shaped her children's behavior with thoughtfulness and love. "She had an excellent way of governing her children," one frequent visitor reported. "She knew how to make them obey her cheerfully. She seldom punished them, and spoke to them using gentle and pleasant words."

Sarah prayed throughout the day for her children. "She bore them constantly on her heart before God," a minister friend said of her.

Meanwhile, Edwards's published sermons and books won praise across the American colonies and in Britain too. The focus of his preaching and writing was the sinfulness of man and the redemption found in Jesus Christ. But most of the people of Northampton seemed unmoved by his faithful preaching. It was frustrating work because many hearts were hardened, and the teenagers and young adults seemed so far from God. Over time, the youth of the town grew more rowdy, disrupting church services, reveling in their drunken "frolics" and "night-walks."

Jonathan and Sarah agonized over the problem and prayed for God to change hearts. Then early in 1734, as Jonathan preached a series of sermons on faith, the young adults began paying close attention and staying after church to discuss what they had heard.

One day a young woman—one of the most rebellious girls in the town—knocked at the Edwards's door. Sarah welcomed her in and got Jonathan from his study. "For the last several days the weight of my sin has crushed me," the girl told them. "Just when I thought I was without hope, the Lord warmed my heart and lifted me up."

As they talked, it became clear that Christ had touched her. "I believe," Jonathan told her, "that God has given you a new heart."

Immediately her life changed. Her selfishness turned to love. She never missed a worship service or prayer meeting. "The news of her conversion," Jonathan said, "was like a flash of lightning upon the hearts of young people all over the town."

Young men and women, some of them the most notorious sinners in Northampton—who used to make fun of Pastor Edwards and disturb the services—now hung on every word of the sermons. Soon people of all ages throughout the town, overwhelmed by their sin, cried out to Christ for forgiveness. Few spoke of anything but the things of God. Nightly throughout the town, neighbors gathered for prayer and Bible reading. "It was never so full of love or joy," Jonathan wrote. "It was a time of joy in families because of the Lord's salvation. Parents rejoiced over their children as newborn, and husbands over wives and wives over husbands."

In the space of six months, over three hundred people found forgiveness in Jesus Christ. The revival spread to several other towns in Massachusetts and Connecticut; it was the dawning of the Great Awakening. Sarah herself felt a renewed discovery of God's mercy, and she rededicated her life to His service and glory. "She was overwhelmed," Jonathan said of her, "in the light and joy of the love of God."

Supportive ministers in England and America, including Isaac Watts, the famous hymn writer, urged Mr. Edwards to write a report on the revival. He did, and in 1737, *A Faithful Narrative of the Surprising Work of God* was read eagerly on both sides of the Atlantic inspiring George Whitefield, John Wesley and other preachers.

But many people in New England stood firmly against the awakening. Some ministers condemned it from their pulpits. Critics complained that Jonathan Edwards was stirring up emotions. "This is not a true work of God," they said. The criticism stung Sarah. She knew that she worried too much about what other people thought of her and her husband. "I desire," she confessed, "to have my own good name and fair reputation among men, and especially the esteem and just treatment of the people of this town."

After a time, the fire of the revival cooled down, but when George Whitefield, the English preacher, arrived in October 1740, the flames leaped up and spread throughout the American colonies. Tens of thousands, broken in spirit and weeping, turned to Christ through his preaching. Not long after Whitefield arrived in America, Edwards invited him to Northampton. Whitefield accepted and enjoyed his visit immensely. He was so impressed by the love between Jonathan and Sarah that it kindled in him the desire to be married. Whitefield wrote in his journal about the Edwards, "A sweeter couple I have never seen."

In 1742 when Jonathan was away for a few weeks, Sarah fell into a deep depression that made her anxious, fearful and withdrawn. Through the black night of her thoughts she tried to press on with her family duties. When Jonathan returned home and found his wife overwhelmed with sadness, he asked her to tell him in detail all of her thoughts and fears. They prayed together and waited on God. Soon her depression lifted, and Sarah reported that she felt full of assurance of God's love and forgiveness. "I could sit and sing this life away," Sarah told her husband.

Jonathan was amazed at the transformation. "Her heart was swallowed up in a kind of glow of Christ's love coming down as a constant stream of sweet light," he said.

Although more and more pastors and laymen in America, Britain and Europe admired his printed sermons and books on theology, trouble was brewing in Northampton. There were men and women who did not like Edwards or his strong sermons. In 1749, a problem erupted over the Lord's Supper. For many years the church at Northampton had permitted people to take the bread and wine, even if they did not have a personal faith in Jesus Christ. Edwards came to believe that communion was only meant for those who openly declared a saving faith in Jesus. When Edwards took steps to change the church's policy toward the Lord's Supper, his enemies accused him of being judgmental and divisive. They spread lies about him and undermined his ministry. Finally, the congregation voted to remove him. For twenty-three years he had served the church as a devoted minister; now the note in the Northampton Church Record Book read simply: "June 22, 1750—The Reverend Jonathan Edwards was dismissed."

A year later, the Edwards became missionaries to the Housatonic Indians at Stockbridge, a tiny settlement on the edge of the Massachusetts wilderness. Their new home sat at the foot of the beautiful Berkshire Hills, not far from a river. The slower pace of life was a boon to the family. Jonathan and Sarah often walked arm in arm through the meadows along the winding river, praising God together for His glorious creation. The younger children loved exploring the hills and valleys. For seven years they worked among the Indians, and Jonathan wrote several books.

In 1757, the College of New Jersey (Princeton) asked him to be their college president. Sarah and Jonathan discussed at length whether or not he should accept the post. They would have preferred to stay in Stockbridge. But in the end they believed he should accept the position. Jonathan left to begin the work while Sarah remained in Stockbridge to prepare to move the family to Princeton. Before Sarah could join her husband there, he died of smallpox. On his deathbed, he turned to his daughter Lucy and said, "Give my kindest love to my dear wife and tell her that the uncommon union which has so long subsisted between us has been of such a nature as I trust is spiritual and therefore will continue forever."

Then he looked around the room and said, "Now where is Jesus of Nazareth, my true and never failing friend?"

Through great grief and many tears, Sarah submitted herself to the will of God in taking her husband. She sent a letter to her daughter: "O my very dear child," she wrote, "What shall I say. A holy and good God has covered us with a dark cloud. O that we may all kiss the rod and lay our hands on our mouths. The Lord has done it. He has made me adore His goodness that we had him so long. But my God lives and He has my heart."

Just six weeks after Jonathan passed away, Sarah suddenly fell gravely ill. She quickly wrote out a will dividing her modest estate evenly between all the children. "Share and share alike," she instructed. When Sarah sensed her death was near, she told those attending her, "I resign myself entirely to God. May He enable me to glorify Him to the last."

Sarah and Jonathan's witness lived on in their children, grandchildren and great grandchildren—among them were scores of missionaries and clergymen who proclaimed the good news of Jesus across the globe, many university professors, medical doctors, thirteen college presidents, thirty judges, four United States senators and three state governors. The family that began with the marriage of Sarah and Jonathan Edwards became one of the most accomplished families in American history.

MISSIONS REAWAKENED

MISSIONARIES AND CONVERTS

Beginning late in the eighteenth century, the missionary zeal of the church awakened after many centuries of slumber. Christians in Britain, Europe and America, impassioned by God's call to proclaim the good news of Jesus Christ to every tongue, tribe and nation, sent pioneering men and women across the globe. From the heart of Africa to the islands of the South Pacific, from the sands of Persia to the jungles of South America, they brought—at great personal sacrifice—the light of Christ to people living in darkness. Before long, there were millions of people praising Jesus Christ who a short time before had never heard His name.

28 ELIZA SPALDING
A Light to the Nez Perce, 1807–1851

In June 1836, Eliza Spalding lay in the back of a Dearborn wagon, her thin body drenched in sweat. Her husband Henry held a cup of water to her cracked lips. Doctor Marcus Whitman listened to her labored breathing and checked her pulse. A few minutes later, the two men stood beside the wagon, looking at the Rocky Mountains looming in the west. Over the last three months, they had crossed the Great Plains of the United States, but the hardest part of their journey to the Pacific Northwest lay ahead. And Eliza's health had steadily weakened. "I don't think she'll make it," Whitman told Henry.

But Eliza held on. One week later she wrote in her diary, "We are expecting in a few days to begin ascending the Rocky Mountains. Only God, who knows all things, knows whether my weak body will survive this undertaking. His will, not mine, be done."

Five missionaries—Henry and Eliza Spalding, Marcus and Narcissa Whitman and William Gray—were bound for the Pacific Northwest to bring the good news of Jesus to the Nez Perce Indians. They were traveling with a fur-trading caravan that was rushing to arrive in time for the summer rendezvous in the Rockies, the annual meeting of mountain men, fur traders and Indians.

Weeks later, when they arrived at the rendezvous, a large party of Nez Perce men, women and children—who had anxiously awaited their arrival—rushed forward to meet the missionaries. They swarmed them, shouted greetings and touched their clothes. "The women were not satisfied short of saluting Mrs. Whitman and me with a kiss," Eliza wrote. "All appear happy to see us. If permitted to reach their country and live among them, may our labors be blest to their physical and spiritual good."

Although weak, Eliza began to get acquainted with the Nez Perce women and learn their language. She started to make a list of Nez Perce words that she heard the women speak by writing the words phonetically and repeating them back to the Indians. Before long, Eliza was able to communicate simple ideas to them in their own language. She loved them at once, and the feeling was mutual. "Mrs. Spalding, feeble as she was," observed William Gray, "seemed to be the favorite with the Indian women."

Indian guides led them through the mountains to the Nez Perce homeland near the confluence of the Snake and Clearwater rivers. After scouting the region, the Whitmans chose to locate one hundred miles to the west at Waiilatpu among the Cayuse Indians. The Spaldings settled at Lapwai with the Nez Perce on the Clearwater River.

With the help of the Nez Perce, the Spaldings built a small cabin and then got right to work. Eager to learn, many Nez Perce gathered near the cabin each morning and evening for prayer and teaching. At first, Henry Spalding spoke through a Nez Perce interpreter who had learned a little English from fur traders, but before long he was preaching in Nez Perce. "Oh that we may point them to the Lamb of God who takes away the sins of the world," Henry said. "May we see souls flocking to Jesus."

The Spaldings used creative ways to teach the message of Christ. Before each sermon, Eliza painted Bible scenes from the passage on which Henry planned to preach. He pointed to the pictures as he spoke. At the end of the sermon, Henry and Eliza asked the people what they had learned. After correcting misunderstandings, they urged them to share the message with their friends. Soon the gist of the sermon had spread to all the people.

Eliza began a school in her home. Before long, she had taught several Indian children and a few adults to read and write in Nez Perce, preparing them to read the Scriptures for themselves. "O blessed privilege," Eliza wrote, "to labor in the vineyard of my Savior and point the lost and perishing to Him—for He is the way, the truth, and the life."

The first Nez Perce Indians to profess faith in Christ were two chiefs whom Henry named Joseph and Timothy. (Because Indian names were hard for missionaries to pronounce and remember, they often gave converts English names at their baptisms.) "Joseph," Spalding said, "urges all the people to give their hearts to Jesus without delay." By 1839, a large number of Nez Perce had confessed their sins. "Many give evidence of a change of heart," Henry reported.

The Spaldings knew that settlers would soon pour into the region and that the Indians could not continue for long their life of hunting and gathering. Henry showed the Indians how to plant crops and dig irrigation canals to water them. The Spaldings harvested the first potato crop in the land that would one day become the state of Idaho. "We point them with one hand to the Lamb of God who takes away the sins of the world," he said.

"With the other hand we point to the hoe, as the means of saving their famishing bodies."

Soon the Spaldings had children of their own. Their first child was a girl named Eliza and the second, a boy named Henry. "Only through Jesus Christ strengthening me," Eliza wrote, "shall I be enabled to educate these precious lambs for Him who has committed them to my care." Later, the Spaldings had two more daughters. The Nez Perce were fascinated by the white children. "Little Eliza is a favorite of the natives," Eliza reported. "They are so determined to take her into their own arms that they sometimes almost rend her from mine, and frequently when I am busy about my work, take her from the cradle. Often, I have the distress to pick a flea or louse from her clothes, but these are little things and I will say no more about them."

Eliza, although often frail and ill, pressed on in the work. Once, when she was laid low by a long illness, Henry suggested that they leave the mission, thinking it put too much strain on her. But Eliza refused to give up. "I like the command just as it stands," she told him. "'Go ye into all the world'—and no exceptions for poor health."

At one point, when she grew so sick that many feared she would die, Chief Timothy stood by her bed and told Henry, "I would gladly die in her place that she might live to teach my people."

Despite good progress through many years, several Nez Perce became hostile toward the Spaldings. Some members of the tribe abandoned their profession of faith in Christ when they realized that it did not make them wealthy. Later, a few Indians from the eastern United States arrived and told the Cayuse and Nez Perce that the missionaries were scheming to poison them and steal their land. Unruly young men disrupted school by bursting in covered with war paint or walking their horses through Eliza's classroom. They stole tools, smashed windows, trampled crops, tore down fences and threatened the Spaldings with violence.

Once when Henry was away, a gang of young Nez Perce men accosted Eliza, demanding that she turn over her supplies to them. "We will kill you and your children and burn the house over your dead bodies," they threatened.

"Do as you please, but you'll get nothing from me!" Eliza said, shutting the door in their faces. One missionary who worked with the Spaldings said, "Mrs. Spalding was considered by the Indian men as a brave, fearless woman, and was respected and esteemed by all."

But the setbacks discouraged the Spaldings. Henry wrote in a letter in February 1847, "What heart have I to replace the windows and repair the roof to the meeting house, when it is almost certain that the windows will be immediately broken again. We are now called upon to pay for the water we use, the wood we burn, the trails we travel and the air we breathe. Our prospects as missionaries have become very dark."

Despite the frustrations, the Spaldings didn't give up. "The promises of God are sufficient to calm and console the heart that is set on Him," Eliza said.

In November 1847, Henry brought their ten-year-old daughter Eliza to Waiilatpu to attend a school for white children which the Whitmans had started. While there, Henry decided to visit some Indian villages about a half-day's ride south. The next day, a band of Cayuse Indians raided Waiilatpu and murdered Marcus and Narcissa Whitman and eleven other men. They took the remaining women and children hostage—including the Spaldings' daughter. This was the first step in their plan to kill the Whitmans, Spaldings and other Protestant missionaries in the region.

Unaware of the killings, Spalding spent two days visiting Indian villages before heading back to Waiilatpu. When he was just three miles from the mission, a Catholic missionary met him on the trail and told him about the murders. "They will certainly kill me too," Spalding said.

Spalding turned his horse and sped for his home at a full gallop. Soon Cayuse warriors were scouring the countryside for him. They probably would have captured Henry quickly, but a thick fog rolled in that made it hard to see. Spalding rode through the night. To avoid getting caught, he stayed away from the main trails, walked his horse in streams to cover his tracks and slept in ravines.

Meanwhile, word of the disaster reached Mrs. Spalding at Lapwai when a stranger burst into her cabin and asked, "Has Mr. Spalding come home yet?"

"No," Eliza answered, "but we expect him any day."

"I have bad news," the stranger said. "They are all murdered at Doctor Whitman's."

No one spoke for a moment, then Eliza replied calmly, "Go on, sir, and let me hear the worst."

"Doctor and Mrs. Whitman are murdered," he said, "and your husband without doubt shared the same fate of all the women and children who I expect are butchered."

Eliza sat down in stunned silence and began to pray. The next day, Eliza got word that her husband had escaped the massacre and that her daughter was alive and being held captive by the Cayuse. After three nights and days of travel, Henry arrived home and was reunited with his family.

A few days later, a large party of friendly Nez Perce escorted Eliza, Henry and their three youngest children to Fort Walla Walla where an officer of the Hudson's Bay Company had won the release of the Waiilatpu hostages. At the fort their daughter Eliza ran into their arms.

After the killings, the Spaldings had to leave Lapwai for their own safety. The Christian Nez Perce mourned Eliza's leaving most of all. "Now my beloved teacher," Chief Timothy said to her as she departed, "I shall look upon your face for the last time in this world. But this Bible in which your hands have written the words of God I shall carry in my bosom until I lie down in the grave."

The Spalding family went to the Willamette Valley in Oregon, thinking that they would be there for a short time until it was safe to return. However, after the massacre the mission board decided to close all their mission stations in the Northwest. It was a crushing blow to the Spaldings who longed to resume their work. "Our hearts seem constantly inclined to return to the Indians," Eliza wrote.

Not long after, in January 1851, Eliza passed away at the age of forty-three. On her tombstone, Henry had chiseled, "She died in peace trusting in her Savior. Rest sweet dust, till Jesus bid thee rise."

Many years later, when Henry Spalding was finally able to preach again to the Nez Perce, a great spiritual awakening broke out. It spread to other neighboring tribes. Soon hundreds of

Indians had confessed faith in Christ and were baptized. "Bless the Lord, O my soul!" Henry wrote in his journal. "My heart overflows with praises to God and joy in his wonderful work."

Some of the Indian churches started during the awakening are thriving today, and Nez Perce believers still sing some hymns translated into their language by Henry and Eliza Spalding.

"Eliza Spalding: A Light to the Nez Perce" is excerpted from Richard M. Hannula's *Lights in the Northwest: Stories from Two Centuries of Pacific Northwest Christians* (Tacoma WA: Sound Summit Books, 2004). Used by permission.

29 SARAH BOARDMAN JUDSON

Pioneer Missionary to Burma, 1803–1845

In the middle of the night the cry rang out: "Rebels!" George and Sarah Boardman awoke to bullets ripping through the bamboo walls of their hut. Sarah grabbed her infant daughter from the bed and lay flat on the floor. Slowly, they crawled toward the back door. Native rebels were attacking the gates of Tavoy, a British outpost in Burma. The Boardmans, Christian missionaries from the United States who lived just outside the city gate, could hear the voices of rebel fighters gathering near their front yard. "Heavenly Father," George prayed, "protect us."

As dawn broke, they saw that the Sepoys—native troops in the service of the British—still held the main gate. With the help of some Christian natives, the Boardmans fled into the town, leaving behind all of their property. Soon rebels controlled most of the city, and the British commander of the Sepoys ordered a retreat to the wharf on the river bank. With fewer than one hundred soldiers to protect them, several hundred people huddled in a large wooden building on the docks. They faced nearly one thousand rebel fighters who soon set fire to the buildings on the wharf. It looked as if the Boardmans would either be massacred by the sword or burned alive. "We lifted up our hearts to God," George Boardman said later, "and He heard us from heaven."

Suddenly, torrential rains poured down, dousing the fires and forcing back the attackers. For two long and frightening days, the defenders held out until a British steamship arrived with re-inforcements. When the rebels were driven off and the town was retaken, the Boardmans found their house destroyed and their belongings stolen or wrecked. British officials urged George and Sarah to leave the region for their own safety, but they were deter-mined to continue sharing Christ with the natives.

Ever since Sarah was in her early teens growing up in Salem, Massachusetts, she felt called to foreign missions. "It is my ardent desire," she wrote a friend at that time, "that the glorious work of reformation may extend till every knee shall bow to the living God. How can I be so inactive when I know that thousands are perishing in this land of grace, and millions in other lands are at this very moment kneeling before senseless idols?"

Just a few years earlier, James Colman, the pioneer mis-sionary to Burma, had died. Nineteen-year-old Sarah wrote a poem about his life on the mission field. A Christian magazine printed her poem. It was read by George Boardman, a Baptist minister preparing to take Colman's place in Burma. He asked to meet the author of the poem. When they met, George and Sarah talked for hours about their Christian faith and inter-national missions. Before long, they fell in love. In 1826, they married and honeymooned on the ship that took them from the United States to Calcutta, India. They remained in Calcutta for a time while the British put down a rebellion by natives in Burma. In the meantime, the Boardmans worked at learning the Burmese language.

In 1827, George and Sarah Boardman and their newborn baby arrived in Maulmain, Burma, and met Adoniram Judson, the head of the mission, who was still reeling from the death of his wife. Several months later, Judson sent them to start a mission in Tavoy, a city about fifty miles away. When they got to Tavoy, the British commanding officer urged them to live inside the fortified walls of the town for protection. "Our goal is to bring the gospel to the Burmese people," George told him, "and to do that we must live among them." They had a small bamboo hut built outside the town walls on the edge of the jungle. Soon Sarah contracted malaria which greatly weakened her. She suffered recurring bouts of the disease for the rest of her life.

One night, as the Boardmans slept, bandits broke into their home armed with knives and machetes. They stood over the bed and would have killed them all instantly if they had awoken, but neither the parents nor their baby stirred as the thieves rifled through their belongings and stole everything of value. Shortly after the bandits left, they awoke. As the Boardmans discovered their loss, they saw knife slits in the mosquito curtains around their bed. "I forgot the stolen goods," Sarah wrote later, "and thought only of the treasure that was spared. In my imagination I saw the assassins with their horrid weapons standing by our bedside, ready to do their worst had we been permitted to wake. Oh how merciful was that watchful Providence which prolonged those powerful slumbers, not allowing even the infant at my bosom to open its eyes at so critical a moment. If ever gratitude glowed in my heart, if ever the world appeared to me worthless as vanity, and if ever I wished to dedicate myself, my husband, my baby, my all, to our great Redeemer, it was at that time."

Tavoy was a stronghold of Hinduism filled with thousands of shrines and hundreds of Hindu priests. As George and Sarah Boardman slowly mastered the language, the natives began to visit them to hear about their God. The people loved to touch Sarah's clothing and her fair white skin. Over time, some of the natives turned to Christ. Many of the converts were Karens, tribal people who lived in the forests and mountains. Other Burmese people called them "wild men." The Karen converts led many of their tribesmen to the Christian faith. George began to venture many miles into the jungle to visit remote Karen villages. The people welcomed him and flocked around to hear him preach the good news of Jesus Christ. He baptized young converts and helped to organize village churches.

While George made trips into the jungle, Sarah cared for their daughter and their newborn son and told those who visited their home about Jesus. Sarah began a women's Bible study and prayer meeting. She opened a school in Tavoy and trained native women to start Christian schools in their villages. "To see so many in this dark land putting on Christ fills me with joy and gratitude," Sarah wrote in a letter home. "It makes us forget the hardships and dangers."

Sadly, Sarah had to face even greater hardships that crashed upon her like tidal waves. Her little daughter died suddenly. Then George fell ill with tuberculosis, a disease that sapped his strength and made him cough constantly. "We must look beyond this frail fleeting world for our true peace," Sarah wrote her sister. "Alas, I know by most bitter experience that it is in vain to seek for true happiness here below. My fondest earthly hopes have again and again been dashed. My heart was almost broken when I stood by the deathbed of my sweet, lovely girl."

Not long after, their eight-month-old son died. Through all the trials, the Boardmans clung to God and worked to bring the Burmese to faith in Christ. Later, Sarah gave birth to another son, but shortly afterward, her husband George died.

"The hours of loneliness and bitter weeping I endured are known only to God," Sarah said. "But still Jesus has sweetened the cup." After the death of her husband, Sarah wondered if she should remain a missionary in Burma or return to the United States. At that time, single women rarely served on the mission field. Her parents and the leaders of her hometown church urged her to return home. "When I first stood by the grave of my husband," she wrote in a letter home, "I thought that I must go home. But these poor Karens and the Burmese would then be left without anyone to instruct them. How then can I go?"

She decided to remain, and she threw herself into the work. "Every moment of my time is occupied from sunrise to ten in the evening," Sarah reported. "Within the last two months, fifty-seven Karens have been baptized."

Two years later, she wrote to a friend, "Our schools are flourishing with sixty scholars in town and about fifty among the Karens in the jungle. I feel desolate, lonely, and sometimes deeply distressed at my great and irreparable loss—but I bless God. I am not in despair."

Because there was not a missionary minister to care for the fledgling churches in the jungle, Sarah, with her little boy in her arms, crossed the mountain passes and jungle trails to the Karen villages. She led worship services—sometimes to congregations of three hundred or more. She performed that duty until native preachers could be trained to take over.

After three years in Burma as a widow, Sarah married Adoniram Judson and moved to Maulmain, the headquarters of Judson's mission. Adoniram had been laboring in Burma for more than twenty years. He had suffered imprisonment, torture and the death of his wife Ann and all of their children. Through those difficult times he preached, organized churches and translated the entire Bible into Burmese. Sarah proved to be as great a blessing to Adoniram as he was to her. "You know I love you more than all the world beside," Adoniram told her.

Through the years, they had eight children. Sarah led Bible classes for women and trained teachers to start Christian schools. One day after a Bible study, an elderly, gray-haired Burmese woman looked at Sarah's little daughter and said, "I am the same age as Abby-Ann."

"What do you mean by that?" Sarah asked her.

"I did not believe in Jesus Christ until the year that Abby-Ann was born, and it was not till then that I began to live."

Sarah had so mastered Burmese that she preferred reading the Scriptures in that language rather than in English. She translated John Bunyan's *Pilgrim's Progress* into Burmese as well as hymns, a catechism and Christian tracts. All the while, Sarah suffered recurring bouts of malaria that laid her low for weeks on end. One day as Sarah worked on her porch on a translation of the life of Christ, she looked up and saw a native man leaning on the rail and staring at her. "Hello," Sarah called, "is there something I can do for you?"

"I was just watching you write," the man said. Sarah put down her pen and invited the man onto the veranda. He sat down, and Sarah explained to him that she had been writing about Jesus Christ. Then she told him about the life, death and resurrection of Christ. "I have never heard about Jesus before," the man told her. After their conversation, he said, "I will pray to the Eternal God and ask Him to give me a new heart that I might believe in the Savior, the Lord Jesus Christ."

Sarah Boardman Judson died at the age of forty-one. In one of her final letters home she wrote, "I can say with gratitude to God that amid all the vicissitudes through which I have been called to pass, I have never for one moment regretted that I entered the missionary field. We are not weary of our work—it is our hearts' desire to live and die among these people."

30 FIDELIA FISKE
Loving in Christ, 1816–1864

In 1843, Miss Fidelia Fiske, a missionary teacher among the Nestorian people of Northwestern Persia, put the girls of her small boarding school to bed. They slept—according to the practice of their people—on comforters on the roof of the house. Exhausted, Fidelia went to her room and fell fast asleep. Working with the girls was a challenge. She kept anything of the slightest value under lock and key because lying and stealing were second nature to the girls. Every day items went missing, and all the girls denied taking anything. "We all lie," one Nestorian woman told her. And nearly all the students had foul mouths. "My little girls swear and use the vilest language," Fidelia reported.

"I feel very weak," Fidelia wrote home, "and were it not that Christ has loved these souls, I should be discouraged, but He has loved them, and He loves them still." With a cheerful heart and prayers for strength, she taught the girls and loved them for Christ. In the classroom, they learned reading, writing, arithmetic, science and the Bible. Every morning and evening Fidelia prayed with them and read the Scripture to them. "Miss Fiske's power was loving," one missionary said of her. "It was the outgrowth of Christ in her—for He lived in her and she in Him."

The Nestorians, a poor persecuted minority living among Muslim Persians and Kurds, lived in tiny houses with dirt floors alive with fleas and lice. The men regularly beat the women and expected them to do the lion's share of the work in the field and all the work at home. They did not teach their daughters to read and write. When Fidelia asked young ladies if they would like to learn to read, they shook their heads saying, "I am a woman."

Fidelia pressed on, asking God to change hearts. "Oh, there is a sweet delight in pointing souls to the Lamb of God!" she said. "Yes, I do love them, and if I can lead them to heaven I shall feel that my joy is full."

Just a few years earlier, Fidelia Fiske had attended Mount Holyoke College, a new Christian college for girls in Massachusetts led by Mary Lyon. After graduating, Fidelia became a teacher there. One day during chapel in 1842, a missionary named Justin Perkins told the students and faculty about the needy women and girls of Persia. "I am praying that a young lady might go with me and my family back to Persia as a missionary teacher," he said. After the service, Fidelia sent Perkins a note. "If counted worthy," she wrote, "I should be willing to go."

Within a year, Fidelia sailed across the Atlantic and Mediterranean to Constantinople. Then she and the Perkins traveled eight hundred miles overland to Persia—all the while she studied the Persian language. When she arrived in Urumiyeh, a city of twenty-five thousand people, she threw herself into the work at once, trying to start a school for Nestorian girls. This was difficult because they did not see a need for education, and by the age of twelve, nearly all the girls were engaged to be married. Fathers did not want their daughters to go to a boarding school for fear that they would grow unaccustomed to work and miss out on opportunities for marriage. "If our daughters remain long with you," parents told Fidelia, "they will not be able to carry heavy burdens in the fields nor use the spade as well as their companions who have never learned to read."

Despite the obstacles, within a few months she had six students. By the start of her second year, she reported, "I have now twenty-five little girls, all under thirteen years. They are a great charge, often wayward and causing my inmost soul to weep. And yet I have so much to encourage me that I am far from sinking. I've enjoyed spending hours each day in reading the Bible with these children. God may yet sanctify them through His truth; though now they seem far from it."

Then during the middle of the school's third year, the sunbeams of Christ's love began to warm the students' cold hearts. One day in January of 1846, after Fidelia had prayed with the girls and given them a lesson to work on in their rooms, two of the girls stayed behind with tears in their eyes. "What is the matter," she asked them, "have you heard bad news?"

"May we have today to care for our souls?" one of the girls whispered. They told her that they felt great guilt about their sins and wanted to pray and seek forgiveness in Jesus. Fidelia happily gave them permission to spend some time in prayer. "Nor did they seek in vain," she reported later. "They were soon trusting in Christ and we hoped for yet greater blessings."

Within a few days, many other students felt weighed down by the burden of their sins. "Any of you who feels that you must now care for your souls," Fidelia told them, "come to my room at five o'clock." That evening, her room was overflowing with girls seeking Christ.

"Miss Fiske talked with us till our hearts melted like wax," one student said, "then in the ardor of her love she knelt with us, committing us to the counsel and guidance of God. There was no heart that would not melt before the fire of her love, unless it was one entirely overcome by Satan."

"I cannot well describe the scene," Fidelia wrote in a letter to America. "One after another bowed under a sense of sin. Every place in our house was occupied for prayer."

Day after day, more students turned to Christ. The girls spent their free time studying the Bible and praying for unsaved family members and friends. "Now there are only two in the school over ten years of age who have not been deeply affected," Fidelia reported a few weeks later. "Many appear to be true Christians. Time alone can show the genuineness of their conversion. But I do believe that God is gathering to Himself a precious band here—sisters in Christ, redeemed by His blood!"

The girls' new life in Christ showed in their speech and behavior. Lying, stealing and cursing disappeared. "Our school is so changed that we could hardly realize it is our school," Fidelia said. "We often pause to ask ourselves—is it possible that those whose voices we now hear in prayer and praise from morn till night are the same individuals over whom we mourned just three months ago as dead in trespasses and sins? What has the Lord done! Oh, I want to love Him more and serve Him better."

One girl named Khanee came to Miss Fiske in great distress and said, "Do you remember the day two years ago when Sawdee's new shoes were taken?"

"Yes," Fidelia answered. Bursting into tears, Khanee confessed, "I took them. I was angry with Sawdee and I threw them into a well where no one could find them. I know Jesus will not receive me till I have confessed to Sawdee. Can I go and tell her tonight and pray with her and then go and work to get money to pay her for the shoes?"

"She did pay for the shoes," Fidelia reported later, "and became a bright and shining light. There were many cases just like this."

However, the Nestorian elders resented the change. They threatened any converts with excommunication from the community. "If you do not come home to us," they told the girls, "we will tear out your fingernails. We will hunt you from village to village and kill you if we can."

With heavy hearts the missionaries sent the children home until the elders calmed down. "Oh, we shall hear the words of God no more!" the girls cried as they left. The Nestorian leaders asked the Persian government to drive the missionaries out of the country, but foreign ambassadors convinced them not to do it. In time, the elders allowed the girls to return to Miss Fiske's school, and their growth in Christ continued.

Since the day Fidelia first arrived in Urumiyeh, she had visited Nestorian women in their homes, trying to share the good news of Jesus Christ with them. "She used to go often to some of the large villages," one of her students said, "visiting from house to house to comfort the poor women. She would not spare herself the melting heat of summer, but would go into the fields to the women and converse with them there." However, Fidelia did not find these women interested in following Christ. But when word of the awakening spread beyond the school, that changed.

Mothers of students and women from the villages began coming to Fidelia for spiritual guidance. She urged them to believe in Christ. "Nestorian women flocked around us," Fidelia said, "and our dear pupils were true helpers. I often had as many as ten or fifteen women spend the night with us. I gathered together all the spare pillows and cushions and quilts in the house and made our sitting room one great dormitory. I often stayed with them until midnight and then from my room heard them pray all night. Quite a few who formerly were intemperate and profane appear now to be humbly sitting at Jesus' feet. They have been made free in Christ Jesus."

Seeds planted by Dr. Perkins, Miss Fiske and other missionaries began to bear fruit in the men too. "Many laboring men are now Christians," Fidelia reported. "With their spades in their hands, they preach Christ and Him crucified from morning until night."

One Nestorian man who became a Christian said, "Oh, Miss Fiske was right when she pointed out the way. Free grace! Free grace! Oh, it was free grace."

More and more of the women from the surrounding villages came for instruction and prayer. "Although they are beaten and turned out of their houses by their wicked drunken husbands," Fidelia wrote to the teachers at Mount Holyoke, "They cling to Christ. I never before witnessed such thrilling scenes."

To her great delight, some of the girls who graduated from her school became missionaries to share the love of Christ with others. "Yesterday, four of our former pupils with their husbands left us as missionaries to the dark mountains of Kurdistan," Fidelia wrote. "I thank my heavenly Father for allowing me to live to see my dear children thus take their lives in their hands and go forth for Christ's sake."

After sixteen years of service in Persia, Fidelia suffered from such painful swelling in her neck and arms that she no longer could perform her duties. So she returned to the United States to recuperate. As her stamina improved a little, she worked part-time as a spiritual counselor for the young women at Mount Holyoke College. Soon an awakening broke out in the college, and Fidelia's room was thronged by students seeking her counsel and prayers. Many gave their hearts to Jesus Christ.

Fidelia longed to return to Persia, but her poor health made that impossible. In 1864, the cancer that had been slowly growing in her body for several years took her life. Near the end, she sent one last word of advice to the students of Mount Holyoke—"Live for Christ."

31 AMANDA SMITH
From Slave to World Evangelist,
1837–1915

In the 1840s no man worked harder in Long Green, Maryland, than the black slave Samuel Berry. During the day, he worked his master's fields, and twice a week he traveled twenty miles to Baltimore to sell his master's produce. In the evening, he made brooms and husk mats to sell for his own profit. During harvest time, after working his home fields, he walked three miles and worked for another farmer for pay, often laboring until well after midnight. After walking back home, he slept three or four hours and got up to do it all over again. Samuel drove himself so relentlessly because he had a goal: to buy his freedom and the freedom of his wife and children. Samuel's wife Mariam was a slave on a neighboring farm. They had five children—the oldest daughter's name was Amanda.

For years, Samuel toiled until he earned enough to purchase freedom for himself and his family. With the emancipation papers in his hands, Samuel Berry moved his family to York County, Pennsylvania, where he found work on a farm. Mariam credited their freedom to the hard work of her husband and the prayers of her mother. "I've often heard my mother say that it was to the prayers and mighty faith of my grandmother," Amanda said, "that we owed our freedom. She'd often pray that God would open a way for her grandchildren to be free. How I do praise the Lord for a godly grandmother as well as a mother."

Remarkably, both Samuel and Mariam had learned to read, even though there were laws against teaching slaves to read and write. On Sunday mornings, Samuel, an earnest Christian, gathered the children and read passages from the Bible. Mariam prayed with each child before bed every night. In Pennsylvania, they taught their children to read and write, although most of them had few opportunities for formal schooling.

The Berry home became a station on the Underground Railroad—a network of people and safe-houses where runaway slaves from the South found help for their escape. Slave-catchers roamed the area like wolves, making their living by capturing escaped slaves and claiming the reward. Samuel Berry gave shelter and aid to many of these benighted fugitives. "I have known him," Amanda said of her father, "to work all day in the field and sleep about two hours. Then he'd start at midnight and walk fifteen or twenty miles and carry a poor slave to a place of security, then get home just before day. Perhaps he could sleep an hour and then go to work. Many times he baffled the slave-catchers who suspected what he was up to. Only once was there a poor slave taken that my father got his hands on."

One summer night, at around one o'clock in the morning, a man knocked at the Berry's cabin door. He was a runaway slave who had been told by some white men that he could find help at Samuel's house. Unbeknownst to the runaway, slave catchers had directed him to the home in order to catch Samuel in the act of sheltering a fugitive slave. Samuel welcomed the man and gave him food and coffee. Early the next morning when all the family was awake, there came a loud bang on the door. "Hello," men shouted from outside. "Hide," Samuel told the runaway. When he opened the door, Samuel saw seven armed white men. "We want that nigger you are harboring," they shouted. "I am not harboring anybody," Samuel said. Cursing and pushing, the men barged into the house and began beating Samuel and roughly handling the children. Mariam, holding a baby, tried to defend her husband. One of the intruders slashed at Mariam with his knife, but it glanced off the open stove door that she was standing next to. "I have thanked God often for that stove door," Amanda said later. "If not for it, my poor mother would have been killed."

The runaway ran upstairs and jumped out the window, but the slave-catchers' blood hounds tracked him down as he ran across the fields. After severely beating Samuel and warning the family to stop helping runaway slaves, they left.

Some time later, when the Berrys were hiding a fugitive slave in their home, Samuel saw four white men riding up to the farmhouse. "Mother," he called inside to Mariam, "I see four men coming; do the best you can."

Mariam quickly hid the man under a stack of straw near the fireplace. Samuel stood outside to greet the strangers. "Good morning, gentlemen, you are out quite early this morning."

"Yes," their leader replied, "we are looking for a runaway slave."

Just then Samuel realized that the leader was the son of his old master. "Why, is that you Mr. E.?" Samuel said. "Yes, Sam," he replied.

Samuel laughed with the man and reminisced about old times. Then Samuel asked, "What in the world is up?"

"Do you know anything about a runaway?" Mr. E. asked. "We have a search warrant and we mean to have him. Have you hid him away?"

"Well," Samuel said, "if I tell you I have not, you won't believe me, so come in and look for yourselves."

The men searched the house from top to bottom. Mariam threw the covers off a bed to reveal her little boy sleeping. "Look everyone," she said, "maybe this is he."

"Well, Sam," Mr. E. said, "we can see you haven't got him."

As they rode off, Mariam brought the man out from under the straw pile. He was shaking from head to toe. After hiding the fugitive and feeding him for two weeks, they sent him safely on his way.

When Amanda was seventeen, she married. Although she had been raised a Christian by her father and mother, she did not feel she had truly accepted Christ until she attended a church meeting and heard an evangelist preach. Amanda felt the terrible weight of her sin and cried out, "O, Lord, if you will help me, I will believe You."

"In the act of telling God I would—I did!" Amanda said later. "O, the peace and joy that flooded my soul! The burden rolled away! I didn't know what to do with myself, I was so happy."

She had put her trust in Jesus and felt wonderfully forgiven. Amanda counted her freedom from the punishment of her sins that Christ bought for her on the cross as far greater than her freedom from slavery that her father purchased for her. "I often say to people that I have the right to shout more than some folks," Amanda said. "I have been bought twice and set free twice, and so I feel I have a good right to shout hallelujah!"

Not long after Amanda got married, her husband was killed in the Civil War fighting for the Union. Later, she married James Smith, an officer in an African Methodist Episcopal church, but he died a few years later, leaving Amanda to care for their daughter Mazie alone. Eventually, Amanda moved to New York City where she worked as a washer-woman. She labored hard to make ends meet—sometimes cleaning and ironing clothes the whole day and through most of the night. Amanda's love for Christ spilled over into everything she did. While she worked, she sang songs of praise and prayed. "Many times over my wash-tub and ironing table," she said, "and while making my bed and sweeping my house and washing my dishes, I have had some of the richest blessings—God in me, supplying all my needs according to His riches in glory by Christ Jesus."

At that time, there was a teaching in some of the Methodist churches called the "Holiness Movement." Its followers taught that those who believed in Christ and were saved by grace through faith in Him could expect a second work of grace by the Holy Spirit known as entire sanctification. "If you believe and ask for it," Amanda was told, "the power of the Holy Spirit will make you holy instantly in the twinkling of an eye. You can live the rest of your life without ever willfully sinning again."

Amanda prayed for it and believed she had received it. "God sanctified my soul," she told anyone who would listen. Many people within the Methodist church and Christians from other denominations opposed the Holiness Movement, arguing that it was contrary to the teachings of the Bible. "Christians must wage war against their sin natures all their lives," they said. "The Scriptures do not teach us to expect a special second work of grace from the Holy Spirit apart from being justified through faith."

Amanda shared the good news of Jesus Christ with anyone who would listen. Although she was poor, she often bought stacks of Christian tracts to give to strangers and friends. "My meat and drink," Amanda said, "was to see souls coming to Christ."

She began to teach a Bible study for women and use her beautiful singing voice to praise the Lord in church. In those days, people crowded into big tents or auditoriums to hear evangelists preach. Amanda began to tell her story of coming to Christ at these meetings and often sang hymns solo. She had a gift for speaking about Christ's love in a way that drew people in. Soon she was being asked to sing and give her testimony in Holiness camp meetings across the eastern United States.

In 1878, when her daughter was grown, Amanda accepted an invitation to speak at meetings in England. For the next thirteen years, she traveled throughout Britain, India and Africa. She sang, shared her testimony and taught about Jesus Christ. "She was a woman of remarkable gifts," said James Thoburn, the Methodist Bishop of Calcutta, India. "The novelty of a colored woman from America who had been a slave attracted attention in Calcutta."

Amanda spoke fearlessly about Christ even in the face of great danger. Her calm trust in God while facing a hostile Hindu crowd in India left a lasting impression on all who witnessed it. "I shall never forget one meeting which we were holding in an open square in the very heart of the city," the Bishop of Calcutta recalled. "It was at a time of no little excitement, and some Christian preachers had been roughly handled in the same square a few evenings before. I had just spoken myself, when I noticed a great crowd of men and boys rushing toward us with loud cries and threatening gestures. But at the critical moment, our good Sister Smith knelt on the grass and began to pray. As the crowd rushed up to the spot and saw her with her beaming face upturned to the evening sky—pouring out her soul in prayer—they became perfectly still and stood as if transfixed to the spot! Not even a whisper disturbed the solemn silence. When she had finished, we had as orderly a meeting as if we had been within the four walls of a church!"

When Amanda Smith returned to America, she wrote her autobiography. It was published in 1893 and was widely read by whites and blacks, men and women. With the royalties from the book, she started a home and school for black orphans in Chicago. She often marveled at what God had done for her—a poor slave girl. "Many times," she said, "I was lost in wonder, love and praise at the Lord's dealings in giving me the privilege to enjoy so much that I never expected could come to one like me. Surely it is His doings, and very marvelous."

MARIA TAYLOR
Co-Founder of the China Inland Mission, 1837–1870

In August 1855, Hudson Taylor, an English missionary to China, shaved his head, leaving a small pigtail in the back which he dyed black. When he wore a satin robe, he looked Chinese from top to bottom. He did it in order to reach the Chinese people for Jesus Christ after he discovered that his English looks and clothing were a barrier to people hearing his message. Although the Chinese welcomed his new appearance, he met stiff opposition from the Englishmen in the International Settlement in Shanghai who laughed at him and shunned him. "He is hurting British prestige in the eyes of the natives," they said.

Other missionaries, disgusted by his appearance, thought he had lost his mind. But Taylor stood his ground saying, "We should seek to make them Christians not Englishmen."

Not long after, Hudson Taylor fell in love with Maria Dyer, a young missionary teacher fluent in Chinese. Maria's parents came from the upper class in England. They were missionaries who raised their children among the Chinese people. Maria's parents died while she was young. Her legal guardian was her uncle in England, but Mary Aldersey, a long-serving missionary, acted as Maria's chaperone while she lived in China. In January 1857, Hudson screwed up the courage to write a letter to Maria, expressing his love and asking permission to court her. Maria's heart pounded as she read the letter because she felt the same way for Hudson. The next day, she told Mary Aldersey about Taylor's letter.

"Mr. Taylor? That poor unconnected nobody!" Mary said. "How dare he presume to think of such a thing? You would not think of accepting him?"

"But—" Maria said.

"But he is not a gentleman!" Miss Aldersey interjected, reminding Maria that Taylor came from a lower class family. "He is without education and without position."

"But—" Maria began again.

"He is a ranter," Mary said. "And he wears Chinese clothes!"

"Now, Maria, sit down," she demanded. "You will write a refusal letter to Mr. Taylor at once."

"May I first write to my uncle?" Maria asked.

"That is quite unnecessary, my dear, he would say as I say."

She made Maria write a curt letter to Hudson, telling him not to pursue her any further. Maria closed with a sentence dictated by Miss Aldersey. "I request you not to refer to the subject again."

"There," Miss Aldersey said with a smile, "he will never return after that."

Red-faced and feeling sick to her stomach, Maria left the room. She wrote a letter to her brother. "It seemed to me that God had manifestly answered my prayers, and it seemed to be His will that Mr. Taylor and I should love each other...Mr. Taylor is just the sort of person as our dear father—were he living—would approve of for me."

Hudson Taylor was crushed when he read Maria's reply. "I am tried almost beyond my strength to bear," he told a friend. But Hudson suspected that Mary Aldersey was behind Maria's letter, so he did not abandon all hope. Other friends recognized the love that Hudson and Maria had for one another and did what they could to bring them together. Then one day a missionary friend arranged for Maria to come to his house at the same time that Hudson would be there. When they met, they made plans to bypass Miss Aldersey and write directly to Maria's uncle. After praying together, they parted, leaving the fate of their relationship in the hands of God.

When Mary Aldersey found out that Hudson had met with Maria behind her back, she exploded. She fired off an angry letter to Taylor, upbraiding him for his "disgraceful" behavior. She spread an ill report of Taylor among all the Englishmen in the International Settlement. An English minister confronted Hudson and told him, "You ought to be horse whipped."

Not everyone in the tight-knit missionary community agreed. Some thought that Hudson was worthy of Maria's hand in marriage. Others suggested to Maria that if Taylor returned to England and earned a university degree, then perhaps he might be more suitable. "Is he to leave his work in order to gain a name for the sake of marrying me?" Maria asked. "If he loves me more than Jesus, he is not worthy of me. If he were to leave the Lord's work for the world's honor, I would have nothing further to do with him."

After months of waiting, Maria received a letter from her uncle expressing his wholehearted approval of the union. They were married in China in January 1858.

The mission society that Hudson worked for was poorly funded and badly managed. It never provided the Taylors with adequate resources. The slow communication with the mission office in London added to the frustration. Hudson Taylor worked long hours preaching, caring for the sick and seeking new ways to bring the good news of Jesus to the Chinese. Maria struggled to make ends meet, as she started an elementary school and cared for their growing number of children. Maria's strong faith and pioneering spirit made her a perfect match for Hudson.

Over time, the strain of Hudson's workload broke his health, forcing the family to return to England while he regained his strength. In the Taylors' little rented flat in London, they hung a wall map of China. Every day as Hudson looked at it, he found his eyes drawn away from the coast to the vast regions of inland China where millions lived without any knowledge of Jesus Christ because missionaries had been forbidden outside of a few coastal cities. But a new treaty between China and Britain gave missionaries the right to go anywhere in China. Driven by the great needs of the inland Chinese, he visited the leaders of all the mission societies in England. "You must open up inland China for the gospel," he urged them. But they turned him away. "We don't have enough missionaries," one told him, "and it is too expensive. Besides, with a civil war raging in China, we wouldn't expand into the interior even if we had the money and the men."

Hudson Taylor refused to give up. He decided to start his own mission organization to reach China. With the support and encouragement of Maria, he traveled the length and breadth of Britain, imploring people in prayer meetings and chapel services to pray, give and go. "More than four hundred million live in the Chinese Empire and only a few thousand know Jesus Christ," he told them. "And in all the inland provinces there is not a single missionary. A million people a month are dying without God."

Maria worked behind the scenes to support her husband and advance the work. One Scotsman who got to know them well said, "Mrs. Taylor is loving, bright and energetic. She does everything so quietly that you seldom see she has done it. She is a great woman of prayer."

Eventually, seven men and women joined Hudson and Maria Taylor, and the China Inland Mission was born. The China Inland Mission, unlike any other mission agency, maintained its headquarters in China. It required all missionaries to dress and wear their hair in Chinese style. Upon returning to China in 1866, the Taylor family and three other missionaries went to Yangzhou where not a single foreigner lived. They threw themselves into the work, preaching Christ and providing medicine for the sick. Maria played a critical role. "Mr. Taylor had so learned to value her judgment and prayerfulness," one of their missionaries reported, "that he never took a step without consulting her."

Not long after they arrived, Yangzhou leaders posted handbills throughout the city, warning: "Beware of Foreigners!" They spread lies saying the missionaries kidnapped and ate Chinese children. One official called Hudson into his office and told him, "I know perfectly well what you plan to do. You want to deceive our hearts and then seize the whole land for yourselves."

Then one night—enraged by a rumor that the missionaries had kidnapped twenty-four Chinese babies—a thousand rioters carrying torches surrounded the mission house. They hurled bricks through the windows and screamed, "Kill the foreign devils!" Hudson knew that he could not reason with the mob. Maria, who was six months pregnant, remained serene as she put their children to bed and comforted everyone in the mission house. "She was as calm as if she were sitting in the parlor in London," Hudson remembered later, "and I'm quite certain that if she could have altered any of the circumstances she would not have done it, for she was satisfied that God's ordering was wisest."

The Taylors decided that their only hope for survival was to get troops from the city magistrate to break up the mob. Hudson offered a short prayer, kissed Maria and ran for help with another man. "The foreign devils are fleeing," someone shouted, as he spotted the two missionaries running away.

With a pack of angry men close on their heels, pelting them with bricks and stones, Taylor and his friend barely escaped to city hall and collapsed inside, bloodied and panting. "Save life, save life!" they called.

The magistrate kept them waiting for nearly an hour while the noise from the rioters echoed across the city. "Ah, Mr. Taylor," the magistrate said with a sly smile, "Tell me, what did you really do with those babies?"

"Your Excellency," Hudson said with a bow, "we are living in your city legally, we have done nothing wrong and you are responsible for maintaining law and order. You will be held accountable for any loss of life."

While Hudson was away, rioters broke into the mission house and began stealing anything they could lay their hands on. Maria confronted one of the looters. "What do you want?" she asked him. "We are only women and children here. Are you not ashamed to harm us?"

The intruder snatched a purse and yanked Maria's wedding ring from her finger. Outside the mission house, rioters had set fire to the buildings. Mr. Rudland, one of the missionaries, came upstairs to help bring out the women and children when he was attacked by a looter. Maria and another woman grabbed the man's arm and kept him from crushing Rudland's skull with a brick. With the stairs full of rioters and smoke filling the house, Maria and the other missionaries tied sheets and blankets together and let down some of the children and women through a window into the alley. Maria had to jump from the second story window. She and the others escaped to a neighbor's house. Although battered and bruised, Maria remained calm. "I was anxious not to let anyone know how much I was hurt," Maria said later, "as I felt it would alarm them."

She led the frightened group in prayer. "God was our stay," Maria said later. "He gave me the confidence that He would surely work good for China out of our deep distress."

After some time, the magistrate reluctantly agreed to send his men to stop the riot, but Hudson feared it was too late. When he returned with armed guards, he found the mission house burned and all his possessions stolen. After a frantic search, he rejoiced to find his family and the other missionaries injured but alive.

The next day, the commander of the city guards told them to leave Yangzhou. "My men cannot keep down the people," he said. "I will send you away under escort by boats. When we have repaired the house, we will invite you to return."

For the three months that the missionaries were away, they prayed for a softening of hearts in Yangzhou. "I shall count our physical sufferings light," Maria said, "if they work out for the further opening up of the country for the spread of our Master's kingdom."

Upon their return, they found the people ready to hear about Jesus Christ. Those who had tried to kill them now sat at their feet to learn from them. Soon many in the city trusted in Jesus for the forgiveness of their sins. The Taylors made plans to send more missionaries further inland.

In the years that followed, the China Inland Mission sent men and women to every province in China. Maria taught the Chinese language to the new recruits and trained the single women who came to China to be missionaries. But Maria contracted tuberculosis and her strength steadily failed. At the age of thirty-three, she lay on her deathbed. "You are going home," Hudson told her. "You will soon be with Jesus."

"I am sorry," Maria said.

"You are not sorry to be with Jesus?"

"Oh no," she said looking into his eyes. "It's not that. You know, darling, there is not a cloud between me and my Savior. I cannot be sorry to go to Him, but it does grieve me to leave you alone at such a time. Yet He will be with you and meet all your needs."

All the missionaries mourned the loss of Maria. "She was the backbone of the mission," one of them said. Hudson Taylor, devastated by the death of his wife, sailed to England to get his bearings and plan the future of the work. He returned to China and labored for three more fruitful decades, eventually overseeing one thousand China Inland missionaries who led countless Chinese to Christ.

33 MARY ANN LYTH AND MARY CALVERT
Missionaries to the Cannibals,
1811–1890 and 1814–1882

For several days, the Fijian tribesmen of Mbua entertained special guests, but they had not yet honored them with a cannibal feast. "We shall lose our renown," said Chief Ngavindi to his men. "We shall not be dreaded. We have provided no food for the visitors. Go! We must have some human beings." Straightaway, warriors launched canoes and paddled across the sea to a nearby island. Quietly pulling their canoes ashore and covering them with leaves, they hid among mangrove branches, lying in wait like a panther to pounce on their prey. Before long, a group of women arrived in the company of one man. They leapt upon the man and killed him on the spot, seized the women and paddled back to Mbua.

The warriors arrived home to great rejoicing. Villagers shouted, sang, danced and beat drums. Soon the news crossed over to the neighboring island and the mission house of the Lyths and Calverts. Dr. Lyth and Mr. Calvert were away, leaving Mary Ann Lyth and Mary Calvert alone with their children. "Fourteen women have been brought to Mbua to be killed and cooked," a Christian native told them. The missionary women—sickened by the horrible fate that awaited the poor captives—wondered what they should do. With their husbands away, what could they do? If they tarried, the captives would die. They knew it was danger-ous to intervene with the Mbuan chiefs during the frenzy of a cannibal feast. Overcome with compassion, they decided to try.

They found some Christian natives willing to bring them, jumped into a canoe and set out. While still a distance from Mbua, the sound of death drums beating and muskets firing echoed across the water. As the missionaries drew nearer, they heard victims shriek and villagers shout, signaling that the kill-ing had begun. "Faster!" they urged the paddlers. When the ca-noe reached shore, a Christian native met them, saying, "Come quickly! Some are dead, but some are still alive!"

With their native escort, they marched through the danc-ing, chanting crowd and headed straight to the house of King Tanoa. Fijian custom forbids any woman—not belonging to the household—to enter the king's home uninvited. But Mrs. Lyth and Mrs. Calvert had no time to spare. Carrying gifts in each hand, the women barged into his house. They bowed be-fore the king and begged him to show mercy to the captives. The startled king hardly knew what to make of the intruders. "Please, for the sake of God, spare their lives," the women said. The old man was hard of hearing, so the women plead-ed louder for the captives. After staring at them for a time, he said, "Those who are dead are dead, but those who are still alive shall live." Then Tanoa sent a messenger to stop the kill-ing—five of the fourteen women were spared.

Grieving over the nine women who had suffered a cruel death and full of indignation, the missionary women went straight to

Chief Ngavindi, the host of the cannibal meal. "You know the evil that you did," they told him, "You will face the judgment of God for your dark deeds."

After seeing to the release of the captives, Mary Ann Lyth and Mary Calvert returned home. The women said little about the tragic affair. But word quickly spread about what they had done. One British naval officer, after visiting the Lyths and the Calverts, wrote, "If anything could have increased our admiration of their heroism, it was the unaffected manner in which, when pressed by us to relate the circumstances of their awful visit, they spoke of it as the simple performance of an ordinary duty."

Richard and Mary Ann Lyth had landed in Fiji several years earlier. Dr. Lyth, the first medical missionary in the South Seas, cared for the souls and bodies of the natives. Tribes often invited missionaries to live with them because they thought their power might rub off on them, and they wanted to trade for iron pots and muskets that Europeans possessed.

It was rough going at the beginning in Fiji. They worked among a people who constantly waged war with their neighbors, strangled widows and practiced human sacrifice. The missionaries endured insults and threats. "I will kill and eat any of my people who follow this new God," a local chief declared. Knowing how revolting the missionaries found cannibalism, the tribesmen often dispatched and cooked their victims in front of the mission house to spite them. When the Lyths pulled the shades to shut out the horrible sight—it only fueled the natives' disdain.

Then one night, tribal warriors surrounded the mission house, howling and shaking spears. The chiefs talked about killing all the strangers. The Lyths and another missionary family staying with them turned to God in prayer. For several hours while the warriors shouted in the darkness, they prayed and prepared their hearts to meet Jesus face to face. "If they come to kill us," one of them said, "let them find us on our knees in prayer." Then suddenly, the tribesmen left, and the missionaries passed the rest of the night sleepless, but in safety.

Not long after, Lieutenant Charles Wilkes, commanding officer of the United States Exploring Expedition, anchored at their island. Seeing the cruelty of the natives and the severe hardships endured by the missionaries, Wilkes offered to bring the English families away aboard his ships. They thanked Wilkes for the offer and explained that they believed that God had called them there to bring the natives to Christ. Touched by the courage and dedication of the missionary women, Wilkes wrote in his report, "There are few situations in which so much physical and moral courage is required as those in which these devoted individuals are placed. Nothing but a deep sense of duty and a strong determination to perform it could induce civilized persons to subject themselves to the sight of such horrid scenes as they are called upon almost daily to witness. I know of no situation so trying for ladies to live in."

A breakthrough happened when the tribal king got deathly sick. It was the custom of the tribe to bury alive people thought to be near death. As his family prepared his grave, the desperate king sent for the missionaries. By the grace of God, Richard and Mary Ann nursed him back to health. This changed his opinion of the missionaries and their God. "Our god has left the island," he said, "because the Christian God can beat him till his bones are sore!"

Before long, many in the tribe trusted in Christ and more and more children came to the mission school. "The king has promised to build the chapel and he appears to be sincere," the missionaries wrote back to England. "We believe the fields are ripe for the harvest."

James and Mary Calvert had arrived in Fiji in 1838. James was a young, single preacher when he felt God calling him to serve in foreign lands. However, the mission board frowned upon sending unmarried men into the field. "Find a wife," they told him. Although he had not thought much about marriage before, he knew just the girl—Mary Fowler—the sister of a college friend. Mary must have been surprised to hear James's proposal. "Will you marry me and live with me among South Sea island cannibals?" After a short courtship, she consented. They married in March and set sail in April. They quickly learned the native language. James preached and Mary taught the women and children the good news of Jesus. Through many hardships she looked to Christ. "It is all peace within," Mary said, "I just leave myself entirely in my heavenly Father's hands and have no anxiety about the future. I know that if He sees fit to send me greater suffering, He will give greater grace to bear it."

While serving in the South Pacific, the Lyths and the Calverts had several children, and each family suffered the loss of sons and daughters who died in childhood. "We must all meet in heaven," Mary said.

Healing sick people almost always opened doors for preaching in a village. Mary Ann assisted Dr. Lyth as a nurse, and she taught nursing skills to native women and led them in Bible studies.

She had the women repeat the Bible stories back to her and then urged them to tell the stories to their friends. Many people came to faith in Christ through her teaching. Mary Ann helped other missionaries in the translation of the Bible into Fijian. "She was a cheerful invaluable helper in all literary work," one translator said, "for her knowledge of the language was accurate and she had the pen of a ready writer."

The Lyths went to England for four years to oversee the publication of the Scriptures in Fijian. Then they returned to the island with Fijian Bibles for the natives. By the time the first generation of missionaries had left Fiji, tens of thousands of natives had believed in Jesus Christ, and scores of churches and Christian schools had been planted across the island chain.

34 LIU WEN LAN AND MRS. KAO
Intrepid in the Face of Death,
c. 1860–1900

I n 1900, secret society members in China, hateful of foreigners and Christians, ignited a fire of persecution. The Boxers, as they were called, spread rumors that Christians used the devil's magic to hurt people. "Christian devils trouble our country," they cried, as they set out to kill every foreign missionary and Chinese Christian in the land. Bands of armed men tore down churches, burned houses and murdered Christians by the thousands.

Beijing Girls' School, a Christian high school, was surrounded by Boxers intent on destroying the buildings and carrying off the girls. The students and faculty remained within the walled compound of the school and prayed. "There seemed to be nothing on which we could depend," one of the Christian students said, "and we resolved to place ourselves body, soul and spirit in the hands of the Lord. All day we gathered in prayer. We sang—but silently in our hearts—for we dared not utter a sound knowing that the Boxers were ready to destroy us at any moment."

When word came that an attack was imminent, the principal gathered all the students and teachers into the chapel. "If we are to die," she said, "we shall all die together." They spent the night in prayer, waiting for the Boxers to pounce. One of the girls in the chapel said, "This a good place from which to go to heaven." But they survived the night. The next morning soldiers from the American Legation arrived to protect them.

"Kill! Kill!" They heard the Boxers screaming at the top of their lungs on the other side of the school wall. When the rioters began setting buildings on fire next to the school, the American soldiers led the students and faculty out of the compound. Dodging bricks and bullets, they managed to escape. As the girls made their way across the city, the stench of the decaying bodies of Chinese Christians killed in the streets filled the air. With the help of the American Board for Foreign Missions, they were able to relocate to a safe place and restart their education. Remarkably, not a single student perished during the ordeal.

LIU WEN LAN

However, one graduate of Beijing Girls' School, Liu Wen Lan, suffered a different fate. Wen Lan was a teacher at a Christian girl's school in Zunhua. Wen Lan's love for the students and her talent for teaching won her students' hearts. "It seemed," one Christian observer said, "that she had been selected by the Lord for His own work as a teacher."

The Boxers overran the Zunhua school and captured Wen Lan and seventeen of her students. Wen Lan knew that the Boxers intended to put them all to death. When they were being led away to the place of execution, she encouraged her girls. "Our Lord and Master Jesus Christ was persecuted," she told them. "He was killed, and afterward ascended into heaven."

"Shut up!" A guard shouted at Wen Lan. "If you don't keep your mouth closed I'll kill you at once."

Ignoring his threats, Wen Lan kept fortifying the girls. "Remember," she told them, "that Christ's disciples had been put to death for their faith in Jesus. Although we are not worthy to die for Him, we are ready and willing to do so. We will depend upon His grace to save us."

When they reached the spot of execution the Boxers pushed Wen Lan forward. Without a quiver or a cry, she calmly laid her head on the block. Her courage in Christ strengthened her students to face death full of faith.

MRS. KAO

Another graduate of the Beijing Girls' School was Jessica Kao. She and her mother were Chinese Christian converts. Mrs. Kao spent her days visiting women in medical clinics and homes, passing out Christian literature and Bibles and sharing her faith in Christ. One day when her husband was away, Boxers banged loudly at the gate of the cluster of houses where she lived. "Kill! Kill!" the Boxers screamed as they kicked in the gate.

"Where are the Kaos?" they shouted.

Trembling women and children cowered in the corner of the yard. Mrs. Kao stepped from her door and said, "We are the Kaos—these other families are not Christians. Please permit my daughter and me to put on our long coats and then we will go with you."

Swords flashed around them. "Take and bind them!" the leader ordered.

"We are women," Mrs. Kao said gently, "why bind us? We are believers in the Lord; if we promise not to run, we surely will not do it."

"Bind them tightly lest they escape," the leader bellowed, glaring at Mrs. Kao.

They tied their thumbs tightly together behind their backs like common criminals and pushed the women from their home. At the gateway, Mrs. Kao turned to her terrified neighbors and said, "Sisters, I have been the cause of great fear coming to you today. Farewell. If I am permitted to see you again, I shall rejoice; if not, I hope that we may meet in heaven. I should be so glad if you all believed in Jesus."

The Boxers shoved them into the dusty street and led them through an angry mob. "Aha!" one man shouted. "See the followers of the foreign devils whom the Boxers have captured! They'll soon be done for."

"Isn't that Mrs. Kao, the woman preacher?" someone called.

"Yes," another answered, "and that pretty girl must be her daughter—the one who has been studying for years with the foreign devils in Beijing."

It was impossible for Mrs. Kao to walk quickly, because she had been crippled by having her feet bound as a child—a custom that kept girls' feet small. "Hurry up!" the Boxers yelled, hitting their backs with the flat edge of their swords. "My mother's feet are small," Jessica protested, "it isn't easy for her to walk. Don't hurry her so."

The men shoved them forward to the courtyard of a pagan temple, forcing them to stand in the scorching sun. Mrs. Kao looked into Jessica's eyes and asked, "Are you afraid?"

"Mother," she answered, "Jesus is with us, there isn't anything to fear."

"Let's pray together," Mrs. Kao told her.

With their hands tied behind their backs, surrounded by a jeering crowd, they knelt in the dust and prayed. When they arose, Mrs. Kao's face was aglow. She turned to her daughter and said, "Jessica, I see Jesus has come. Do you see Him?"

"Mother," she answered, "I believe that Jesus is always with those who love Him."

They separated mother from daughter and hustled Mrs. Kao through a sham trial, sentencing her to death. After guards marched her to the place of execution, she said to the leader, "I am only a condemned criminal, but I ask of you one favor. Please give me a little time to pray to my Heavenly Father."

He granted her a moment, and she knelt and prayed, "Father, forgive these men. They don't understand what they are doing."

An executioner beheaded her on the spot. Jessica, spared from the sword, died from disease a few months later. She told her father on her deathbed, "Father, now I am going before you to see my mother's face. The one important thing is that you hold fast to the holy truth of God, and go, as I am going, to the heavenly home."

Tens of thousands of other Christians suffered the most horrible deaths imaginable. Eyewitnesses reported that many met their end singing the praises of the Lord who had saved their souls. In the years following the Boxer Rebellion, the Chinese turned to Christ in vast numbers, and flourishing churches sprang up in every province. The old saying proved true in China: "The blood of the martyrs is the seed of the Church."

35   PANDITA RAMABAI
The Widow's Friend, 1858–1922

As a young student in India in the 1830s, Ananta Shastri was astonished to meet a woman who could read and recite Sanskrit, the language of the sacred scriptures of Hinduism. He had always been told that only men's minds were capable of learning it. Ananta, a high-caste Brahman, made up his mind that when he married and had children he would teach Sanskrit and the sacred writings to his sons and daughters. He did just that, and his youngest daughter Ramabai proved to be the best student of all. She mastered Sanskrit and learned the Hindu classics. Before she reached her teens, she had memorized eighteen thousand verses from the holy books of Hinduism—a feat usually accomplished only by Brahman men studying to be priests. Eventually, she mastered eight languages.

When a prolonged famine devastated India in 1866 and 1867, her family lost everything—their home, money and jewels. They set out in search of work and food. "We went to several sacred places and temples to worship different gods and bathe in sacred rivers," Ramabai said, "to free ourselves from the sin and curse which brought poverty on us. We prostrated ourselves before the stone and metal images of the gods and prayed to them day and night. But nothing came of all this futile effort to please the gods—the stone images remained as hard as ever and never answered our prayers."

Sick and starving, Ramabai's father, mother and sister died within a few weeks of each other. Only sixteen-year-old Ramabai and her brother survived. They traveled across India, getting a little work when they could and living off the charity of others. As they wandered and saw many sacred places, they grew disenchanted with their Hindu faith. One day they traveled to a famous sacred lake in the foothills of the Himalayan Mountains. Hindu priests taught that the lake had seven floating hills, representing seven immortal sages. If earnest pilgrims came to worship at the lake, the hills floated toward them to accept their offerings and give a blessing, but wicked pilgrims would find the hills immovable. When Ramabai and her brother bowed down and prayed at the lakeshore, the hills did not move. "Do not go into the water," a Hindu priest warned them, "it is filled with crocodiles."

But early the next morning, her brother swam out to the hills in the middle of the lake. He discovered that the hills were heaps of rock and mud, sitting on wooden rafts. Hidden behind the hills were boats that were used to push the rafts forward. If a pilgrim made a sufficient donation of money to the priests, a signal would be given for a boatman to push the hills forward to the delight and comfort of the worshiper.

Far worse than the fraud and deception of the priests was the cruelty of the high-caste Hindus. They had it in their power to relieve some of the suffering of the poor lower classes, but they did nothing. In particular, the plight of child-widows broke Ramabai's heart. Very young girls were married to older men, and then lived with their parents until they came of age to live with their husbands. If the husband died, the young girl was blamed for the death and considered bad luck. Child-widows were often beaten and had their heads shaved to shame them and then cast out from their homes to fend for themselves.

After seeing the horrors of infanticide and abuse of child widows across India, Ramabai said, "Hell has become a horrible reality to me."

To Ramabai's delight, her parents had not arranged a marriage for her. When she was about eighteen years old, she married a kindly high-caste gentleman, but he died two years later, leaving her alone to care for her infant daughter. Not long after, Ramabai began to promote education for women and protection for child-widows. Whenever she spoke, a crowd quickly gathered, amazed by her great learning and eloquence. Soon, she gave lectures in packed halls and wrote books, encouraging high-caste Hindus to educate their daughters and stop child marriage. Her great learning won her the title "Pandita," a Sanskrit word that means learned master.

At that time, India was a colony of the British Empire, and Ramabai thought she would benefit from additional study in England. With the support of some English friends in India, she sailed to Britain in 1883. Deeply disillusioned with Hinduism, Ramabai wanted to learn more about Christianity. A congregation of the Church of England welcomed her. Through their love and encouragement she read the Bible and attended worship. Before long, she put her trust in Jesus Christ and was baptized along with her daughter. "I believed on Christ and prayed in His name," Ramabai said. "I prayed earnestly to God to pardon my sins for the sake of Jesus Christ. And when I had done this, my burden rolled away. I realized that I was forgiven and was freed from the power of sin. There was not a shadow of doubt that I was saved through Jesus Christ."

Ramabai then went to America and studied education in Philadelphia. While in the United States, she wrote a book that described the horrors of child marriage and widowhood in India. American Christians were appalled at the sorry state of women in India. When Ramabai shared her goal of starting schools for child-widows, hundreds of American women rallied to her cause, raising funds to support a school.

With aid from Christians in the United States, Ramabai returned to India and opened a boarding school for widows. "I'm crying for joy that my dream of years has become a reality," Ramabai said.

She wanted to teach Hindus, and she knew that few Hindus would send girls to a school designed to make them Christians. So Ramabai did not include religious instruction in the classroom. Her students could become Christians if they wished or practice their Hindu faith.

The witness of Western countries like Britain had left a bad impression on the Hindus of India. "Christianity does not mean going into other countries and taking possession of them," Ramabai wrote, "and taxing the people and introducing the infamous traffic in rum and opium." Many people in India who became Christians wore the clothing and ate the food of Westerners. Ramabai decided to wear traditional Indian clothes and eat a vegetarian diet to show the Indian people that they did not have to forsake all of their culture in order to become Christians.

As soon as Ramabai opened the doors of her boarding school for widows, she attracted several child-widows as students. Before she arrived at the school, one girl had tried to kill herself three times. The only thing that kept her from succeeding was her fear that she would be reincarnated as a woman again. Ramabai strove to make the school welcoming and beautiful. She filled the grounds with colorful flowers, vines and trees. "They come from homes where they have been treated as outcasts," Ramabai said. "A great many of these dear little people have never known love or happiness; and one just longs to be a comfort and joy to them."

With many tears, she prayed for the child-widows and worked for their good. Ramabai's instructors taught reading, writing, math, science, literature, and vocational skills such as nursing, weaving, sewing, cooking and oil-making. Soon there were fifty widows living and studying with Ramabai—the youngest was seven, but most were in their later teens. "I was a mere baby when I was married," one of them explained. "Yet people call me a 'widow' and 'unlucky' and say I have killed my husband."

"I also am a widow because my parents say so," another said. "They say I shall have to suffer much as I grow older because I killed and swallowed my husband, but I never saw him. I do not know who he was. My father was a strict Hindu and did not love me because I was a widow. Since I came to this school, all the teachers loved me. They try to make me happy. They never say unkind words to me or think I am unlucky."

"There are thousands of priests and spiritual rulers for the people who suppress widows and trample the poor, ignorant, low-caste people under their heels," Ramabai wrote. "They sell young and helpless widows to wicked men and when the poor, miserable slaves are no longer pleasing to their cruel masters, they turn them out into the street to carry the burden of shame and finally to die a death worse than that of a starved street dog!"

At first, it was hard to break through the girls' misconceptions because they had been fed lies about Christians all their lives. "Many of them have a great fear," Ramabai wrote, "that one day after they have been fattened up, they will be hung over a great fire and oil will be extracted from them to be sold for a large price for medical purposes. Others think they will be put into mills and their bones ground. They cannot understand that anyone would be kind to them without some selfish purpose."

Every morning from five to six, Ramabai studied the Bible and prayed with her daughter. She kept her door open for anyone who wanted to join them. Before long her room was crowded with students learning about the love of Jesus Christ. Over time, many of her students believed in Christ. "Since their conversion to Christ they are so changed," Ramabai said, "that one who knew them before they were Christians could hardly recognize them now. God be praised for His wondrous love, which can turn the selfish, unruly, and devilish heart, into the beautiful image of His meek and loving Son!"

As more of Ramabai's students turned to Christ, opposition from the Brahmans grew. They spread rumors that Ramabai was forcing all her girls to become Christians. Newspapers printed vicious lies about her and the school. Efforts were made to shut it down. Local Hindus confronted her. "The students need to go to Hindu temple," they demanded. "No students should be permitted to attend any Christian service."

"Do you think I've gone against the religion of the girls?" Ramabai replied. "No, not in any way. I have not taught the girls any religious system. If they wanted any religious training, they might go out of the school to the Christian missionary, or to the Hindu teacher. But I'm glad to say that light came to them—not from ourselves, but from God. I let my girls do what they like, but I have freedom in Christ. Why should I keep my light under a bushel? When I had my family worship in my own room, some of the girls began to come in, and we gave them freedom to come if they wanted to."

Ramabai trusted God to protect the school and bring the girls of His choice. Through the years, she founded other schools and homes, protecting and educating thousands of poor girls and women. She prayed that those who accepted Christ would bring the good news of Jesus to all of India. "I hope someday that a great army of Christian apostles among our people will eventually regenerate the whole Hindu nation through their lives and their teachings," she said.

Until her dying day, Ramabai challenged people to serve the poor and abused. "It seems a sin," she wrote, "to live in a good house, eat plenty of good food and be warmly clothed, while thousands of our fellow creatures are dying of hunger and are without shelter. If all of us do our part faithfully, God is faithful to fulfill His promises, and will send us the help we need."

20TH AND 21ST CENTURIES

TRIAL AND TRIUMPH OF THE WORLD-WIDE CHURCH

Over the last 150 years, Christians have faced great assaults from the hostility of tyrannical governments and the rampant unbelief that infected large parts of the modern church. Yet God raised up bright and bold men and women to stand for Him and the trustworthiness of the Scripture. Many shined the light of Christ while suffering torture and imprisonment for their faith. By the power of the Holy Spirit, they and hundreds of thousands like them helped to spread the praises of Jesus Christ to every corner of the world.

36 ARMENIAN NURSE
A Follower of Him Who Said, "Love Your Enemies," Late 19th to Early 20th Century

There are many stories of loving and courageous Christian women for whom we have no names. Christ made it a point to praise the faith of several unnamed women: the woman who in faith touched Jesus' robe and was healed, the generous widow in the temple giving her last penny, the one who poured out her expensive perfume to anoint the Lord's feet, and others. The Puritan preacher Richard Sibbes once said, "As Christ lived a hidden life—that is, He was not known for who He was so that He might work our salvation—so let us be content to be hidden ones." This story is about one of the hidden ones.

The mountainous land where Asia meets Europe in the shadow of Mt. Ararat, where Noah's Ark landed after the flood, is the homeland of the Armenians. Christianity came to Armenia long ago: it was the first kingdom to adopt Christianity as its religion. For seventeen hundred years Armenians have followed their unique practice of Eastern Orthodox Christianity. To many of them their faith was merely cultural—they thought of themselves as Christians because they were Armenians. For others, their faith involved a living trust in Jesus Christ and a desire to obey His commandments.

For centuries, the Armenians lived under the thumb of the Islamic empire of the Ottoman Turks. In the best of times, the Muslim Turks treated the Armenians with contempt. In the worst of times, they plundered, pillaged and murdered them. In one brutal campaign of terror, the Turks killed hundreds of thousands of Armenians and drove hundreds of thousands more from their homes.

During one such wave of violent persecution, a Turkish army captain and some of his men descended upon the farm of an Armenian couple and their teenage daughters. They were a Christian family who loved the Lord and strove to follow in His steps. Kicking open the front door of the farmhouse, the men ransacked every room and looted all the valuables. Then the soldiers dragged the mother and father into the yard and shot them dead on the spot.

The Turkish captain and his men took up residence in the house, enslaving the girls and abusing them. The officer kept the eldest daughter for himself, forcing her to wait on him hand and foot and mistreating her in every way. Some time later, the girls escaped. Eventually, the oldest sister made her way to a city where she trained as a nurse. She found work in a hospital, serving sick men, women and children in need of care. Her conscientiousness and sympathy for her suffering patients made her an excellent nurse.

Then one night, she was assigned to a ward of severely wounded Turkish army officers. When she came to the bed of one of the patients placed in her charge, she recognized by the light of a lantern the face of the officer who had enslaved her and murdered her parents. Recoiling in horror, an avalanche of dark memories crashed down upon her. Her stomach roiled like it was being twisted inside out. She felt as if her racing heart would leap out of her chest. Fleeing the ward, she collapsed in a quiet corner and sobbed. Minutes later, as she caught her breath, she began to pray.

The Turkish officer lay in a coma, unaware of his surroundings and unable to respond. His condition would require exceptional nursing to keep him alive. But the sight of the man sickened her and the thought of touching him was more than she could bear. "O Lord," she prayed, "What am I to do?"

Several weeks passed, and the officer awoke from his coma and began to regain his strength. One day, the doctor who oversaw the ward stood by the officer's bed with the Armenian nurse beside him. "If not for her devotion to you and your care," the doctor told him, "you would be dead."

The Turkish captain leaned forward in his bed and looked carefully at her. He knew who she was. "We have met before, haven't we?" he said.

"Yes," she answered, "we have met before."

"Why didn't you kill me?" he asked.

"Because," she said, "I am a follower of Him who said, 'Love your enemies.'"

37 KANG CHENG "IDA KAHN"
Chinese Missionary Physician,
1873–1931

In 1873 in Jiujiang, China, a baby girl, Kang Cheng, was born into a poor family. Her parents already had five children—all girls. They had longed for a son, but now their sixth child was a girl too. "What shall we do?" they asked an old blind fortuneteller. "The baby brings bad luck," the old man said. "You must either end her life or give her away. As long as she remains in your home, you will never have a son."

Hoping to avoid killing the infant, the parents cast about trying to find someone willing to take a baby girl. When word reached Gertrude Howe, a Methodist missionary from America working in Jiujiang, she rushed to save the child and adopted her at once. Miss Howe called her Ida Kahn. Later, she adopted another girl, whom she named Mary. She showered the girls with loving kindness and raised them to trust in Christ. "There was no one like her in the world," Ida said of her.

Howe and another American missionary ran a school for girls in the city—the first girls' school in that region of China. When Ida and Mary were old enough they went to the mission school and proved to be bright and hard-working students. They did not fit in with most other Chinese girls their age because they had not had their feet bound as infants. Upper and middle class parents bound their daughters' feet as a sign of beauty and prestige—those who did not need to work for a living could afford to have their feet bound.

Through Ida's teen years, the poverty and misery of the Chinese people—especially Chinese women and girls—deeply touched her heart. Ida decided to become a doctor to help relieve the suffering of her people. In 1892, when Ida and Mary were nineteen years old, they went to the United States and passed the entrance exam for the University of Michigan medical school. With financial support from the American Methodist Church, they spent the next four years studying medicine in Michigan.

Ida and Mary graduated with honors. After serving a short internship in a Chicago hospital, they sailed back to China to heal sick bodies and point lost souls to Christ. Before Ida left America, a man said to her, "I am glad you are going back to your country as a physician. Your people need physicians more than they need missionaries."

Not wanting to contradict the man in public, Ida turned to her friend and whispered, "Time is short—eternity is long."

Ida and Mary returned to Jiujiang as the first foreign-trained female doctors in the province. They hoped to spend several weeks visiting friends and getting re-adapted to life in China. But just two days after they arrived, four patients knocked on their door asking for treatment. The next day, six people came for help. They quickly rented a small office and began their work in earnest.

A few weeks later, the servant of a rich family asked the young doctors to come and see his master's sick wife. When they reached the large house, Ida and Mary met a well known Chinese doctor in the entryway. Turning to the woman's family he said, "I can do nothing more for her, but she will be in good hands with these two. They have crossed mountains and seas to study about these matters."

Before they saw the patient, the head of the house said, "You must assure us that she will live."

"No," Ida answered, "we cannot guarantee any such thing."

When the family insisted that the doctors guarantee that the woman would survive before they would let them see her, Ida and Mary told them that under those circumstances they would not be able to help them. As they turned to leave, the family members clung to them like beggars pleading for help saying, "Please stay and do whatever you can for her."

The medicine they gave the sick woman quickly restored her health. The reputation of the young doctors spread through the city, and more and more patients came to them. The doctors told their patients that they did their work in the name of Christ. "One thing which pleases us very much," Ida wrote to supporters in America, "is that those whom we have treated when they get well almost invariably come and call on us, and even go with us to church."

Soon they were performing surgeries and dispensing medicine to more than six thousand people each year. In their clinic's waiting room, they had a Christian evangelist talk to the patients about the good news of Jesus Christ. The doctors worked closely with other Christian missionaries who did evangelistic work in Jiujiang and the surrounding villages. "People are awakening everywhere," Ida reported, "and crowds flock to us to hear the truth and receive medical treatment. Everywhere they beg us to come and visit them again."

Before long, gifts of land and money were given to build a small hospital and clinic. But just as the building was completed in 1900, the Boxer Rebellion erupted in China. Bands of armed men, seeking to kill every foreign missionary and Chinese Christian in the land, murdered Christians by the thousands. When the carnage reached Jiujiang, Mary and Ida and all the missionaries fled for their lives. Brave Christians risked everything to shelter them and sneak them out of the country. For many months, Ida and Mary waited in Japan until it was safe to return.

At that time, a number of old customs persisted in China that harmed girls and women—including foot binding and the enslavement of girls. Wealthy families bought young girls to use and abuse as household slaves. Ida boldly spoke out against this. Once, she was asked to speak on girl slavery to a large women's conference in Shanghai. She told them how slave girls were often brought to her clinic with broken bones, burns and other injuries inflicted upon them by cruel masters. "My best friend in school," Ida said, "had a mind as beautiful as her person. We were baptized together and she confessed to me that she would like to devote her life to Christian work, beginning with helping her father who was addicted to opium. But all her longings and aspirations were gone when her father sold her to a sixty-year-old man! We, the more favored ones, must plead with all our might that all these unnatural customs shall be swept away with the last relics of our country's barbarism."

One day, a high official in Nanchang sent a request for Ida to come and help his very ill wife. After examining her, Ida determined that she must return with her to Jiujiang for treatment. After several weeks, she recovered completely. The healed woman spread the word of Ida's medical skills, and soon many well-to-do ladies from that city came to her hospital in Jiujiang. The wealthy of Nanchang asked Ida to start a clinic there. Before this, the leaders of the city had not been friendly to missionaries, but now they urged Ida and her helpers to come. Although she did not want to leave Mary and the new hospital, she pitied the three hundred thousand people of Nanchang without a single educated physician. In 1903, she opened a clinic—it was busy from the start.

Ida related well to the rich and the poor, and she treated them equally since they were all created in the image of God. "She is magnificent from the officials' houses to the mud huts," a co-worker said of her. She used her friendships with influential people to advocate for better healthcare for women and children. She also told them about Jesus Christ. "The only hope of China's regeneration," she said, "is in her becoming a Christian nation, and only the love of Christ can bring out the best qualities of any people."

Soon, government officials told Ida that they would provide the land and the money for a hospital on the condition that it would not be a Christian institution. Ida refused—she would not compromise her faith. But before long, a fine hospital was built through the gifts of wealthy citizens and the contributions of American supporters. The Women's and Children's Hospital in Nanchang became the most important medical center in the region. Ida rigorously trained Chinese nurses to assist her in the work. "Always abide in the Spirit of Christ," she told them. They treated thousands of patients each year, and Ida rejoiced to see a growing number of patients believing in Jesus.

She pushed for modern medicine in China, urging that medical schools for men and women be established throughout the land. "Contemplate China's four hundred millions," she wrote, "with barely two hundred physicians using effectual modern medical practice. What would the English-speaking world think if there was only one physician available for the city of New York?"

In 1911, a civil war broke out in China. Most missionaries left to avoid the violence, but Ida stayed. She and her hospital staff cared for hundreds of wounded soldiers and sick and starving citizens. The chaos of war and revolution spilled over into the hospital. At times, military officers took over the administration of the hospital. For a while, Ida's home was occupied by soldiers.

Although she endured many trials, Ida always remained grateful to God. "When I think what my life might have been," she said, "and what, through God's grace, it is, I think there is nothing that God has given me that I would not gladly use in His service."

38 BETSIE AND CORRIE TEN BOOM

The Rescuers, 1885–1944 and 1892–1983

Andrew
ll of Holland was in shock. The peace and freedom that the Dutch people had known for generations vanished with the arrival of the Nazi war machine. In a matter of hours, German planes, trucks and tanks overran the country. No wonder the Germans called it "blitzkrieg"—lightning war. In the spring of 1940 the people of Holland found themselves prisoners in their own land.

The Nazi occupation forces brought their hateful beliefs with them. Their leader, Adolph Hitler, told them: "The German people are the master race. All other peoples are destined to serve us." But the people Hitler hated most were the Jews. "The Jews are people of the devil," he said. "We will not rest until they are wiped off the face of the earth."

Hitler meant what he said. The Nazis in Germany rounded up Jews and sent them to concentration camps. They murdered some immediately, and many others died slowly from disease and malnutrition. As the German army swept over the countries of Europe like the Black Plague, they deported Jews from those lands to death camps. Sadly, most people did not lift a finger to help the Jews. They looked the other way while their Jewish neighbors were hunted down and sent off to their deaths. "We have to look out for ourselves," they reasoned. "It is none of our business."

But in every land some people risked their lives to save the Jews. The ten Boom family in Holland did just that.

Casper ten Boom and his two middle-aged daughters lived in a tall, narrow house in the old part of Haarlem. A steep staircase led up to the tiny bedrooms on the second and third floors. The first floor of the house was a watch shop where Casper ten Boom had worked for most of his eighty years. He was known for his godly character almost as widely as for his skill as a precision watchmaker. Every morning and evening Father ten Boom read a chapter from the large family Bible and led Betsie and Corrie in prayer. His daughters trusted in Christ and strove to serve others.

When they saw their Jewish neighbors in danger, it seemed only natural and right to help them. One day German soldiers broke into the store across the street which was owned by a Jewish family. They roughed up the owner and stole most of his merchandise. Corrie and Betsie raced over and brought the man into their house. Over the next three years, the ten Booms worked tirelessly to rescue as many Jews as they could from the Nazis.

Soon their home was filled with Jews hiding from the Gestapo, the German secret police. Once when Corrie met some of her underground contacts, she was told, "I understand that your building lacks a secret room. This is a danger for you and those you are helping. In the coming week we will build you one."

Within a few days, workmen built a tiny secret room in Corrie's third-floor bedroom. It could be entered only by crawling through a small hole hidden behind the bookshelf, but it had enough space to hide eight people. They also installed alarm buzzers throughout the house to warn if soldiers or policemen entered.

Once, a young Jewish mother and her two-week-old baby came to the ten Boom's home. Their house was full, so Corrie decided to ask a pastor for help who had stopped into the shop to have his watch repaired. Holding the infant in her arms she asked him, "Would you be willing to take a Jewish mother and her baby into your house? They will almost certainly be arrested otherwise."

"Miss ten Boom!" the pastor exclaimed. "I do hope you are not involved with any of this illegal concealment and undercover business. It's not safe! Think of your father and sister."

Corrie pleaded with him. But he said, "No. Definitely not! We could lose our lives for that Jewish child."

Neither the pastor nor Corrie had noticed that Mr. ten Boom had entered the room. "Give the child to me, Corrie," he said.

He held the baby close and looked intently at the infant's face, and then he turned to the pastor. "You say we could lose our lives for this child. I would consider that the greatest honor that could come to my family." The pastor said nothing and left.

They found a safe place for the mother and child, but as the number of rescues increased, so did the chance of being caught. More and more people knew what was going on in the ten Boom house. Mr. ten Boom, Corrie and Betsie prayed earnestly for wisdom and courage, believing that God wanted them to continue.

Then one morning the alarm sounded. In less than two minutes six people and all their things were hidden in the secret room. Just seconds after the hidden panel shut closed, a Gestapo agent rushed into Corrie's bedroom.

"Who are you?" he demanded.

"Corrie ten Boom."

"Where are the Jews?" he asked.

"There aren't any Jews here," she answered.

He slapped Corrie hard across the face. "Where do you hide the ration cards?"

"I don't know what you are talking—" before Corrie could finish, he hit her in the face and kept striking her over and over again. "Where are the Jews? Where is your secret room?"

When he realized that Corrie would say nothing, he began to question and hit Betsie.

The sound of breaking plaster and splintering wood filled the house as a group of trained searchers used sledge hammers to find the secret room. But try as they might they could not find the hiding place. The Gestapo arrested Corrie, Betsie and their father. In the crowded police holding room, Mr. ten Boom prayed a prayer from the psalms: "You are my hiding place and my shield. Hold me up and I shall be safe."

The Germans sent them to a prison in southern Holland where Mr. ten Boom soon took sick and died. Later, Corrie and Betsie were loaded on trains and sent to Ravensbruck, a death camp in the heart of Germany where tens of thousands of prisoners were jammed into barracks. A large brick building housed the gas chambers where prisoners were killed by poison gas.

When they arrived in their barracks, they discovered the place was crawling with fleas. "Betsie," Corrie cried, "how can we live in such a place?"

"Show us, Lord Jesus," Betsie prayed.

Then suddenly Betsie said excitedly, "Corrie, He has given us the answer. In our Bible reading this morning remember it said: 'Give thanks in all circumstances.' That's it, Corrie! That's His answer. We can start right now to thank God about every single thing about this new barracks."

The two sisters thanked the Lord for being together, for their Bible, for the women with whom they shared the barracks. Betsie closed the prayer: "And thank you Lord for the fleas!"

Prison life at Ravensbruck was dark and ugly, but the love of Christ—shining through the ten Boom sisters—helped to bring some light and beauty. Corrie and Betsie began an evening meeting in the barracks near their bunks for prayer, worship and Bible reading. Many women came to gather strength from God's Word. To the prisoners' surprise, no guards ever entered the barracks, and so they were free each evening to worship the Lord to their hearts' content. Later, they found out that no guards wanted to enter their barracks because of the fleas. The Lord had brought blessing through the fleas!

Every night, Betsie and Corrie read from the Dutch Bible and translated it aloud into German. And then the wonderful truths were passed along from woman to woman and translated into French, Polish, Russian, Czech and other languages. Many women believed in Jesus Christ through those nightly gatherings. The sisters saw these meetings as a foretaste of heaven when the Lord will bring His people together from every language and tribe and nation.

Betsie's love extended even to her captors. She encouraged the women to pray for the guards and all of the German people.

Betsie would tell them: "Jesus said, 'Love your enemies and bless those who persecute you.'"

Corrie and Betsie dreamed of starting a home after the war for people whose lives were shattered by the concentration camps. In the home they could find healing and a new beginning. They also hoped to minister to the German people. "Corrie, if people can be taught to hate," Betsie said, "they can be taught to love. We must help them. We must tell people what we have learned."

But Betsie's strength ebbed away, and she died at Ravensbruck. Later, the commandant released Corrie. Years later, Corrie learned that she was supposed to have been sent to the gas chambers—her release was due to a clerical mistake.

By God's grace, Corrie fulfilled the dreams that she and her sister had while in the death camp. Home for healing were started in Holland and in Germany. Corrie became an author and an international speaker, traveling all over the world telling people about Christ's love and forgiveness. While speaking at a church in Munich, Germany, in 1947, Corrie had to face the challenge and joy of forgiveness. "When we confess our sins," she told the congregation, "God casts them into the deepest ocean—gone forever." As she spoke, Corrie recognized in the audience a man who had been one of the brutal guards at Ravensbruck. After her talk, the former guard came up to speak with her. Suddenly, Corrie flashed back to the concentration camp and pictured the man wearing his old Nazi uniform with his leather whip swinging from his belt. Her heart raced and her body stiffened when the man stood in front of her, stuck out his hand and said, "A fine message, Fräulein! How good it is to know that, as you say, all our sins are at the bottom of the sea! You mentioned Ravensbruck in your talk—I was a guard there. But since that time, I have become a Christian. I know that God has forgiven me for the cruel things I did there, but I would like to hear it from your lips as well." Then, reaching his hand further forward, he said, "Fräulein, will you forgive me?"

"My blood seemed to freeze," Corrie said later. "And I stood there—I whose sins had again and again to be forgiven—and could not forgive. Betsie had died in that place—could he erase her slow terrible death simply for the asking?"

For several seconds the man stood with his hand held out, but to Corrie it seemed like hours. She knew that Christ called her to forgive her enemies. She had preached that message to thousands of others. But now, face to face with one of her old tormentors, she struggled. "Help!" she prayed silently. "Lord, I can lift my hand. I can do that much. You supply the feeling."

When she rigidly stuck her hand in his, something wonderful happened. "The current started in my shoulder," Corrie reported later, "and raced down my arm and sprang into our joined hands. And then this healing warmth seemed to flood my whole being, bringing tears to my eyes. 'I forgive you, brother!' I cried. 'With all my heart!' I had never known God's love so intensely, as I did then."

The book that tells the story of her life during the war, *The Hiding Place*, was one of the most widely read Christian biographies of the twentieth century, and it remains popular today. Corrie ten Boom lived to be ninety-one. She was an active servant of Christ to the end.

39 SABINA WURMBRAND
In Christ's Underground, 1913–2000

During the Second World War, German troops occupied Romania. As they did in every country that they controlled, the Nazis rounded up Jews for execution. Sabina Wurmbrand, a Romanian Jew who had converted to Christianity along with her Jewish husband, lost her entire family to the Nazi murderers. Sabina and her husband Richard, a well-educated Lutheran pastor, tried to shine the light of Christ to their fellow Romanians and to the German invaders.

In August 1944, one million Russian troops attacked the Germans in Romania, forcing the German army to retreat. In the confusion of battle, some German soldiers were left behind. When Romanians discovered these hated German soldiers, they turned them over to the Russians who shot them on the spot or sent them to starve to death in prison camps. It happened that Richard and Sabina came across three German officers. Instead of turning them in, they risked their lives by hiding them in a snow-covered shed in their backyard. One day, as Sabina brought food to the hunted men, a German captain said, "You know that it is death to shelter a German soldier. Yet you do it—and you are Jews! I must tell you that when the German army recaptures Bucharest, which it surely will, I'll never do for you what you have done for us."

Sabina looked into his eyes and said, "My family was killed by the Nazis, but even so, as long as you are under my roof, I owe you not only protection, but the respect due to a guest. You will suffer. The Bible says, 'Whosoever sheds man's blood, by man shall his blood be shed.' I will protect you as much as I can from the police, but I cannot protect you from the wrath of God."

"Humbug," he scoffed. Then he caught himself and added, "I just wondered why a Jewess should risk her life for a German soldier. I do not like Jews. And I do not fear God. You see us as men who have committed crimes against Jews. And you forgive them all?"

"Even the worst crimes are forgiven by faith in Jesus Christ," she answered. "I have no authority to forgive. Jesus can do so, if you repent."

With help from the Wurmbrands, the three German soldiers safely escaped the country.

Soon, the Russian army installed a communist government in Romania that took its orders from Moscow. Like the government of the Soviet Union, it was a brutal regime, jailing and murdering tens of thousands of innocent people. Hoping to control and eventually wipe out Christianity, the Communists confiscated church property and forbade ministers to work without licenses from the government. Sabina and Richard invited Russian soldiers into their home to share a meal and the love of Christ with them. The Wurmbrands took the opportunity—wherever a crowd would gather at a train station or a bus stop—to speak a short message about Christ and then disappear into the crowd before the police arrived. As the authorities grew more suspicious of the Wurmbrands' activities, friends urged them to flee the country. But they decided to share the fate of their Christian countrymen and spread the gospel as long as they could. "We're here to stay," they told their friends.

Soon after taking power, the communist government convened a congress of all the Christian church bodies in Romania. Four thousand priests, bishops and ministers assembled in the great hall of the Parliament building before a huge portrait of Stalin, the Russian dictator. Under fear of imprisonment, torture and death, one Christian leader after another praised the new communist rulers, declaring that communism and Christianity shared similar goals and could thrive together.

Sitting in the meeting were Richard and Sabina Wurmbrand. Sabina turned to her husband with flaming eyes and furrowed brow saying, "Richard, stand up and wash away this shame from the face of Christ! They are spitting in His face."

"If I do so," Richard whispered, "you lose your husband."

"I don't want to have a coward as a husband," Sabina replied.

So Richard arose, walked to the rostrum and requested permission to speak. Looking out over the sea of faces, he spoke into the microphone which broadcast the message live to the whole country. "It is our duty as ministers," Wurmbrand reminded the audience, "to glorify Christ. Our loyalty is due first to Him and not to earthly powers."

As Richard talked, applause broke out from every corner of the hall. Many jumped to their feet cheering. "Your right to speak has been withdrawn!" a red-faced official shouted from the platform. Officials cut off the microphone, and the day's meeting ended in an uproar. Richard and Sabina knew that he would pay for his boldness, but they believed it was worth it. Not long after, on a beautiful Sunday morning as Pastor Wurmbrand walked to church, agents of the secret police seized him and hauled him off to prison. Day after day, Sabina tried to find out what had happened to him, but every government official told her the same thing, "We have no record of him." Sabina and their son Mihai did not know if he was alive or dead.

While she prayed for her husband, Sabina led secret worship meetings and Bible studies. Government agents harassed her often. They refused to grant her a work permit or a ration card to buy food. "How are I and my son to live?" Sabina asked an official. "That's your problem," he answered. Despite her own poverty, she worked with others to help families whose husbands had been arrested. Then one day in 1950, the secret police burst into her house at five o'clock in the morning. "Sabina Wurmbrand!" shouted the officer, "we know you're hiding weapons here. Tell us where the arms are hidden or we'll tear this place apart!"

Holding up her Bible, Sabina said, "This is the only weapon we have in our house." After ransacking her home, the officers arrested her. For weeks, they pulled Sabina into the prison's interrogation rooms trying to get her to reveal information they could use against Richard and others. "You could go home to your family," they said. "Just tell us about these counterrevolutionaries."

"I know nothing," she said.

They put her in solitary confinement and fed her a starvation diet to get her to talk, but she refused. "Mrs. Wurmbrand," one interrogator said, "you are only thirty-six years old. The best years of a woman's life are before you. Why do you refuse to co-operate with us? You could go free tomorrow, if you'd only give us the names of these traitors."

Then he promised to release her and Richard and provide them with money and good jobs if she would give them the information they sought. "Thanks, but I've sold myself already," Sabina said. "The Son of God was tortured and gave His life for me. Through Him I can reach heaven. Can you offer a higher price than that?"

Shortly thereafter, Sabina—along with hundreds of thousands of her countrymen—was sentenced to forced labor without ever being brought to trial. They sent her to Jilava, a huge prison camp. When she entered her overcrowded cell, an inmate asked, "Who are you?"

"Sabina Wurmbrand, the wife of a pastor," she answered.

"Religious, eh?" a gray-haired woman said. "Tell us a Bible story—it is so boring here."

Sabina told them the story of Joseph and his brothers. "God can turn the most hopeless circumstances into a blessing," she said. This began two years of bringing the hope of Christ to her fellow prisoners.

By this time, the communists had begun to turn against some of their own members. Many early supporters of communism had been arrested. Elsa had been an important communist of-ficial—now she was a prisoner, but still loyal to the Communist Party. "Don't start that preaching in here again or I'll hammer on the door until the guard comes," Elsa warned Sabina.

"Do you still believe in the Communist Party?" Sabina asked her.

"Certainly," she answered. "I haven't changed my beliefs. My arrest was all a mistake."

"Nor has my arrest altered my faith," Sabina said. "In fact, it is stronger. I want to tell people what a friend they have in Jesus."

"Your God hasn't helped you much," Elsa sneered.

"What is your idea of God?" Sabina asked her.

"God is a fanatic who won't let science tell the truth," she said. "The myth of God exploits the working class and abuses the poor."

"What you call God is certainly very unlovable," Sabina said. "The God I love is quite different from that. He shared the poverty of the workers. He was brought up among the oppressed. He fed the hungry and healed the sick. He teaches love. He died for us."

"Love!" Elsa bellowed. "I'm all hate! How I loathe those treacherous comrades who put me here. I wish them in hell! I gave my whole life to the Communist Party, and this is what they do to me?" With tears streaming down her cheeks, she added, "I don't accept forgiveness—it's all lies."

Then she looked up and with a slight grin said, "Sabina Wurmbrand, you are sly. I tell you to stop preaching and in five minutes you are preaching to me."

In her years as a Christian, Sabina had memorized many passages from the Bible. Other Christian prisoners knew verses too. New Christian inmates added more verses. "We repeated daily those passages we knew," Sabina wrote later, "they brought riches to prison. While others quarreled and fought, we'd repeat these verses to ourselves through the long nights. So an unwritten Bible circulated through all Romanian prisons."

The prison guards put the women to work moving wheelbarrows of earth and stone to build a canal. It was back-breaking labor, especially for the malnourished prisoners. When the guards weren't looking, the prisoners ate grass to survive. Sabina's hands were cracked and bleeding after each day's labor. Beatings were common. "You wanted to be martyrs, so now suffer!" the guards shouted at those imprisoned for their faith. Once, a guard threw Sabina off an embankment into the shallows of a river. The fall broke several ribs and badly bruised half her body.

Many prisoners confided in Sabina and sought her prayers. One woman told her how she had killed her own child from neglect in order to win the favor of a man who didn't like children. "I long to be good," she told Sabina. "No one is really good," Sabina said. "But if we confess our sins Jesus is righteous to forgive."

One day, Sabina was moved to a new prison. A guard brought her to the commandant's office. "In this place, Mrs. Wurmbrand," he told her, "you must know that I am more powerful than God. Now—have you seen through the sham of religion? Have you realized that in a communist society, you don't need God anymore?"

"I see that you are powerful," Sabina answered, "and probably you have documents there about me that can decide my fate. But God keeps records, too, and neither you nor I would have life without Him. So whether He keeps me here or sets me free, I'll accept that as best for me."

Banging his fists on the desk, he shouted, "I'm sorry to see that you failed to learn your lesson, and I shall make a report to that effect."

To Sabina's surprise, she was let out of prison a few days later and dropped off on the outskirts of Bucharest. She trembled as she knocked on the door of her old flat, but soon she was in the arms of her son. "Don't cry too much, Mother," he said as he wiped tears from her cheeks. Later, he told her that he thought it would be good to kill the communist tyrants who were destroying Romania. "It's not the best way," Sabina told him, "we should try to kill the tyranny, not the tyrant. We should hate the sin, but love the sinner."

The authorities had ordered Sabina not to engage in any religious activity, but as she regained her strength, she resumed her work with the underground church. She taught Bible studies and, if there was no pastor, preached a message. "We simply did our Christian duty," Sabina said. "We paid no heed to communist laws."

In June 1956, after nearly nine years of incarceration and torture, Richard Wurmbrand was suddenly released under a general amnesty. When he limped home to the loving embrace of Sabina and Mihai, he said, "Don't think that I have come from misery to happiness. I've come from the joy of being with Christ in prison to the joy of being with Him in my family."

Right away, Richard began preaching to hidden groups of Christians huddled in basements, attics or fields. After two years of freedom, the secret police took him away for five more years of torture. When he was released the second time, he went right to work again preaching Christ. He wanted to remain in Romania, but the leaders of the underground church urged him to leave the country. "Be the voice of persecuted Christians to the free world," they told him.

An international Christian group paid a ransom to the communist government to bring the Wurmbrand family out of Romania. They came to America and founded *The Voice of the Martyrs*, a ministry to persecuted Christians throughout the world. They sent Bibles and supplies to the families of Christian martyrs and informed the world about atrocities committed against Christians.

In 1989, when the communist government in Romania collapsed, Richard and Sabina returned to their homeland, bringing the message of Jesus Christ to overflowing churches. "Forgive the communists and turn to God," they told their hearers. "Love your persecutors. Love their souls, and try to win them for Christ."

40 AHN EI SOOK
Imprisoned for Christ, c. 1914–1997

In 1938, Imperial Japan forced its will on the conquered Koreans. Japanese overlords built Shinto shrines in all the cities and villages of Korea. They forced the people to set up little shrines in their homes and schools, and the Japanese placed an idol in every Christian church. Policemen spied on Christian congregations during Sunday services to see that every person bowed to the pagan god as they entered the sanctuary. Hundreds of pastors and parishioners suffered imprisonment and torture for refusing to bend the knee.

Ahn Ei Sook, a young teacher in a Christian girls' school, had steadfastly refused to bow to the Japanese idols in church, but so far she had escaped detection by the authorities. However, that was about to end. Japanese officials had ordered a mass pilgrimage to a shrine dedicated to the sun-goddess at Namsan Mountain. Everyone in the region—including the students and faculty of Ei Sook's school—were under orders to worship the Japanese idol there on the appointed day. "As we made our way up the mountain," Ei Sook said later, "I determined that with God's help I would never bow before the Japanese idol. I was saved by Jesus. I could bow only before God, the Father of my Savior."

As Ei Sook walked past the Japanese guards at the mountain her heart thumped like a drum in her chest. "O Lord," she prayed, "I am so weak! But I am Your sheep so I must obey and follow You. Lord, watch over me."

"Attention!" a man's voice cried over a loud speaker. The immense crowd stopped talking and straightened into line. He then directed them to worship the idol in unison. "Let us make our profoundest bow to the sun goddess!" Altogether, everyone in the great crowd bowed deeply to the idol, except Ei Sook. She stood erect, looked to heaven and prayed. "I've done what I should have done," she prayed. "I commit the rest to You."

As she walked down the mountain she said to herself, "I am dead. Ahn Ei Sook died today at Mount Namsan."

When she got back to her school, waiting policemen shoved her into a car and drove to the office of the district chief. "Who do you think you are?" he demanded in Japanese. "Do you realize what you did at Namsan Mountain today? Why were you so reckless? Don't you know about our great Imperial Japanese police power, you miserable woman!"

Ei Sook knew he would cast her into prison, but just then he received a phone call, and he quickly stepped out of his office. Ei Sook believed God was providing a way of escape, so she calmly walked out of the room, down the hall and out of the building. When she reached home and told her mother what had happened, her mother urged her to flee. Ei Sook smeared ash on her face and hands, disguised herself in peasant clothing and caught an evening train out of town. A few days later, she phoned her sister who arranged for Ei Sook to meet her mother. In the hope of escaping the police, they rented a tiny straw-thatched house in the country not far from her sister's home. Through spring and summer, while they enjoyed the quiet of the country house, Ei Sook prepared for prison by fasting and memorizing whole chapters of Scripture.

Then one day, her sister arrived and warned Ei Sook that the police had been at her home asking where she was hiding. Ei Sook disguised herself again. She walked over a mountain pass to a small town and caught a bus for Pyongyang, the largest city in the north of Korea. In Pyongyang, she met many Christians hiding from the authorities and heard horror stories of Christians tortured for their faith. "Terrible things go on behind bars," she was told. "How long will I be able to endure?" Ei Sook kept asking herself. "I knew it would be impossible for me to keep my faith in my own power," she said. "God would have to work through me if I was to stand firm." She prayed and fasted and asked for God's grace and strength.

Day by day, Ei Sook passed the train station and saw train-loads of young men heading off to war. "Someone must tell each one the good news that Jesus Christ had come to save," she said to herself. "If only someone in a high position would stand up to the Japanese leaders and make them see that they are sending these young men to death and hell."

Then suddenly a voice spoke to her heart saying, "You are the one! You must do it!"

"But I am a weakling, a child of sin," she thought. From that day forward, she couldn't get the thought out of her mind that she was to warn the leaders of Japan. She believed that Japan would be judged by God like Sodom and Gomorrah when sulfur fire rained down from the sky.

When she wasn't praying or studying her Bible, she went to the open market and passed out Christian tracts. "Believe in Jesus," she told anyone who would listen. Then one morning a bearded old man in tattered clothes came to the house where Ei Sook was staying. "O thank You, Lord!" he said when he met Ei Sook. "I finally found her."

The man's name was Elder Park. To Ei Sook's surprise, he told her that he had heard about her unwillingness to bow to the mountain idol and that she spoke Japanese fluently. "God directed me to find you in Pyongyang," he said.

"What did God tell you to do when you met me?" she asked Elder Park.

"God wants us to warn the Japanese," he said.

After several days of prayer and fasting and seeking the counsel of her Christian friends, Ei Sook decided to go to Japan with Elder Park. The words of Queen Esther rang in her ears. "I will go into the King, which is not according to the law; and if I perish, I perish."

They booked passage on a ship leaving Pusan. As the ship set sail for Japan, Ei Sook said, "I will surely die at the hands of the Japanese." In Tokyo, they made an appointment to see a retired Japanese government official who had been the governor of Korea some time before. Ei Sook told him about the persecution of Korean Christians and the brutal treatment of Koreans at the hands of the Japanese. "God has clearly told me," Ei Sook said, "that Japan will be punished and destroyed by sulfur fire unless she repents and turns from this course of action."

The man nodded in agreement. He lamented the behavior of Japanese officials, and he feared that they were plunging Japan headlong into a world war. "At present I have no power," he said, "but some of the authorities of the present government are my friends. They will listen to me. I think I will be able to help you."

Although he introduced Ei Sook to a few members of the Diet, the Japanese Parliament, who stood against the actions of the Japanese military, nothing came of it. Elder Park decided that they should go to the Diet and pass out papers that urged the Japanese government to change its ways or face the wrath of God.

On March 23, 1939, during the final session of the Imperial Diet, Ei Sook and Elder Park sat in the balcony overlooking the assembly hall full of Japanese legislators. Suddenly, Mr. Park stood up and shouted, "Jehovah's great commission!" Then he flung papers over the railing that warned the Japanese to repent. Representatives looked up and caught the floating papers in their hands. Guards seized Elder Park and Ei Sook and whisked them away to Tokyo police headquarters.

They led Ei Sook into an interrogation room where detectives questioned her. "You lawless Koreans disturbed the Diet of holy, Imperial Japan!" he shouted. "Why did you come to Japan? Speak up! Why did you come to Tokyo?"

"Mr. Detective," Ei Sook answered, "Japan is rebelling against God, the Creator of the universe. God has to punish Japan. I have been sent here to tell the national leaders that Japan is going to be ruined by sulfur fire!"

"You fool! How could you think such a crazy thing?" he bellowed. Turning to the other detective, he sneered, "Sulfur fire? She's crazy!"

After the Japanese imprisoned Ei Sook and Elder Park for a month in Tokyo, they expelled them from the country under armed guard. Not long after she returned to Korea, Ei Sook was arrested in a widespread roundup of Christian leaders. In the harsh conditions of prison, Ei Sook looked to Jesus Christ, and she was often filled with His peace. "Why are you so calm?" one of the jailers asked her.

"I'm beginning to understand what faith really is," she told him.

Whenever she had an opportunity, Ei Sook shared the good news of Christ with her jailers and interrogators. Once, when she was questioned about her family, she answered, "My grandmother worshiped idols and consulted soothsayers all the time. I saw that idols and demons are unable to do any good for their worshipers. I knew how unhappy and powerless my grandmother was. But my mother—who was saved by Jesus Christ and believed in the true God—was the happiest person, living a life of peace and victory in spite of miserable circumstances. I became a Christian not because somebody told me to do so. Rather, I made up my mind and believed after seeing the facts with my own eyes."

Ei Sook barely survived on a scant ration of millet mixed with sand, and she had to endure the filth and stench of overcrowded cells. But on several occasions, sympathetic Korean jailers gave her extra food and encouraged her to hold on. A few days after telling one female Korean guard about Jesus Christ, the guard came to Ei Sook's cell and said with a smile, "Now I am a believer."

Once, Ei Sook was interrogated by the Japanese superintendent of the prison. After she boldly proclaimed her faith in Christ he asked her, "Do you mean that our emperor, who is a living god, must also believe in Jesus?"

"Yes," she answered, "unless the emperor, who is just a man like we are, is saved by Jesus, he will go to hell when he dies."

"That is an unpardonable blasphemy!" he roared, his cheeks flushing red. Then the superintendent lit a cigarette and said, "You seem to have been made fearless. Do you know what misfortune is going to befall you for what you are saying?"

"Yes, of course," Ei Sook said. "But I can't tell a lie, for Jesus never tells a lie."

Not long after, Ei Sook's mother came to visit her. Her eyes flooded with tears when she saw the condition of her daughter. "You are going to die for certain this time," her mother said. "Follow Jesus Christ completely. Let's meet at the gates of heaven. Whichever one gets there first, she shall wait there for the other."

When her mother left, Ei Sook prayed, "Lord, I am a weakling. Unless I live each day holding Your hand, I will become too frightened. Lord, hold my hand firmly so I won't part from You. Jesus, I love You."

For six long years, Ei Sook expected to die in prison, but her emaciated body lived on. Then suddenly in August of 1945, word came that Japan had surrendered to the United States. For two years, American B-29s had rained fire bombs down on Tokyo and all the major cities of Japan. Hundreds of thousands of Japanese perished in the flames and the nation lay in ruins. The final blow came when the American military dropped atomic bombs on the Japanese cities of Hiroshima and Nagasaki. In seconds, tens of thousands of people and large sections of the cities evaporated in the fiery blasts from the air. Ei Sook's warning of destruction by fire had come true.

After the war, Ei Sook toured the United States and many other countries, telling her story of Christ's love and His upholding power that preserved her through the horrors of the Japanese prisons.

41

DARLENE DEIBLER ROSE
Missionary, Prisoner of War, 1917–2004

One morning in 1942 on Celebes Island, Russell and Darlene Deibler and their fellow missionaries in Indonesia heard the roar of approaching trucks. Darlene looked up to see Japanese soldiers, rifles at the ready, shouting, "We're taking the men. Move quickly!"

The missionaries had been expecting this ever since Japan attacked Pearl Harbor in December 1941 and overran the islands of Southeast Asia. Darlene rushed into the house and stuffed a pillow case with her husband's Bible, a notebook, pen, shaving gear and clothes. She ran to the driveway where soldiers with bayonets prodded Russell and the other men into the back of a flatbed truck. As the driver started the engine, Darlene reached up and gave Russell the pillow case. He leaned over the tailgate and said, "Dear, remember one thing: God said that He would never leave us nor forsake us."

Then the truck sped away to a prisoner of war camp for men. "I believe that all things work together for good," she told God in prayer after Russell was taken. "But what about now, Lord? It seems like You have left me and forsaken me."

It wasn't long before the soldiers returned, rounded up the women missionaries and brought them to Kampili, a large internment camp for women. They crammed the women in dirt-floored barracks with walls lined with double-decker bamboo sleeping racks. The first night in the barracks, Darlene and the other missionaries invited everyone to pray and listen to the reading of a Bible passage. "I believe," Darlene said later, "that this practice was responsible for maintaining the high level of compassion and cooperation."

As Darlene worried about her husband, she thought about their arrival in Indonesia in August 1938. Darlene and Russell Deibler had started to bring the good news of Jesus Christ to the natives of the interior of New Guinea. But not long after they began, the Second World War broke out. Now they were separated and languishing in prison camps.

Life in Kampili was difficult. The women inmates fought a constant battle against lice, fleas and mosquitoes. But far worse than the bugs were the rats and the rabid dogs that roamed the prison at night. The inmates worked from sunup to sundown, sewing soldiers' uniforms, hoeing gardens, clearing land, pumping water, cooking and cleaning. "The sweat of our bodies and the craft of our hands were required to keep ourselves alive and to advance the Japanese military machine," Darlene said.

Poor food and filthy conditions caused dysentery, malaria, and other diseases to sweep through the camp, crowding the infirmary with the sick and dying.

A brutal officer named Mr. Yamaji ran Kampili. Once he flew into a rage and kicked a prisoner to death. One time when Darlene made a suggestion to him about improving the efficiency of the cooking stoves, Yamaji cracked his cane across the back of her neck. "You talk too much," he yelled. As he marched off, Darlene collapsed to the ground, trying to suppress the hatred welling up in her heart. She limped back to the barracks and stretched out on her mat. Then phrases from the Gospel of Matthew went through her mind: "Love your enemies. Do good to those who despitefully use you." "Alright, Lord," Darlene prayed. "I don't want the man to be lost eternally—but I really would like it if You would curdle the food in his stomach tonight and stretch him on the rack of his conscience at least for a while."

Then she turned away from thoughts of revenge. "Without you, Lord," she prayed, "what might I have become? Forgive me, Lord."

Near the end of November 1943, when Darlene had been in the camp for over a year, a fellow missionary told her, "Your husband has been very ill." Then tears filled her eyes, and she choked on her words. Darlene grabbed her shoulder and cried, "Oh, no! You don't mean he's gone!"

"Yes," she answered, "three months ago he died in the prison camp."

Darlene walked away, her chest pounding and her head swimming. Looking up to heaven, she cried out, "But God...why?"

Immediately, Darlene felt God speaking to her soul. "My child," the Lord seemed to say, "did I not promise that when you pass through the waters I would be with you?" Later that afternoon, Yamaji called her to his office. "This is war," he said.

"Yes, Mr. Yamaji, I understand that."

"What you heard today about your husband, women in Japan have heard."

"Yes, sir, I understand that too," Darlene replied.

"You are very young," Yamaji said. "Someday this war will be over and you can go back to America and you will marry again.

You have been a great help to the other women in the camp. Don't lose your smile."

"Mr. Yamaji may I have permission to talk to you?" Darlene asked. He nodded and motioned for her to sit down.

"Mr. Yamaji," she said, "I don't sorrow like people who have no hope. I want to tell you about Someone of whom you may never have heard. I learned about Him when I was a little girl in Sunday school back in Iowa in America. His name is Jesus. He's the Son of Almighty God, Creator of heaven and earth." Then Darlene told the prison commander the wonderful news of Jesus Christ. Tears began to run down his cheeks. "He died for you, Mr. Yamaji," she said. "He puts love in our hearts—even for those who are our enemies. That's why I don't hate you. Maybe God brought me to this place and this time to tell you that He loves you."

As he dismissed her, he stepped into a side room crying and closed the door. Darlene walked back to the barracks grateful that she could tell about her Savior even in the midst of her sorrow.

Sometime later, the Japanese secret police came to Kampili and took Darlene to another prison to torture her for information. A guard confiscated her Bible saying, "You can't have that! All you'll do is sit there and think of that book instead of your evil deeds against the Imperial Japanese Army."

As an officer led her to a cell, she could hear the screams of a prisoner being tortured. Darlene knew that she would likely be executed as a spy. After the officer locked her in, she prayed, "O Lord, whatever you do, make me a good soldier for Jesus Christ."

The next morning a guard brought her to the interrogation room. Two men were waiting for her—an interrogator and a torturer. "How long have you spied for the American military?" the interrogator asked.

"I have never spied for the Americans," Darlene answered.

Crack—came a swift karate chop to the base of her neck. Darlene reeled from the sharp pain that coursed down the side of her body.

"How do you make contact with American military personnel?" he demanded.

"I have never made contact with the American military," she said.

For several hours they pressed her with questions about her alleged spying. If they weren't happy with her answers, the torturer would deliver a karate chop to the neck or hit her between the eyes, leaving her forehead and eyes bruised and swollen.

Every few days for weeks, they hauled Darlene to the interrogation room and put her through the ordeal all over again. "You are a spy!" the interrogator said. "You contacted the Americans with your radio. We will be lenient if you confess."

Darlene knew that if she confessed the Japanese would execute her as a wartime spy. "I am not a spy," she said. "I never had a radio, and I never contacted the American military."

To all their questions Darlene gave truthful answers, but they refused to believe her. She was determined that her tormentors would never break her nor see her cry. "Lord, help me," she prayed silently. Through every session—despite the pain—she never shed a tear. But once back in her cell alone, "I wept buckets of tears," Darlene said.

With a tiny portion of dirty rice each day as her only food, she quickly lost weight and strength. Although she suffered from malnutrition and dysentery, she tried to keep her mind and spirit sound by reciting Scripture. In her youth and young adulthood, Darlene had memorized many verses and whole chapters of the Bible. Starting with the letter A she said aloud a verse that began with that letter and went through the entire alphabet. She also found great comfort in singing Christian hymns softly in her cell.

Darlene discovered that if she pulled herself up and put her foot on the doorknob, she could look out the barred window and see the prison courtyard. One day, as she struggled to peek out the window, she saw a woman prisoner near the fence. When the guards weren't looking, someone on the other side handed a bunch of bananas to her. "Bananas!" Darlene thought as she dropped to the floor of her cell. Soon she couldn't get the thought of bananas out of her mind. She seemed to be able to smell and taste them. Kneeling down she prayed, "Lord, I'm not asking you for a whole bunch like that woman has. I just want one banana. Lord, just one banana."

"But that is impossible," Darlene said to herself. "There is more chance of the moon falling out of the sky than that my captors would bring me a banana."

Then she prayed again, "Lord, there is no way for you to do it. Please don't think I'm not thankful for the rice. It's just that those bananas looked so delicious!"

The next day—to Darlene's surprise—Mr. Yamaji, the camp commander from Kampili, came to visit her. She did not find out until later that he had told the secret police that Darlene was not a spy. "You're very ill, aren't you?" he asked.

"Yes, sir, Mr. Yamaji, I am."

He tried to encourage her, and then he said, "Would you like me to bring any word back to the women?"

"Yes, sir," she replied, "when you go back, please tell them for me that I'm alright and still trusting the Lord. They'll understand what I mean, and I believe you do too."

"Alright," he said as he turned and left. A few minutes later, a guard unlocked her cell and threw in several bunches of bananas saying, "These are yours—they're from Mr. Yamaji."

Darlene could hardly believe her eyes—on the floor of her cell she counted ninety-two bananas! Then, overwhelmed with shame, she pushed the bananas into the corner and began to weep. Through her tears she prayed, "Lord, forgive me; I'm so ashamed. I couldn't trust you enough to get even one banana for me. Just look at them—there are almost a hundred."

Then in the quiet of her heart, she felt the Lord answer back. "That is what I delight to do, to give exceeding abundant above anything you ask or think."

Darlene carefully portioned out a few bananas to eat each day, saving the green ones for last. Her strength revived from the life-giving nutrients of the fruit.

After six weeks of interrogation, the secret police brought Darlene back to Kampili. For the next year, Darlene and the other prisoners struggled to survive. With each passing month more and more American planes flew overhead, often dropping bombs in the area. The women knew that Japan was losing the war. Then one day in late August 1945, Mr. Yamaji appeared before the prisoners wearing his full dress uniform. "His Imperial highness, the Emperor Hirohito," he said, "has announced by radio that the war is over. Japan has surrendered." Then he saluted and left.

Not long after, Darlene—weighing just eighty pounds, little more than skin and bones—sailed home to the United States. Three years later, she married a missionary named Jerry Rose. Soon, they left for New Guinea to establish a mission outpost in the interior of New Guinea in the very place that Darlene and Russell had started to work a decade earlier. For thirty years, Jerry and Darlene taught the native people about Jesus Christ. Hundreds of them put their trust in Christ, and several native churches were formed.

After the war, Mr. Yamaji was sentenced to life in prison for his war crimes. After a few years, his sentence was commuted, and he returned to Japan. Many years later, Darlene learned that an American man visiting Japan had met Mr. Yamaji. "During the war," Yamaji told him, "I was commander of Kampili, a women's prisoner of war camp in Indonesia. If you ever meet any of the women who'd been in Kampili, tell them that I am sorry I was so cruel. I am a different man now."

Darlene hoped and prayed that Mr. Yamaji's change came from Jesus Christ creating in him a new heart.

42

EDITH SCHAEFFER
Guide to the Searching, 1914–2013

In 1955 at a Swiss mountain chalet in the village of Champery, Francis and Edith Schaeffer faced a crisis. They knelt with their children in prayer. The Schaeffers were American missionaries who had come to Europe after the Second World War to teach children about Jesus Christ. For seven years, they organized children's Bible classes and wrote Bible study materials for young people. While living in Switzerland, they rediscovered the joy of walking daily with Christ. "It is moment by moment communion, personal communion, with God Himself!" Francis said. By God's grace, Francis and Edith determined to live each day in fellowship with the living God.

They began to realize that their work was changing as more and more visitors came to their chalet. Students from nearby boarding schools, friends of their children and people they met in the village seemed to be open to the message of Christ while enjoying the hospitality of the Schaeffers' home. Conversation which began around a cup of tea often extended into an evening-long discussion about the existence of God and the truth of the Bible. As time went on, an increasing number of young people came for spiritual help. Francis and Edith poured more time and energy into showing the love of Christ to visitors, answering their questions and presenting them with the good news of Jesus. One by one, a few children from the neighboring school, some adults from the village and college students on holiday came to a living faith in Christ.

One day Francis said to Edith, "Let's call our work L'Abri,"—French for shelter. "Let's let people know that they are welcome to come back and bring their friends with them."

"We started to pray that God would unfold His will and send us the people of His choice," Edith said. "We asked one basic thing—that this work would be a demonstration of God's existence—that God would help us to answer honest questions with honest answers."

Unbeknownst to the Schaeffers, not everyone was happy with their work. Some of the citizens of Champery did not like their Christian activities, and they did not want to see any villagers change their faith. They voiced their objections to local officials who then complained to the immigration office in Berne, the capital of Switzerland. A few weeks later, the Schaeffers received devastating news from the government: "You must be out of Switzerland within six weeks," the notice read.

"Why?" they wondered. "What about our dream for L'Abri? Where will we go?"

They knelt in prayer in the living room of their rented home, asking God to change the minds of the Swiss officials. The Schaeffers sent letters to Christian friends in America and Europe, asking them to pray. Through a Swiss friend they learned that they could appeal the order to leave Switzerland, but to do so they had to leave Champery and move to another canton. They had to set up a home there and have officials in the new village appeal the Swiss government to cancel the order to leave the country—all in the space of a few days. It seemed nearly impossible to Edith and Francis. "Where would we find a house?" they asked one another. "Why would a village that doesn't know us want to be bothered with helping us with the appeal?"

For two days they tramped through waist-deep snow looking for a chalet for rent. With time running out, Edith set out one last time to search for a place. This time, she stumbled upon a real estate agent whom they had talked to a few days earlier. "I have a home to show you," he said. He brought Edith to a large old chalet, but a thick fog obscured the view of the surrounding countryside. After looking through the house, Edith thought it could meet their needs. "Oh, I almost forgot to ask," Edith said to the man as he hopped into his car to leave, "how much is the rent?"

"Oh, it is not for rent," he answered, "it's for sale." With that he drove off.

"For sale," Edith said to herself. "For sale! We have no money and even if we were millionaires, who would buy a house in a country without having a permit to live there?"

As Edith made her way back home, she prayed, "Oh Lord, please show us your will about the house. If we are to buy it, send us a sign that will be clear enough to convince Francis as well as me—send us one thousand dollars before ten o'clock tomorrow morning."

The next day a letter arrived from a couple in the United States who had never contributed money for the work before. "We both feel certain," they wrote, "that we are meant to send you this money to buy a house somewhere that will always be open to young people." The envelope contained exactly one thousand dollars!

God graciously answered many other prayers too. Shortly thereafter, the Swiss government permitted them to stay, and more money came, allowing them to buy the chalet. When they moved in, they discovered to their delight that the property had a sweeping view of the Rhône River Valley and snow-covered peaks with glistening glaciers. They also found that the road below their property had a bus stop. And that bus connected to a nearby town with trains to the major cities of Switzerland. It would be easy for visitors to reach L'Abri even though it was nestled in a rural mountainside.

They had guests from the very beginning—on the first night they hosted a German musician, a Swiss peasant and an English travel guide. After a few days, the English woman told Edith, "I always thought Christians were dull, unhappy people, but you all seem to be so excited about it—and your life is anything but dull!"

Soon young people—hearing about L'Abri by word of mouth—came from all over the world. Edith loved each guest as a unique individual with special needs. Some came with open hearts ready to hear the truth and some came angry and resistant. "So you believe all those myths in the Bible really took place?" a visitor asked Francis Schaeffer.

"Wait a minute," Francis answered, "you have to start further back. Let's not ask first of all 'Is the Bible true?' Let's first see what the basic questions are, and find what the Bible has to teach in the way of answers."

Visitors were astounded to discover that the thoughtful, well-educated Schaeffers believed that the Bible was God's infallible Word. "Why, I thought belief in the Bible went out with the Dark Ages," one young woman said. "I didn't know anyone believed it to be true today."

While Francis led the large group discussions, Edith popped in and out while cleaning dishes, checking on her children, washing sheets, preparing meals and doing the hundred and one other tasks necessary to keep the home humming. Through it all, Edith lent a listening ear and spoke about Christ to guests as she enjoyed a meal with them or worked alongside them. She encouraged them to live moment by moment in communion with Christ and in obedience to the Word of God. "We are meant to live in the Scriptures," she said.

Hilary, a Jewish woman with no real faith in God, was one of their first visitors. She had tried to find fulfillment in music and work, but all in vain. Over the course of a few days, her heart opened to Francis's teaching and the kindness of Edith. On the afternoon she was scheduled to leave, Hilary asked Edith, "Can we talk?" They went upstairs and sat on a couch. "How can I be sure that I really believe?" she asked. "I want to know how it can become personal to *me*."

"Look Hilary," Edith said, "There are four questions you need to answer. Do you believe that God exists? Do you acknowledge that you are a sinner and cannot get rid of the guilt of your sin by yourself?" Hilary nodded her head in agreement. "Yes," she said, "I really can say 'yes' to those two questions."

"Do you believe that Jesus came in space, time and history to be born of a virgin and to live a sinless life and to die on the cross for the sins of men?" Edith asked.

"Yes, all of this is certain to me now," Hilary answered, "but how do I know that I am truly right with God?"

"It is true that a person can believe these first three areas and yet not really be a Christian," Edith said. "This last question involves bowing before God. Do you submit to God and personally accept what Christ did for you, that he took your deserved punishment for your individual sins, as he died outside Jerusalem?"

Over the course of a two-hour conversation, the light suddenly broke through on Hilary's face. She prayed softly, accepting Christ as her Lord and thanking God for His great gift. Then word came that Hilary's ride was departing. With a beaming smile, she gave Edith a quick hug, rushed downstairs and out the front door. Thousands of young people would follow in Hilary's steps—coming to L'Abri estranged from God and leaving as believing Christians. In describing God's wonderful work at L'Abri, Edith wrote, "We wept, we laughed, we thrilled, we agonized, we squealed with surprise."

But the ministry was not trouble free. It involved a great deal of hard work, frustration and disappointment—but through it all young people kept coming and kept turning to Christ. "Was I now going to have no faults?" Edith wrote. "Would I be really dead to self all the time, and have no frustrations as I cooked, weeded gardens, and washed dishes for an endless stream of people? No, a million times no! But God is very patient and gentle with His children as they attempt to live in close communion with Him."

As the number of visitors grew, so did the chalet. They added a large living room with a fireplace and more bedrooms. Over the years, they bought more chalets in the neighborhood, and leaders trained by the Schaeffers started L'Abri homes in Italy, England, the United States and Holland.

Francis Schaeffer's talks to young people became the basis of several popular books that presented the Christian faith to un-believers and challenged Christians to shine the light of Christ to a dark world. Edith began writing books too—award-win-ning and best-selling books. Her most influential works en-couraged Christian women to reject feminist ideas that dispar-aged marriage, motherhood and home life. "There needs to be a homemaker exercising some measure of skill, imagination, and creativity," she wrote, "with a desire to fulfill needs and give pleasure to others in the family. How precious a thing is the human family. Is it not worth some sacrifice in time, energy, safety, discomfort, and work?"

Edith thought of God's work in the world as a tapestry. Each human being is a thread in His hands. By God's sovereign power, He designs and weaves the threads into a tapestry of His artistry. Through her writings and her work at L'Abri, Edith called people to give their lives to Christ and become part of God's beautiful tapestry. "You must come to know," Edith told them, "the ex-citing greatness and kindness and creative imagination of our marvelous God."

43 DAYUMA OF THE WAODANI (AUCAS)

First to Carry the Name of Jesus to Her People, c. 1932–2014

In February 1955, a drunken native woman—a worker on Don Carlos's remote hacienda in Ecuador—staggered into her boss's office. "Sell me a gun, Señor Carlos," Dayuma said. "Teach me how to use it. I want to go back to my home and kill Miopa."

Carlos did not sell her the weapon. But Dayuma's hatred and lust for revenge against Miopa, the tribesman who murdered her father and sister, churned in her gut and never left her mind. Dayuma came from the Waodani tribe, a violent people living deep in the jungles of eastern Ecuador along the Curaray River. Their only encounters with outsiders had been bad ones. In the early 1900s, rubber hunters invaded the jungle, destroying villages, and killing or enslaving natives. The Waodani learned to fear the deadly power of white men's guns. But the greatest danger that they faced came from themselves. They murdered one another through a never-ending cycle of revenge killings.

After her father was speared to death, Dayuma fled for her life. She canoed down the Curaray for several days and then hiked through jungle trails until she reached Don Carlos's hacienda. For eight years she had worked there, cutting and hauling firewood and washing clothes. She learned Quechua, the language of the other native workers. The Quechuas called Dayuma's people "Aucas" meaning "savages who speared."

A few days after Dayuma left Don Carlos's office without a gun, Rachel Saint came to the hacienda. Rachel, a missionary from America, had heard about Dayuma, and she came with the hope that Dayuma would teach her the Waodani language. She wanted to share the good news of Jesus Christ with the Waodani. Her brother, Nate Saint, was a missionary pilot in Ecuador, flying supplies to missionaries scattered throughout the region. Nate and his friends, Jim Elliot, Pete Fleming and others, also hoped to bring the message of Christ's forgiveness to the Waodani.

At first, the dark-skinned Dayuma was suspicious of the white woman who wanted to learn her native language. But over time, Rachel's kindness broke through the barriers of distrust, and they became friends. Dayuma taught Rachel Waodani words and phrases. She learned about the Waodani's life in the jungle—living in clusters of thatched huts, harvesting yucca and bananas, spearing sunfish and hunting monkeys with poison blow darts. What shocked Rachel most was their cruelty and disregard for human life. "We throw away babies when we don't want them anymore," Dayuma said, thinking nothing of it. As she told Rachel about her family and friends, she would often conclude with the phrase, "Being speared, he died." Many of them had been murdered by rival tribesmen.

"Once, when my father was gone for many days," Dayuma said, "my mother told me, 'If your father does not return tomorrow, I will kill you.' That night, I trembled with fear in my hammock. The next morning, I asked my mother, 'Are you going to kill me?' 'If your father doesn't come by this afternoon,' my mother answered, 'yes, I will kill you.'"

Fortunately, her father returned that day and Dayuma was spared.

"Why do the Waodani kill?" Rachel asked her.

"Because they are killers," she answered.

Rachel discovered that the Waodani knew nothing of a loving heavenly Father, and that they lived in fear of evil spirits. "The devil of the forest sucks our blood and we die," Dayuma told her.

A few years earlier, Dayuma had married a Quechua worker. They had two children, but shortly after their second son was born, measles took the lives of her husband and baby boy. "I tried to drown myself in the river," Dayuma told Rachel, "but I couldn't do it. 'Why can't I die?' I wondered."

Over time, Rachel told Dayuma about Christ's love and sacrifice for sinners. She was particularly curious about the Bible— "God's carving"—she called it. Dayuma sat spellbound as Rachel read her stories from the Scriptures, and she remembered them all. Rachel introduced her to Nate and his missionary friends, Jim Elliot and Pete Fleming. They asked her to teach them words of greeting in her language, explaining that they wanted to visit the Waodani and tell them about Jesus. "Never, never trust them," Dayuma warned them. "They appear friendly and then they will turn around and kill."

Then in September 1955, Nate spotted a Waodani village from the air. Together with his missionary partners, he started to make regular flights over the village to drop gifts, hoping to convince the Waodani that they wanted to be friends. After a few months of dropping gifts and shouting greetings in Waodani that

Dayuma had taught them, the men decided to meet the tribesmen on the ground. In early January 1956, Nate, Jim, Pete and two other missionaries landed the plane on a stretch of beach along the Curaray River about five miles from the Waodani village. The men had brought pistols with them that they hid in duffel bags, but they vowed that if attacked, they would not shoot the Waodani. If threatened, they planned to fire warning shots to scare them away.

They called out Waodani words of welcome in hopes that the natives were watching them from the jungle. Before long, a Waodani man and two women stepped out from the trees. Jim smiled and said, "*Puinani!* —Welcome!" They spent several hours showing the visitors objects and sharing food with them. In the evening, the natives left. The next day, Waodani warriors attacked the five missionaries and speared them all to death. The five men had fired warning shots over their heads to frighten them, but the warriors kept charging anyway. Rather than shoot their attackers, the missionaries let the Waodani kill them.

Rachel wept and wept when word came of the death of her brother and his four friends. Dayuma wondered if Rachel might kill her to avenge her brother's death. When Rachel told her that she forgave the people who killed her brother and that she still wanted to go and tell them about Jesus, Dayuma began to glimpse the transforming power of Christ. Soon she believed in and prayed to Jesus. "Are you trusting the Lord Jesus?" another missionary asked her.

"Yes!" Dayuma answered with a smile. "I think of him day and night!"

When Rachel needed to return to the United States for a few months, she asked Dayuma to join her. Rachel wanted the opportunity to learn more Waodani from her without the interruption of Dayuma's work on the hacienda. In America, Dayuma met family members of the five missionaries killed by the Waodani. Tears flowed down her cheeks when they told her that they had no intention of retaliating against the Waodani. "We pray that your people will follow Jesus," they said.

When Billy Graham heard that Rachel Saint and a Waodani Christian were in the United States, he invited them to speak at his evangelistic crusade in New York's Madison Square Garden. A few days later, Dayuma stood on a platform before thousands of people. She told the story of Jesus raising the official's daughter from the dead. Dayuma energetically acted out the scene Waodani style while Rachel translated it into English.

After Billy Graham preached, he invited people who wanted to trust in Jesus to come to the front of the platform. As hundreds came forward, Dayuma was amazed that so many Americans did not know Jesus. "But they have God's carving in their own language!" she said to Rachel.

When they returned to Ecuador, Dayuma met with her two aunts who had come out of the jungle and were staying with the missionary Elizabeth Elliot, the widow of Jim Elliot. "God lives high in the sky," she told her aunts. "Long ago His Son was born as a child. We did not live well, we sinned. It is true that before I did not live well. I didn't know about God; I didn't understand. Now I understand, and now I am happy. When we did not live well, God's Son came to earth. He died in exchange for us. After three days, He came to life. Now He lives high in the sky. If we love God when we die, we will go high in the sky where He is thatching a beautiful hut for us."

It had been twelve years since Dayuma fled from the tribe, and she was anxious to hear news from home. The Waodani women told her about many family members and friends who had been murdered. Dayuma rushed away in tears saying, "I will never go back!"

After she had time to grieve, Rachel told her, "If the Lord Jesus had not left heaven, we would never have heard of Him. You're the only one of your people who knows God. How will they hear if you don't go and tell them? You may be the only one who can tell them about Jesus."

Dayuma took it to heart. A few days later she said, "Now I have finished crying for my brothers. I will go back to my forest home with my aunts." But Dayuma wondered if her people would accept her or see her as an outsider wearing strange clothes. Before they returned to the Waodani village, both of Dayuma's aunts believed in Christ and began to pray for the first time to the one true God in heaven. Several weeks later they came back, bringing other relatives with them. They brought good news—an invitation for Rachel Saint and Elizabeth Elliot to live among them. Trusting in Christ for wisdom and protection, Dayuma led the missionary women and her relatives back into the jungle. They received a warm welcome from the Waodani who wore nothing but colorful headdresses of bird feathers and jewelry made of animal bones. The Waodani had built round thatched huts for them to live in.

As the missionaries adjusted to jungle life, they continued to learn the language and tried to share bits of the gospel with the people. However, Dayuma was the main evangelist. Dayuma, a natural-born storyteller, followed the Waodani tradition of introducing the name of the main character first. "Jesus," she told her relatives, "His name is Jesus."

As they gathered fruits and caught fish, Dayuma told them about Adam and Eve, David and Goliath and Christ and his disciples. Every Sunday, the villagers would crowd into Dayuma's hut to listen to her teach about God's Son. "After people sinned," Dayuma told them. "God said, 'Now what will I do that they may live well? I will send my Son to die in exchange.' Yes, He became like a child and was born. Then He died high on the tree, His very good blood dripped."

Over time, the message began to sink in, even though it was hard to believe. "Once, Jesus walked on water," she told them, "just as if it were a beach."

"No man can walk on water!" one woman objected.

"But Jesus did," Dayuma said. "He is the Son of God. He made the water, and He walked on it. If we don't believe in Jesus, our hearts are black like the blackest night. If we believe in Jesus, our hearts become like light. Do you understand? Who will live well? Who will follow God's trail to heaven?"

The people talked about Dayuma's teaching as they lay in their hammocks each evening.

As they began to realize that Jesus was the ruler of all nature, some believed in Christ.

Eventually, Rachel and Elizabeth talked with the people about the day that they killed the five missionaries. "We thought the men in the wood-bee (the airplane) had killed Dayuma and eaten her when she went out of the jungle to the foreigners. We were afraid. We thought the foreigners would kill us and eat us."

"That is just what the foreigners think about you!" Dayuma said.

Later, one of the men laughed and said, "Our ancestors told us that big woodpeckers created the mountains and hills. They were talking wild."

"Talking wild?" Rachel asked. "What do you mean?"

"Now we know better," he said. "Dayuma has come and told us that God created everything! Now we know the straight story."

Rachel Saint and other missionaries worked among the Waodani for many years, translating the Bible into their language and teaching them to read. In 1992, the printed New Testament in Waodani was presented to the tribe. For decades, Dayuma kept telling her people about her Savior. Many put their trust in Jesus Christ. The tribe's endless cycle of warfare and revenge killing grew weaker.

Rachel rejoiced in what Christ did through Dayuma. "In God's planning," Rachel wrote, "Dayuma was the first one to carry the name of Jesus to her people."

44   BILQUIS SHEIKH
She Dared Call Him Father, 1912–1997

One evening in 1966, Bilquis Sheikh, the most prominent citizen of Wah, Pakistan, ordered her chauffeur to bring her car around. Then the fifty-four-year old Bilquis drove to a place where she, as a high-caste Muslim, never imagined she would go—the home of a Christian missionary. But her dreams had driven her to distraction; she had to find some answers.

Despite the comfortable life she enjoyed raising her grandson Mahmud on her large estate, Bilquis was restless. As she read the Koran she found little comfort in it, especially when she read the ease by which it let men cast off their wives—a few years earlier Bilquis's husband had coldly informed her that he was leaving her for a younger woman. Although she had been taught, as all Muslims are taught, that the early Christians had falsified much of the story of Jesus Christ, she purchased a Bible and began to read Paul's letter to the Romans. Shortly after she began reading the New Testament, Bilquis had two strange and vivid dreams. One night she dreamed that she was having dinner with Jesus in her home. "He sat across the table from me and we ate dinner together in peace and joy," Bilquis said. Then suddenly, the dream changed. "Now I was on a mountaintop with another man," she said. "He was clothed in a robe and shod with sandals." Somehow she knew that he was John the

Baptist, even though she had never read or heard of him before. "I found myself telling John the Baptist about my recent visit with Jesus. 'But now he's gone, perhaps you, John the Baptist, will lead me to him?'"

She kept reading the Bible and the Koran and was struck more and more by the forgiveness and mercy of Christ. "The words burned in my heart like glowing embers," she said. Not long afterward, Bilquis dreamed that a perfume salesman came to her home and sold her a beautifully fragrant perfume in a golden jar. He set it on her bedside table and said, "This will spread throughout the world."

When Bilquis woke up the next morning, she looked at her bedside table and saw the Bible. "What do these dreams mean," she asked herself, "are these messages from God?"

Desperate to find an answer, Bilquis drove to the home of Mr. and Mrs. Mitchell, Christian missionaries who had once visited her garden. Mrs. Mitchell was startled to see Bilquis standing on her front porch. "Why, Begum Sheikh!" she said. "Please come in." She led her into the living room and asked, "Would you like tea or coffee?"

"Neither," Bilquis answered bluntly. "I've come to talk, not to drink tea. Where is your husband?"

"He is away on a trip."

"I see," Bilquis sighed. "Well—do you know anything about God?"

"I don't know as much as my husband knows about God," she said, "but I do know Him."

Bilquis told her about her dreams, and then she asked, "Tell me, who is John the Baptist?"

Mrs. Mitchell leaned back in her chair and said, "John the Baptist was a prophet, a forerunner of Jesus Christ, who preached repentance and was sent to prepare the way for Him. He was the one who baptized Jesus and pointed to Jesus and said: 'Look, the Lamb of God who takes away the sins of the world.'"

"That is what I was afraid of," Bilquis said.

"What are you afraid of?" Mrs. Mitchell asked.

"I was afraid that John the Baptist was pointing me to Jesus. If I choose Jesus, I lose everything!"

"Mrs. Mitchell," Bilquis said, staring intently into her eyes, "forget I am a Muslim. Forget the problems we have with Jesus being called the Son of God. Forget our believing that the Bible has been changed. Just tell me one thing—what has Jesus done for you?"

Mrs. Mitchell smiled and told her how she was wonderfully forgiven when she asked Christ into her heart. When she finished Bilquis said, "Could you pray for me?"

As the two women knelt on the floor, Mrs. Mitchell prayed, "O God, I know that nothing I can say will convince Begum Sheikh who Jesus is. But I thank You that Your Spirit can take the veil off our eyes and reveal Jesus to our hearts. So Holy Spirit, do this for Begum Sheikh. In Jesus' name. Amen."

When she finished her prayer, Bilquis added, "Yes, God, that is exactly what I want."

Then Mrs. Mitchell told Bilquis about the dream that God gave the wise men warning them to avoid Herod on their homeward journey. "God does speak in dreams, then!" Bilquis said. "If the Bible tells about God speaking in dreams—then I know He has spoken to me in my dreams. What do you think my dream about the perfume means?" she asked. "Let me think about that," Mrs. Mitchell answered.

As she walked Bilquis to the door, she gave her a Bible in modern English. "Start with the Gospel of John," she advised. "He makes the role of John the Baptist very clear."

The next morning, Mrs. Mitchell sent Bilquis a note. It contained the words: "Second Corinthians chapter 2, verse 14." Bilquis opened the Bible to the verse and read it. "Thanks be to God who leads us, wherever we are, on Christ's triumphant way, and makes our knowledge of Him spread throughout the world like a lovely perfume!"

"The knowledge of Jesus is like a lovely perfume!" Bilquis told herself. "In my dream the salesman had put the golden jar on my bedside table and said that the perfume 'would spread throughout the whole world.' The next morning I found my Bible in the same spot where the perfume was laid!"

A few days later, Bilquis knelt in her bedroom. With tears streaming down her cheeks, she confessed her sin and believed in Jesus Christ. "I am sorry my Father," she prayed, "for not having known You before."

From that moment on, Bilquis could not get enough of the Bible. Beginning with the Gospel of Matthew she read straight through the New Testament. She began to attend a Christian worship meeting on Sunday evenings in the home of another missionary. But the excitement she felt for her new life in Christ was tempered by her concern for her family. "I knew for certain," she said later, "that everyone I loved would advise me to turn my back on Jesus."

She did not want to break the hearts of her family members. She especially worried that her conversion to Christianity would lead to losing her guardianship of her grandson. "Could you really want me to lose my family?" she asked God in prayer. Then she remembered Christ's words: "Anyone who puts his love for father or mother above his love for Me does not deserve to be mine, and he who loves son or daughter more than Me is not worthy of Me."

Bilquis determined to openly follow Christ. The final break from Islam comes when a convert is baptized. Many Muslims who trust in Christ never take this step out of fear of rejection or violence from family and friends. But Bilquis believed she must be baptized. "I'm sure that the Lord has told me to be baptized," she told a Christian minister.

"Bilquis are you prepared for what may happen?" he asked. "They could label you an unfit guardian and take Mahmud away from you."

"Yes, I know," she said. "I realize many people will think I'm committing a crime. But I want to be baptized; I must obey God."

On January 24, 1967, Bilquis was baptized. Soon word spread through the town and to all her relatives in Pakistan that Bilquis had become a Christian. When her daughter heard the news, she rushed to Bilquis's home. With tears in her eyes she asked, "Oh mother, did you really have to go so far?"

"My dear," Bilquis told her, "there is nothing I can do but be obedient."

"You know what people are saying?" her daughter cried. "You'll be attacked. My friends say you'll be murdered!"

Bilquis received threatening phone calls in the middle of the night. People called her "infidel." "O Lord," Bilquis prayed, "You know that I don't mind dying. But I'm an awful coward. I cannot stand pain. I guess I'm not made of the stuff of martyrs, Lord. I'm sorry. Just let me walk with You through whatever comes next."

Her family and friends shunned her. They sent an Englishman who had converted from Christianity to Islam to show her the error of her ways. "Begum Sheikh," he said, "one thing really disturbs me about Muslims who convert to Christianity. It is the Bible. We all know the Christian New Testament has been changed from what God gave."

"I've heard often that the Bible was changed," Bilquis said, "but I've never been able to learn who changed it. Tell me, why were the changes made and what passages were corrupted?"

The Englishman stared at her with a blank expression; he couldn't give her an answer.

"You see," Bilquis said, "in the British Museum there are ancient versions of the Bible which were published nearly three hundred years before Mohammed was born. The experts say that in every basic essential these old manuscripts are identical to today's Bible. For me, the Bible is an alive Word. It speaks to my soul and feeds me and guides me."

"You talk about the Word almost as if it were living," the Englishman said.

"I believe that Christ is living, if that's what you mean," she answered. "The Koran itself says that Christ was the Word of God. I would love to talk with you about it sometime."

"I must be going," the man mumbled as he made his way out the door.

Bilquis became all the more determined to share her faith. She bought one hundred copies of the Bible and started giving them away.

In 1968, a missionary friend told her that the Billy Graham organization wanted her to speak at a crusade in Singapore. "Singapore?" she asked.

"Yes," he answered, "Billy Graham is holding evangelistic meetings there. It will be for Asian Christians of all kinds—Indonesians, Japanese, Indians, Koreans, Chinese and Pakistanis. Your testimony will be an inspiration."

After some thought and prayer Bilquis agreed to go. As she spoke to the thousands of men and women who filled the conference hall and told them how she came to faith in Christ, she sensed a warm presence of the Lord.

When she returned home, she kept telling the good news of Christ and hosting Christian meetings in her home. Then one day her maid said, "I simply must warn you, Begum Sheikh. My brother was in the mosque yesterday. A group of young men began talking about the damage you are doing. They kept saying that someone had to shut you up."

Not long after, someone set fire to her home. If Bilquis hadn't happened to go outside and smell the smoke, the house would have been destroyed and everyone in it. When the threats increased, she fled to the United States with her grandson. She wrote a book about her coming to faith in Christ, and she traveled throughout the United States and Canada. She told her story and led many Muslims to Jesus Christ. After sixteen years away, Bilquis returned to Pakistan where she lived confident in her Savior until her death in 1997.

45 ETA LINNEMANN
From Criticism to Christ, 1926–2009

I n 1978, Eta Linnemann, the world's most renowned woman in New Testament studies, stood in her university office in Braunschweig, Germany. She looked over the shelves lined with books and articles that she had written. She scanned the volumes containing thousands of pages of her writings on Jesus and the Scriptures. These works represented nearly thirty years of toil. They had earned her a professorship, a comfortable living and the respect of her academic peers. She became the first woman to hold a chair in theology in a major German university. Scholars from across Europe and North America consulted her works and invited her to lecture at their universities. Now as she looked over her life's work, Dr. Linnemann shook her head and sighed. One by one, she picked up each book and journal article—and threw them in the trash!

Why? Why would a woman at the pinnacle of her career throw away the work that got her there? Because Christ came into her life—and this is how it happened.

Although Eta Linnemann went to church as a girl, her pastors did not teach the Bible as the Word of God because they had been trained in the historical-critical method. Historical-critical theology rejects the Bible's accounts of miracles and prophecies—anything that is outside ordinary human experience.

When Eta entered Marburg University just after the Second World War, she studied under the famous theologian Rudolf Bultmann. Bultmann trained her to be a historical-critical theologian. For Bultmann and the other theology professors in all the German universities, the virgin birth, the miracles of Jesus and Christ's resurrection were all legends not historical facts. "You must study the New Testament as if there were no God," her professors taught her. Eta embraced this way of viewing the Scriptures and went on to earn a doctorate in historical-critical theology.

As a professor, she taught her students to read the Bible with skepticism and unbelief. But over the course of many years, she began to doubt that her teaching had any real value. She came to see that much of what she taught was not truth, but simply opinion based on the assumption that supernatural events cannot happen. The realization that her life's work was hollow and served no helpful purpose threw her into a deep depression. "I reacted by drifting toward addictions which might dull my misery," Eta said. She began drinking alcohol heavily and wasted her evenings and weekends watching countless hours of television. But then a series of events led her to Christ.

Part of her work as a university professor was to read the papers of graduate students. One day, she came across a paper that referred to supernatural events in the African churches. "I was deeply impressed with its truthfulness," Eta said later. "It gave so much honor and glory to God."

About a year later, when Dr. Linnemann was giving her usual lecture full of skepticism about the miracles reported in the Bible, to her surprise she suddenly began telling her students about the reports of miraculous events in Africa that she had read about. There were some evangelical Christian students in her class who were delighted to hear her speaking about miracles as if they had actually happened. These students began to pray for their professor, and they asked other believers to pray for her too. Soon many people were asking God to bring Eta Linnemann to Christ.

The Christian students began to speak with her after class. One young woman invited her to come to their student prayer meeting. "This group of students had been unusually nice to me," Eta said later, "so I wanted to be nice to them."

As a favor and a gesture of kindness, she went to the prayer meeting, but she didn't understand what was going on, and she never went back. Another student asked her to attend their monthly Christian meeting. Month after month, the student invited her. Month after month, Dr. Linnemann didn't go. Finally, after six months of invitations, she reluctantly went to a meeting. "I was deeply impressed with the atmosphere of joy and love," she said. She found the message on justification by faith stimulating, and she decided to go again.

After Dr. Linnemann had attended the meetings for a year, a speaker preached on the abundant life that believers enjoy in God. "I was so hungry for this life with Christ," Eta said later, "so when the speaker asked, 'Who is willing to surrender his life to Christ?' I knew it was for me. I lifted my arm and, by God's grace and love, I entrusted my life to Jesus. And my life was changed."

Her destructive addictions disappeared, replaced by a hunger and thirst for the Word of God and for fellowship with Christians. For the first time in her life, she saw what sin really was and what Christ had suffered to pay the penalty for her sin. "As a holy God," she wrote later, "He must take sin very seriously and cannot forgive us just like that! He had to send His beloved Son to carry our sins on the cross and die for our salvation. That is the real love of God that these theologians miss."

One month later, she went to a Christian conference and heard a missionary from Nepal speak about his language helper named Paul. The missionary said that Paul had been imprisoned for leading others to Christ, which was a capital crime in Nepal. Then the missionary told how Paul had boldly and clearly defended the gospel in front of the judge. Dr. Linnemann couldn't believe that a poorly educated, inarticulate man could have spoken like that. But then she remembered Jesus' words in Mark 13:11, "Whenever you are arrested and brought to trial, do not worry beforehand about what to say. Just say whatever is given you at the time, for it is not you speaking, but the Holy Spirit." Eta recognized that the language helper's testimony before the judge was a fulfillment of that prophecy of Jesus. "But I had always been taught that there was no such thing as true biblical prophecy," she said.

One by one, she realized that the things she had learned as a university student and had taught as a professor were not true. The old god that she had taught about could neither hear, nor speak, nor act. "But now I became aware of the living God!" she exclaimed. "I had been a blind teacher leading my blind students. I repented of my wrong teaching. I also realized that despite all my years of study, I knew nothing of God. I resolved that now I must get to work learning about this God."

Although Eta Linnemann was a world-renowned New Testament theologian who had mastered Greek and Hebrew and could describe in minute detail the contents of the gospels and epistles, she decided to go to Bible school. Sitting in a small class that included teenagers and seventy-year-olds, she heard the Scriptures taught straightforwardly as the true Word of God. "It was in this Bible school that—for the first time in my life—I learned the basics of Christian belief," Eta said.

She began going to church, and she asked her new brothers and sisters in Christ to pray for her. "Then I found myself faced with a momentous decision," she said. "Would I continue to control the Bible by my intellect, or would I allow my thinking to be transformed by the Holy Spirit? By God's grace, I experienced Jesus as the one whose name *is* above all names. I was permitted to realize that Jesus *is* God's Son, born of a virgin. He *is* the Messiah and the Son of God."

Dr. Linnemann radically changed the way she instructed her university courses. "I began to investigate all the arguments of the historical-critical theologians and found that none of the arguments for doubting the Scriptures was valid," she wrote. "So I said, 'No!' to historical-critical theology and 'Yes!' to my wonderful Lord and Savior Jesus Christ and to the glorious redemption He accomplished for me."

She started to teach her students that the Scriptures are the divinely inspired Word of God—showing them that the New Testament's accounts of Jesus' words and deeds were convincing. Dr. Linnemann taught that Jesus was the Son of God, born of a virgin, performed miracles, prophesied the future, was killed on the cross and rose on the third day. When her fellow professors heard of her new approach to teaching the Scriptures, they recoiled, rejecting her arguments out of hand. They shunned her and considered her hopelessly lost in the irrational world of faith.

Eta began writing papers that argued that the historical-critical method was unreliable and rested on a shaky foundation of opinions. "I regard everything that I taught and wrote before I entrusted my life to Jesus as refuse," she wrote. "I pitched my books and writings into the trash. I ask you sincerely to do the same thing with any of them you may have."

Eventually, she stepped down from her professorship and became a missionary to Indonesia. Eta spent most of the rest of her life there teaching the Scriptures to young men training to be pastors. And she wrote books that exposed the bankrupt theories of liberal theology.

"You can trust your Bible," Eta said. "You cannot trust historical-critical theology. It is not trustworthy. I praise God for bringing me out of it, and pray that He will use me to bring others from criticism to Christ."

46 ANNGRACE TABAN
Sharing the Gospel with Women in Need, 1965–

I n the last fifty years, a great awakening of faith in Christ
has swept across Africa. Since the start of the twenty-first
century, more than thirty thousand Africans have become
Christians every day. Millions of African Muslims have converted to Christianity, and many of them face the threat of death
for rejecting Islam. Civil war, famine and radical Islamists make
life very hard for countless African believers. In South Sudan,
Nigeria and other nations, Islamist raiders attack Christian
villages and kidnap women and children. They carry them off
into slavery or forced marriages to Muslims. In many countries,
Islamist gunmen shoot worshipers and burn down churches
and Christian schools. Armed groups force children into being
child soldiers trained to kill. Anngrace Taban is one of millions
of African women who have found Christ and clung to Him in
the midst of great trials.

One night in 1990 in Yei, South Sudan, Anngrace Taban
heard a loud banging on her front door. Her husband Elias, a
Christian pastor, was away from home preaching the good news
of Jesus in the villages of the surrounding countryside. When
Anngrace peeked through the window and saw an Arab soldier
in a green uniform standing in the dark outside her door, her

heart leapt to her throat. She knew this Muslim soldier was part of the forces sent by the Islamic government in northern Sudan, and that meant trouble for Christians like the Tabans. When he pounded the door again, Anngrace slowly opened it. "Where is your husband?" he barked. Before Anngrace could answer he shouted, "You'd better tell me the truth, woman. Lying won't do you any good."

When Anngrace caught her breath, she said, "My husband is out preaching the gospel. He has permission from the government to go out and preach in the countryside."

"We think your husband could be spying for the enemy," the man said. By the enemy he meant the SPLA, the Sudan People's Liberation Army. It was formed in South Sudan to fight the soldiers from Khartoum who attacked their people and tried to force Islamic law on Christians and animists.

"My husband went to share the gospel of Jesus Christ," Anngrace insisted.

After questioning her at length about her husband's activities, he left saying, "I'll be back."

During the day, Anngrace could hear gunfire and exploding grenades in the distance. And night after night Muslim soldiers pounded on her door, demanding to know Elias's whereabouts. "My husband went to preach the gospel with the permission of the local authorities," she always answered.

Anngrace breathed a deep sigh of relief when, at last, Elias got home. "There is great trouble brewing in the area," he told her. "A big battle will be fought here soon. Quickly pack some clothes and food. We need to get out of town at once."

They grabbed what they could carry and fled into the bush. Millions of others in southern Sudan had also run away to try to escape the violence. The Tabans, like the other refugees, survived in the wild, eating roots and plants, and trapping rats and birds. Finding drinking water was a constant challenge, and their only shelter was a grass roof held up by bamboo poles. Eventually, they made their way to a large refugee camp on the border of the Democratic Republic of Congo. Elias began preaching to the frightened and confused people, and Anngrace organized the women to assist one another and to help new folks who arrived nearly every day.

When soldiers of the SPLA saw how well Anngrace led the women and learned that she was well educated and a skilled typist, they came to Elias and said, "We need your wife. We want to give her military training. She'll be back after twenty-one days."

Anngrace had no choice—she had to go with them. The SPLA assigned Anngrace to type secret battle plans. She lived the rough life of a soldier, constantly on the move. She often wondered if she could go on. "Jesus, help me!" she prayed over and over again. After more than a year with the army, she was allowed to return to her husband in the refugee camp. She took up her work among the women, and she and Elias kept pointing people to Jesus. Many put their trust in Christ.

After years of fighting, the SPLA gained control over most of southern Sudan, and the Tabans were finally able to go back to their home in Yei. They resumed their ministry at once. Hundreds of thousands of Sudanese had been killed or had perished from starvation during the war. The people who returned to their homes had suffered greatly. War orphans abounded, desperate to be taken in by families. Over time, Elias and Anngrace adopted five children, and they helped to find homes for hundreds more. Elias became an important preacher and leader in the Evangelical Presbyterian Church in South Sudan. Elias and Anngrace worked with a Christian organization from the West to distribute Bibles to thousands of families that had no copy of the Scriptures. "We want to distribute Bibles," Elias said. "Our goal is for every literate Christian household to have its own personal Bible."

The Tabans also began a pastor's training school to help the many men who were preaching without any training in the Bible or theology.

Anngrace ministered to the women who had suffered so much in the war. Her heart ached and her tears flowed as women recounted the horrible abuses they endured at the hands of the soldiers. With nearly everyone mired in poverty, women wondered how they would feed their families. Widows faced the direst circumstances of all. Anngrace gathered a group of women together and said, "Let us set aside time to fast and pray for God's guidance and help."

When peace came to the region, international aid agencies arrived to help the South Sudanese construct roads and repair buildings. Anngrace organized teams of women to gather sand from the riverbank to sell to the construction companies. She named this work the Women's Project. The women threw themselves into the work, and they soon had a small mountain of sand to sell. With the profits, Anngrace paid her women workers and invested the money in other projects.

Anngrace observed that a growing number of international aid workers and officials from many countries visited the region, but there were few places for them to lodge. The women began to build guesthouses for the visitors to rent. As more money came in, they built more guesthouses. Many women were employed in cleaning and maintaining the houses and caring for the guests.

When Anngrace heard about a Christian organization that gave away vegetable seeds, she contacted a representative and said, "Please may I have some bags of seed? Growing vegetables can generate more income for the Women's Project."

Soon hundreds of women were growing vegetables to feed their families and selling the surplus at market. The women started thinking of more ways to generate income. Some raised goats and chickens. Others dyed fabrics or made bricks. Others sold homemade candy or soap. As word spread, women from across South Sudan came to Anngrace for advice on how to start women's projects in their areas. She taught them how to train leaders and empower them to develop ideas and put them into practice.

But Anngrace's goal was not primarily to help the women make a living for themselves and their families. "My main aim in starting the Women's Project," she said, "was to share the gospel with women in need. Our primary focus should be on preaching the Word of God."

The Tabans founded an organization—with support from Western Christians—to dig wells for clean drinking water. Many hundreds of wells have been built across South Sudan, bringing healthy water to towns and villages. Anngrace and Elias praise God for all that He has done to improve the living standards and change the hearts of so many. And they press on to do more. "This is a miracle," Elias said, "and for a miracle no one takes the glory. It belongs to God." As he spoke, Anngrace smiled, nodded her head and said, "Glory to God in the highest!"

FOR FURTHER READING

The work of the historian and biographer is highly selective—especially for the writer of biographical sketches. Far more is left out than can be included. To learn much more about the women introduced in this book, explore the following sources. Many of the older works are available free of charge through websites like books.google.com and archive.org.

EARLY CHURCH

What we know about some early Christians comes to us through short, fragmentary accounts. The believers who endured the persecution of the Roman Empire often wrote down short testimonials of the arrest and execution of their martyred brothers and sisters. These accounts circulated widely. What we know about Anthusa comes from her son Gregory Nazianzen's sermons or funeral messages. The letters of the Church Father

Jerome are a primary source for the life of Marcella. In the case of Monica, her son Augustine revealed many interesting aspects of her life and character in his book *Confessions* and some other of his writings.

- *Confessions of St. Augustine by Augustine*, Oxford University Press, 1992.

- *Letter CXXVII: To Principia from the Writings of St. Jerome. The Principal Works of St. Jerome* posted by the Christian Classics Ethereal Library, www.ccel.org.

- "St. Gregory's Funeral Oration for His Father," *Fathers of the Church Volume 22: Funeral Orations by Saint Gregory Nazianzen and Saint Ambrose*, translated by Leo McCauley, 1953.

- "The Martyrdom of Perpetua" and "The Martyrdom of Crispina," included in *In Her Words: Women's Writings in the History of Christian Thought*, edited by Amy Oden, 1994.

MIDDLE AGES

The lives of saints was a popular genre of Christian literature in the Middle Ages. Detailed accounts of men and women—often of monks and nuns—told their stories replete with many tales of miracles that they were reported to have worked. Readers who can wade through the fanciful and recognize the beliefs and practices of the age that were unscriptural will be rewarded with some beautiful examples of devotion to Christ and sacrifice for others.

- *Bertha, Our First Christian Queen and Her Times* by Elizabeth Hudson, 1868.

- *Life of Princess Margaret, Queen of Scotland* by Samuel Cowan, 1911.

- *Life of St. Claire* by the monk, Thomas of Celano, translated by Pascal Robinson, 1910.

- *Life of St. Leoba* by Rudolph, Monk of Fulda, www.fordham.edu/halsall/basis/leoba.asp.

- *Lives of the Primitive Fathers, Martyrs, and other Principal Saints* by Alvan Butler, 1799.

- *Lives of the Queens of England from the Norman Conquest Vol 2: Anne of Bohemia* by Agnes Strickland, 1841.

- *The Saint's Tragedy: Or, The True Story of Elizabeth of Hungary* by Charles Kingsley, 1851.

REFORMATION AND BEYOND

During the Reformation and afterward, Christian chroniclers—like John Foxe—carefully gathered written evidence and eyewitness accounts and recorded the trials and triumphs of Christ's people during those challenging times. In the last generation, fine biographies have been written on key individuals from the era.

- *Erdmuth Dorothea: Countess von Zinzendorf, Noble Servant* by Erika Geiger, 2006.

- *Katharina Von Bora: A Reformation Life* by Rudolf and Marilynn Markwald, 2002.

- *Ladies of the Covenant* by James Anderson, 1890.

- *Ladies of the Reformation* by James Anderson, 1855.

- *Marriage to a Difficult Man: The Uncommon Union of Jonathan and Sarah Edwards* by Elisabeth D. Dodds, 2005.

- *Queen of Navarre: Jeanne d'Albret* by Nancy Lyman Roelker, 1968.

- *The Acts and Monuments of John Foxe* by John Foxe, 1870.

- *The Nine Days' Queen, Lady Jane Grey and Her Times* by Richard Davey, 1909.

- *The Pearl of Princesses: Life of Queen Marguerite of Navarre* by Hugh Williams, 1916.

- *Women of the Reformation in France and England* by Roland Bainton, 1973.

MISSIONS REAWAKENED

When the modern mission movement accelerated in the nineteenth century, Christians in Britain and the United States developed an insatiable appetite for details about the lives of the missionaries and the progress of the gospel. Hundreds of missionary biographies were written during the era, inspiring countless Christians in the English-speaking world.

- *Autobiography of Amanda Smith* by Amanda Smith, 1893.

- *Fidelia Fiske: The Story of a Consecrated Life* by William Guest, 1870.

- *Hudson and Maria: Pioneers in China* by John Pollock, 1996.

- *Life of Sarah B. Judson* by Fanny Forester, 1860.

- *Memoir of Mary Calvert* by Mary Calvert and George Rowe, 1882.

- *Pandita Ramabai: The Story of Her Life* by Helen Dyer, 1900.

20TH AND 21ST CENTURIES

Over the last 150 years, people from nearly every tribe and tongue have come to faith in Christ, and some have written their personal testimonies—deepening the understanding of Western Christians of the world-wide Kingdom of God. These years also witnessed two world wars and the rise of modern totalitarian governments, violently hostile to Christianity. The stories of faithful Christian men and women who—by the power of the Holy Spirit—stood for Christ and suffered torture and imprisonment have inspired Christians across the globe to praise their Savior and walk more closely with Him.

- *Dayuma: Life Under Waodani Spears* by Ethel Wallis, 1996.

- *Evidence Not Seen: A Woman's Miraculous Faith in the Jungles of World War II* by Darlene Deibler Rose, 2003.

- *Historical Criticism of the Bible: Methodology or Ideology? Reflections of a Bultmannian Turned Evangelical* by Eta Linnemann, translated by Robert Yarbrough, 2001.

- *I Dared to Call Him Father: The Miraculous Story of a Muslim Woman's Encounter with God* by Bilquis Sheikh and Richard Schneider, 2003.

- *If I Perish* by Ei Sook Ahn, 1977.

- *L'Abri* by Edith Schaeffer, 1969.

- *Singing through the Night: Courageous Stories of Faith from Women in the Persecuted Church* by Anneke Companjen, 2007.

- *The Hiding Place* by Corrie ten Boom, 1971.

- *The Pastor's Wife* by Sabina Wurmbrand, 1979.

CPSIA information can be obtained at www.ICGtesting.com
Printed in the USA
BVOW08s0801140415

396009BV00005B/10/P